Wakefield Press

More than Miners

More than Miners

*Cornish Essays from
South Australia*

EDITED BY

JAN LOKAN and PHILIP PAYTON

Wakefield
Press

Wakefield Press
16 Rose Street
Mile End
South Australia 5031
www.wakefieldpress.com.au

First published 2023

Copyright © in this selection Jan Lokan and Philip Payton, 2023
Individual essays remain the copyright of the respective authors

All rights reserved. This book is copyright. Apart from
any fair dealing for the purposes of private study, research,
criticism or review, as permitted under the Copyright Act,
no part may be reproduced without written permission.
Enquiries should be addressed to the publisher.

Typeset and edited by Michael Deves, Wakefield Press

ISBN 978 1 74305 995 1

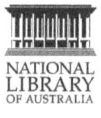 A catalogue record for this book is available from the National Library of Australia

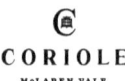 Wakefield Press thanks Coriole Vineyards for continued support

Contents

Introduction	vii
Before the mines: Early Cornish Emigration to South Australia *Philip Payton*	1
Captains of the Kapunda Mine *Greg Drew OAM*	25
Thomas Roberts: From Greenwith via Montacute to Burra *Keith Johns OAM*	37
'Songs of the Old Home': Cornish Carols in South Australia *Kate Neale*	47
Thomas Ninnes of Clare *Moira Drew*	74
Fire and Grain: Stephen and Elizabeth Goldsworthy, Farming Pioneers *Kerryn Goldsworthy*	89
William Abraham (1847–1922): A mine inspector's response to industrial disaster *Cheryl Hayden*	98
The Cornish Influence on Music in Broken Hill *Robynne Sanderson*	112
Local Cornish and their Choirs: Cornish Connections of South Australia's Metropolitan Male Choir *Jan Lokan and John Brimson*	147
H. Lipson Hancock and the 'Betterment Principle': Health and Wellbeing at Moonta and Wallaroo Mines *Philip Payton*	160

Sir John Langdon Bonython, a Rich and Successful Life:
But South Australia or Cornwall? **170**
Jean Prest

One False Move: The Bravery of Leon Goldsworthy GC, DSC, GM **186**
Jan Lokan

Creative Cornish: An Australian Literary Heritage **203**
Rosanne Hawke

Cousin Jack and his Economic Niche **221**
Cheryl Hayden

Acknowledgements **233**

Contributors **234**

Introduction

The Cornish have long been associated with hard-rock mining, mainly copper and tin in Cornwall itself, and a range of base and precious metals across the globe, from gold in California and South Africa to silver in Mexico and Peru. In South Australia in particular, the Cornish connection with the state's copper-mining communities and landscapes is well-known and deservedly celebrated. So too is the influence of the South Australian Cornish in other parts of the continent, not least neighbouring Broken Hill and the Victorian goldfields.

Yet even in South Australia the Cornish dominance in the mining industry was only part of the story. Technology transfer and the application of Cornish mining skills were certainly critical in the successful establishment of what was Australia's earliest mining era. But the distinctive characteristics of Cornish impact went beyond mining machinery, organisation and practices to embrace a wealth of recognisably 'Cornish' cultural and social signifiers, notably in music and Methodism. Besides, not all Cornish immigrants were miners or connected with mining, with many Cornish men and women involved in a variety of occupations, not least farming. Indeed, many Cornish mining families aspired to 'go on the land'. Those miners who had done well on their 'tribute' contracts, rewarded for amassing large quantities of high-grade ore, might save enough to purchase property, as might those who had profited from a successful sojourn on the Victorian goldfields.

This collection of essays reflects this diversity. It begins with Philip Payton's contribution, which shows that South Australia had emerged as an attractive destination for Cornish migrants, even before the first mineral finds, with Cornwall identified already as an important source of potential settlers for the new colony. The discoveries of copper in the Adelaide Hills and at Kapunda and Burra in the 1840s attracted highly skilled mine managers or 'captains', as Greg Drew and Keith Johns indicate in their chapters, and later discoveries on northern Yorke Peninsula led to the growth of vibrant Cornish communities at Moonta and environs. The three Peninsula towns became a major focus for Cornish musical activities, especially – as Kate Neale notes in her ground-breaking chapter – for the composition and performance of Cornish carols.

As Moira Drew relates, an early departure from Burra for the goldfields of Victoria was Thomas Ninnes, originally from Towednack in Cornwall, who after eighteenth months returned to South Australia wealthy enough to purchase land at Spring Farm, Clare, an exemplar of the 'miner-turned-farmer' phenomenon. Similarly, as Kerryn Goldsworthy describes in her chapter, Stephen Goldsworthy from Sithney and his wife Elizabeth Higgs from Lanlivery also came back to South Australia from the goldfields with sufficient funds to acquire land on Yorke Peninsula, first at Black Point and then at Curramulka, establishing a Cornish presence on the Peninsula well before the first copper discoveries. A somewhat different trajectory was that of William Abraham (a west Devon miner) who, as Cheryl Hayden explains, emigrated to Moonta but soon found his way across to Victoria where he became an inspector of mines. Alongside Victoria, Broken Hill was a significant destination for South Australia's mobile Cornish population, and Robynne Sanderson demonstrates the extraordinary extent of the Cornish contribution across a broad spectrum of the district's musical activities. Likewise, in Adelaide, as Jan Lokan and John Brimson show, the Cornish made an important contribution to the growth of the city's Metropolitan Male Choir.

The Cornish cultural influence on northern Yorke Peninsula extended to the sophisticated welfare system developed in the mining communities, as Philip Payton argues, but H. Lipson Hancock's 'Betterment Principle' also reflected the latest thinking in Australian mine management. Similar hybridity was apparent in the life and work of John Langdon Bonython, a passionate and prominent Cornishman in South Australia but also a newspaper magnate and a politician on

Introduction

the national stage, as Jean Prest indicates in her chapter. The enduring influence of Cornish heritage was likewise evident in the extraordinary wartime achievements of Leon Goldsworthy, the most decorated officer in the Royal Australian Navy, as Jan Lokan shows. Similarly, the importance of Cornish heritage is a central theme in Rosanne Hawke's contribution, where she notes that, especially in contemporary fiction for young people, writers are increasingly discovering and asserting their Cornish-Australian identities.

Finally, Cheryl Hayden dares to ask the 'elephant in the room' question in her second chapter in this collection. Why is Cornish heritage in Australia being celebrated so passionately today? Part of the answer, she discovers, is the power of Cornish mining history to enthuse those with Cornish elements in their family trees, even when other ethnicities are genealogically more prominent. Other Cornish occupations, including farming, were far less attractive to Australians of Cornish descent, she found. Women, in particular, were more likely to be interested in their Cornish family stories if they involved mining. Here, Hayden contends, we may detect the attraction of the 'myth of Cousin Jack', as it has been termed, the Cornish claim to economic superiority in the mining districts of Australia and elsewhere on the international mining frontier. Paradoxically, then, while we may wish to stress that the Cornish were 'more than miners', it is nonetheless the seductive allure of the Cornish miner that remains most prominent in their descendants' memories today.

While Moonta was a highly significant presence during the 19th and early 20th centuries in South Australia, its dominance waned shortly after the Great War when the world had less use for its copper and Kadina grew to become more important administratively. Many of Moonta's citizens left for other areas after the mines closed almost exactly 100 years ago. Those who stayed mostly found other kinds of employment, especially farming, which kept the town alive. Some, however, felt that its uniqueness as a Cornish, and Celtic, community would fade as the exodus continued and the town's population became diluted by immigrants of other descent. Miner and journalist Oswald Pryor was key in keeping Cornish and Celtic issues in the local public's consciousness for several decades; he was concerned at how quiet and sleepy the town had become and lamented that even carol singing at Christmas, entrenched as the 1900s unfolded, had lapsed some decades later.

By the time of Pryor's death in 1971, Donald (Don) Dunstan AC had become Premier of South Australia for the second time, an office he held from 1970 to 1979. Dunstan was very aware of his Cornish antecedents and thought that the state should be doing much more to celebrate its own Cornish heritage, unique in Australia in terms of the concentration in one region of people of Cornish descent. It is fitting that, 50 years from 1972 when Dunstan provided a grant of $1000 as seeding money to set up a festival honouring the Cornish, this book has grown out of several of the most recent of them. The festival, known as 'Kernewek Lowender' (using the old Cornish language) has taken place every second year since 1973, even in Covid-constrained 2021 – in the main growing in strength with every indication of continuing to survive. It is supported by the state government, Copper Coast Council, the National Trust, local businesses and the Cornish Association of South Australia (CASA). Kate Neale has described in her chapter how CASA began in 1890, with many notable local citizens, including John Langdon Bonython, among its inaugural members. Although CASA's membership numbers have waxed and waned over the years, it is the oldest continuously-operating Cornish Association in the world, the next oldest being St Ives which started 25 years later – as confirmed by recent former Grand Bard of Cornwall Maureen Fuller.

CASA has arranged some kind of seminar associated with the Kernewek Lowender each time since the third festival in 1977. At first these were more like mini-conventions, held in Adelaide over three days, Tuesday to Thursday, during the week before the events of the festival itself on the Copper Coast. Unfortunately, the program for 1977 was not kept, but the 1979 and 1981 versions each had a topic: 'The settlement of the Cornish people into the United States of America' and 'Methodism and the Cornish', respectively. There was a theme-related lecture on the first afternoon, interspersed with lunches and dinners and a bus tour on the third day to a site of Cornish interest: Adelaide Hills mine sites in 1979 and several Methodist churches in 1981. In that year a fourth day was added, involving travel to Yorke Peninsula and a 'Meet the Cornish'

Introduction

evening in Kadina. Participants paid $3.50 or $4.00 for the bus trip and $4.50 or $5.00 for the dinner in 1979 and 1981 – how times have changed!

The four-day pattern continued in 1991, with lectures, meals, excursions and a newly-introduced Cornish language workshop, but the lectures each time were on different topics according to the expertise of the speakers. By 1993 the event was down to two days' duration, still with a bus tour (to the Talisker mine site that year – $20 including lunch) and a hotel dinner ($17.50). The first day featured several talks, most of them relating to growing up in a Cornish community (Moonta Mines, New Zealand and Cornwall were featured). The 'Meet the Cornish' component was no longer part of the event's program. In 1995 the two-day pattern in Adelaide, with talks on the first day and a bus tour plus dinner on the second, was repeated. There were four talks on the first day, on topics related only in that they were based on matters of interest to people of Cornish descent (for example, the Victorian gold rush and Cornish pilot gigs).

In 1997 the shape of the event changed markedly, with a move of location from Adelaide to the Copper Coast, and the first of five single-day seminars, up to and including 2005, was held at the Kadina Golf Club during the festival week. This proved to be a very congenial location, with facilities that allowed both lunch and dinner to be catered at the Club. By this time the seminar was evolving to become more like those that have been held in recent years, but it was not until 2001 that a single unifying theme for the papers presented was specified. The first time a bound book of the day's talks was given to participants to take home was 1999. These two practices have been followed ever since. After 2005, however, another change of venue was needed to accommodate larger attendance numbers and a dinner at the end of the day was no longer feasible. In 2007 the venue was the Kadina Town Hall, but this was needed for other events from 2009 and the seminar was moved to the Wallaroo Town Hall. These two larger venues are both used for other events in the evening of the seminar day and so the dinner was discontinued.

Since 2001, each seminar has occupied a full day, from 9 am to 4 pm, with an introduction, eight to ten papers presented and a summary session. Lunch, morning and afternoon refreshments and a bound copy of the papers are provided to attendees, who each pay a registration fee to cover the expenses. The themes to 2009 focused on Australian Federation (particularly the part played by Sir John Quick of Bendigo), participation in wars, notable Cornish women, migration to Australia and the communities established.

The main intention of the seminar series, after the first three, has been to highlight the contributions made by people of Cornish descent to Australian society in a wide range of areas – no other regular event similar in nature has been held elsewhere or in relation to another country. Cornwall itself has not been completely ignored, of course, and has often been mentioned in contextual or sometimes comparative terms in the papers featured.

This book contains chapters from selected papers presented at the most recent half dozen seminars, held over eleven years from 2011 to 2021. The variety of theme topics means that we can illustrate wide-ranging contributions of Cornish settlers from South Australia's earliest days until roughly the middle of the 20th Century. The themes were:

2011 – The Ingenious Cornish: Inventions, Enterprises and Exploits
2013 – Cornish Life Beyond the Mines
2015 – The Cornish Were Here Earlier Than You Think
2017 – Another Side of Cornish Life – Music!
2019 – Cornish Australians Who Changed Our World
2021 – Cornish Contributions to Medicine, Health and Welfare.

The 2017 seminar was honoured in Cornwall in 2018 by the presentation of an Awen ('Inspiration') award from the Cornish Gorsedh, in recognition of its contribution to preserving creative heritage, traditions and the 'Celtic spirit of Cornwall'. Of 24 such awards earned that year, it was the only one given to a person or entity outside Cornwall itself.

Jan Lokan and Philip Payton

Before the mines: Early Cornish Emigration to South Australia

PHILIP PAYTON

Introduction

Not without reason, Cornish emigration to South Australia is generally associated with the development of the State's nineteenth-century copper-mining industry, and the growth of mining communities such as those at Kapunda, Burra and northern Yorke Peninsula, with their strong Cornish heritage. Even 'Australia's earliest mining era', the discovery and exploitation of first silver-lead and then copper in the Adelaide Hills in the 1840s, is linked inextricably to early Cornish immigrants in what was then the colony of South Australia. However, this emphasis, understandable and welcome as it is, serves to obscure part of the story – that Cornwall had been identified as an especially suitable source of emigrants *before* the mineral discoveries in South Australia, and that a significant number of the colony's earliest European settlers were Cornish.

This chapter examines the South Australian recruiting campaign in Cornwall after 1836. It asks why it was so successful, what types of immigrants applied for free passage, and from what parts of Cornwall. It notes Cornish collusion in the recruiting process – not least letters written home from early colonists, which appeared in newspapers and posters devoted to the campaign. It concludes by making the obvious point that, although these Cornish emigrants were attracted before the mineral discoveries were made, there were sufficient numbers with mining experience resident in the colony to facilitate the rapid exploitation of the silver-lead and copper deposits when they were located. Indeed, they were to play an important role in those early discoveries.

Radicals and emigration

The foundation of South Australia in 1836, a radical project initiated by Edward Gibbon Wakefield and his circle, coincided with (and was a product of) the 'Reforming Thirties', the movement for political change that swept Britain during that decade. The Great Reform Act of 1832 extended the franchise and abolished the worst excesses of the 'pocket' and 'rotten' boroughs. But for many the Act was merely the first step on the road of social, economic, religious and political reform, not least in Cornwall where Nonconformity – especially Methodism – lent moral authority to a growing popular radicalism in the 1830s.

In capturing the attention of the Cornish populace, radical Nonconformists had been aided by the *West Briton* newspaper.[1] Established in 1810, by 1831 the *West Briton* had achieved a substantial lead in circulation over its rival, the Tory *Royal Cornwall Gazette*, and had done much to articulate and mobilise radical opinion in Cornwall in the run up to the 1832 Act. Its first editor was Edward Budd, a schoolmaster and Wesleyan local preacher at Liskeard in east Cornwall. As Budd made clear in the first issue of the *West Briton*, published on 20 July 1810, the newspaper's purpose was 'to give the calumniated advocates of a temperate and constitutional reform an opportunity of explaining their real sentiments', for 'Reform of some kind is not only expedient but absolutely necessary'.[2] He chose his words carefully. But this did not prevent political opponents from denouncing him as a 'Satellite' of Richard Cobbett, the radical agitator, and from insinuating that he favoured the subjugation of Britain to 'the power of France', that he advocated rampant 'democracy', and that he expressed dangerous opinions that 'would produce a commotion that shall terminate in a turbulent republic or a military despotism'.[3]

The *West Briton* busied itself in the election years of 1812, 1818, 1820 and 1826 with its vigorous pursuit of Parliamentary Reform, drawing particular attention to the illegal activities of the 'Borough Mongers' in Cornwall. But it did not neglect other issues deserving of radical support. In particular, the *West Briton* supported the agricultural community in its opposition to tithes, high rents and high taxes, and did much to highlight the rural distress then widespread across Cornwall. After 1832, the newspaper continued to press for further reform in a variety of areas. As

Before the mines: Early Cornish Emigration to South Australia

Budd put it: 'Unless the abuses of the corrupt system which have so long cursed this country be rectified, the privilege granted by the Reform Act will be worthless'.[4] Abolition of slavery, reform of the Church of Ireland, poor law reform, and the admission of Nonconformists to universities were among the prominent causes championed by the *West Briton*.[5] As the *Royal Cornwall Gazette* complained in 1841: 'The *West Briton* has committed itself to those who glory in the name of Radical'.[6]

Isaac Latimer and South Australia

The *West Briton* was also a 'Dissenting Newspaper', according to its critics, reflecting the overwhelmingly Methodist-Nonconformist affiliation of its subscribers.[7] In particular, as Brian Elvins has observed, 'the *West Briton* emerged as a supporter of emigration', not least in the 1830s 'for those Cornish desirous of leaving for economic, political or religious reasons'. Like its Methodist readership, the *West Briton* embraced emigration as a radical 'improving' cause, Elvins explained, and 'when it referred to "the rage for emigration", as it frequently did, it did so in sympathetic terms'.[8] This was especially so after Isaac Latimer joined the staff of the newspaper as chief reporter in 1837. An accomplished journalist, Latimer had worked previously in the Midlands and in London for the *Morning Chronicle* (where among his colleagues was Charles Dickens), and he arrived in Cornwall in the midst of the 'Reforming Thirties'. He moved into Rosewin Row, a fashionable street in Truro, the *de facto* capital of Cornwall where the *West Briton* was published, and immediately turned his attention to the cause of emigration.

For many, the Great Reform Act of 1832, welcome as it was, left too many key issues unaddressed or unresolved. Some, fearing that further reform at home was unlikely or even impossible, decided that emigration was the only alternative. After 1815, Cornish miners had been attracted to the developing copper and silver mines of Latin America, and by the 1820s and 1830s Bible Christians from rural north Cornwall were already finding their way to Prince Edward Island and other parts of maritime Canada, as well as to the United States. Likewise, some Cornish families had been attracted by the offer of assisted passages to Cape Colony in the 1820s, and there were similar attempts to entice would-be 'free' emigrants (as opposed to convicts) to New South Wales and Van

Diemen's Land. Latimer swiftly immersed himself in this emergent 'emigration culture', carefully examining the motives and aspirations of those who chose to move overseas.

Typical of the grievances that sped many abroad were those articulated by Samuel James, a Methodist yeoman farmer on the Lizard peninsula of west Cornwall. He had decided upon emigration, he explained: 'To escape the heavy charges of supporting certain useless institutions'. There was also the desire to 'escape from supporting a State religion' and to 'live under free and useful institutions'. He wished to avoid, he said, 'supporting the abominable oppression of the Poor Law Bastilles [the workhouses]', and wished to 'go where the light of heaven, the vital air, the fish of the sea and the produce of the earth, necessary for the sustenance of man, are free for all as intended by their Great Creator'.[9] Eventually, Samuel James went to America, the 'land of the free'. But he might as easily have decided upon South Australia, given its early reputation as a 'Paradise of Dissent'.[10]

Isaac Latimer, meanwhile, had been drawn to the prospects of the new colony. He had studied Wakefield's scheme of systematic colonisation, and had observed the deliberations of the South Australian Commissioners. He arrived in Cornwall immediately after the foundation of South Australia, and was duly impressed by the enthusiasm that the new province had excited, especially (as he reported in the *West Briton*) when John Marshall, South Australia's Emigration Agent in London, visited St Austell 'at the request of numerous applicants in this part of Cornwall [to] hold a meeting . . . for the purpose of affording information as to the terms and conditions on which free passage may be obtained'.[11] Marshall was followed shortly by Rowland Hill, Secretary to the South Australian Commissioners, who held a similar public meeting at Falmouth intended to recruit a 'number of persons of the labouring classes' for the new colony.[12] A few months later, in March 1839, Isaac Latimer announced, once again through the pages of the *West Briton*, that he himself had now been appointed Special Agent for Truro and neighbourhood by the South Australian Commissioners.[13]

In explaining his role to the newspaper's readers, Latimer emphasised that 'the many evils necessarily generated under the old system of Colonial misgovernment will be avoided by the wise and judicious plans pursued by the promoters of the Colonization of South Australia'. Not putting too fine a point on it, he added that 'emigrants to South Australia will not come in contact with the mass of iniquity that prevails in the other Australian Colonies, as no convicts are permitted to be sent to this part of Her Majesty's dominions'.[14] Indeed, he insisted, 'NO CONVICT SHALL EVER BE TRANSPORTED THITHER ... the vice and demoralization of Australia has reference only to New South Wales, Van Diemen's Land, and Norfolk Island ... the morality of South Australia is secured in every way that can be thought of.'[15]

Turning to the other advantages of the colony, Latimer explained that there were free passages available for workers from a wide variety of occupations – shepherds, wheelwrights, farriers, brickmakers, and a host of others – as well as their families. As he put it: 'Every kind of laborer [sic] and artisan may, if married, of good character, and within the age prescribed by the Commissioners, obtain a free passage to this flourishing colony'.[16] There was also land to be bought in the colony, and he was 'ready to negotiate sales ... at a uniform price of £1 per acre, in sections of 80 acres each'.[17] Latimer issued posters to advertise the attractions of South Australia.[18]

Several posters listed the many other occupations of interest, elaborating the eligibility criteria for potential emigrants, as well as

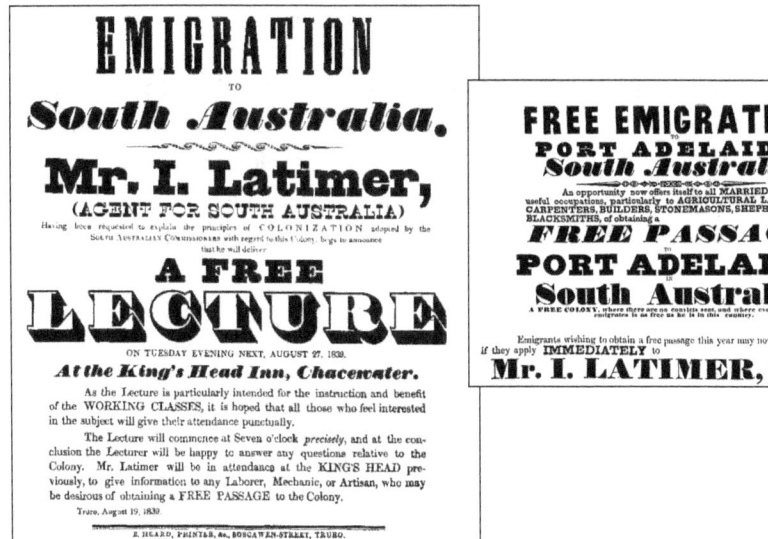

extolling South Australia as 'a delightfully fertile and salubrious country in every respect well adapted to the constitution of Englishmen'.

An experienced lecturer accustomed to speaking on 'improving' subjects – such as his talk on the art of printing at the St Austell Useful Knowledge Society in December 1839 – Latimer held a series of public meetings up and down Cornwall to advocate emigration to South Australia. He spoke at Bodmin, at the 'King's Head' in Chacewater, and at the Market House in St Austell. The latter, it was reported, 'was extremely crowded, by persons from a great distance', and many 'letters of the most pleasing nature were read, which had been received from Cornish emigrants, who all spoke in most flattering terms of the province'.[19] In publicising South Australia, Latimer was assisted by emigration agents appointed elsewhere in Cornwall – A.B. Duckham at Falmouth, G. Jennings in Penzance, John Geake at Launceston, and W.B. Wilcocks across the border in Plymouth. He was also helped by John Stephens' recently published volume, *The Land of Promise*, designed to advocate emigration to the new colony. Stephens was a Methodist of Cornish descent – his father was born at St Dennis, near St Austell – and his brother Joseph Rayner Stephens was a leading Chartist radical as well as Wesleyan minister. John Stephens would later emigrate to South Australia himself, arriving in January 1843, and under his editorship the *South Australian Register* became the leading radical voice in the colony, the province's equivalent of the *West Briton*.

In the pages of *The Land of Promise* Stephens explained the principles of the Wakefieldian system under which South Australia was to be settled. 'Land, capital, and labour, are the three grand elements of wealth', he wrote: 'the art of colonization consists of transferring capital and labour from countries where they are in excessive proportion to the quantity of fertile land, to countries where there is plenty of fertile land, but neither capital nor labour'.[20] If all this sounded rather hypothetical, then he was keen to emphasise that:

> The superiority of South Australia, not only over the British colonies in North America, and Africa, and Asia, but also over New South Wales, Swan River, King George's Sound, and Van Diemen's Land, themselves, appears to be established on testimony that cannot be disputed. Persons

who have had experience of all the other colonies in question agree in awarding the palm of decided excellence to the new settlement.[21]

As Latimer was quick to add, South Australia was:

> well-watered – and there have never been any complaints from the colonists of want of this valuable element; on the contrary, the letters from Cornishmen who have written home are very satisfactory on this point. It should be borne in mind that complaints of a scarcity of water do not relate to Port Adelaide, but to other settlements not connected with South Australia.[22]

Some ten percent of all applications in the United Kingdom for free passage to South Australia in the period 1836-1840 were lodged in Cornwall, such was the success of Latimer's publicity efforts and Stephens' purple prose.[23] But fine words were not always enough, and on occasion Latimer found himself negotiating with the South Australian Commissioners, those responsible for managing emigration and setting the rules, to accommodate the concerns of those considering applying for passages to the colony. In 1839, for example, many would-be emigrants complained to Latimer that, despite securing free passages to South Australia, they could not afford to pay the charges for accompanying children. As Latimer explained:

> there are hundreds of families, said an intelligent labouring man to me on Monday last at St Austell, across the water (alluding to the parishes of Fowey, Tywardreath, Lanteglos and their neighbourhood) who would be glad to emigrate, who would do anything to pay for their children, but who could not remove from their parish if it cost them a shilling.[24]

To his credit, Latimer took this up with the Commissioners, arguing successfully for a change in the regulations, and soon he was able to announce that free passages would now be awarded to children, so long as they were under one, or seven years and over, at the time of emigration.

'the attention of the enterprising Cornish of all classes'

Enthusiastic letters written back by early Cornish settlers found their way into the hands of Isaac Latimer and the other emigration agents, and some were reproduced in the *South Australian News* and the *South Australian Record*, newspapers published in London by the Commissioners and circulated throughout Britain to promote emigration to the colony. No doubt suitably edited before publication, they spoke eloquently of the advantages of the new colony. Religious and political freedom were frequent themes. 'We have a [Methodist] chapel as large as Budock Chapel', wrote Samuel Bray from Falmouth, with 'about one hundred in society'. Thomas Sleep, also from Falmouth, added that 'none of us desire to return to the bondage which holds our fellow countrymen', while John Holman insisted that 'I am freer than when I was in England … we would not be back to South Petherwin for £500'. John Oats agreed, writing pointedly from Adelaide to his relations in Cornwall: 'if you mind to bind yourself in the chains of slavery all the days of your life, you had better stay where you are'.[25] As the *Register* put it, reviewing a decade's progress in March 1847, 'enough has transpired through the press or the private communications of those who have cordially sent home their favourable impressions to arouse the attention of the enterprising Cornish of all classes, from one end of the county to the other'.[26]

Sometimes these letters were reproduced as handbills or posters, such as that published by A.B. Duckham in Falmouth on 24 June 1839. Addressed to tradesmen and labourers, the main text of the poster was a lengthy letter from one Marmaduke Laurimer, a Falmothian whose application for free passage had been successful, and who subsequently emigrated in the *Trusty*, which put into Falmouth harbour to collect its Cornish passengers on 9 December 1837. The ship arrived in Port Adelaide a little over five months later, on 19 May 1838, where Laurimer later penned his missive. Ostensibly candid in its description of the colony, Laurimer's letter was ultimately very persuasive, its apparent sincerity and telling insights a valuable tool in Duckham's hands. 'I should have written before', Laurimer confessed, 'but it takes some time for a person to be in a new colony to know its ins and outs'. Moreover, he explained, in 'the first place, no farming has yet been done in the colony; not an acre of corn planted; nothing but a few sections of 80 acres each, has been ditched'. He added that 'the colonists were not in possession of their country lands before last May; they have lived on their means the while ... shoes are dear, earthenware very dear ... Cornish ploughs would be broken to pieces in our soil'.[27] But if all this sounded unpromising, then Laurimer was quick to add that Adelaide,

> which only 2 years ago was a desert, is rising rapidly, some of the buildings would grace London itself; there is no colony that has risen so fast as South Australia. Work, I expect, will be very brisk near winter; the ground then, is soft: plenty of rains fall in the winter, and there is neither frost nor snow ... it is a fine climate, and very healthy.[28]

For those back in Cornwall who were nervous about the reaction of Indigenous people to European intrusion, Laurimer explained reassuringly that the Aboriginal population was harmless: 'I was out the other day with three others, unarmed, and met two natives ... I walked up to them and shook hands, they were pleased as you like ... I tell you this to show you how friendly they are with us'. There were also those at home who feared that the emigrants would be bonded on their arrival to the South Australian Company which, it was rumoured, had a monopoly of employment in the colony. Again, Laurimer offered reassurance, asking his mother 'to inform Dr Simmons of Flushing what I have said of the colony'. In particular:

> I am happy to tell him he was quite mistaken in his opinion that the South Australian Company are the only commercial body of individuals; the Emigrants are sent out by government, the company has no control over any person but such as choose to live under them; an Emigrant is free the moment he lands.

Indeed, Laurimer added, a newly arrived emigrant 'is allowed a home to live in for six months, with 14 days rations; his luggage is brought from the ship to Adelaide, free of expense, to his very door'.[29]

Marmaduke Laurimer's fulsome conclusion was that:

> South Australia is one of the most beautiful countries in the world; all the splendid descriptions of it at home were strictly true: its fine rich plains without a tree upon them; its trees are evergreens, its mountains forming a boundary at the eastern direction of the town [Adelaide]; its soil rich as nature can make it.

Finally, in a flourish that – as A.B. Duckham well understood – would create a stir in Cornwall, Laurimer offered his opinion (prescient, as it turned out) of the potential mineral wealth of the new colony. He predicted that South Australia's 'slate, stone, copper, silver ... in a few years will make it as rich as any country in the world'. As he explained:

> I saw a piece of silver ore about 28lbs weight, last week, that was picked up by a young man of the name of James Nichols, who was a shipmate of mine; on the mountains he traced the load [sic] for a mile, and picked up about thirty pieces as big as a hens egg, all of which he showed me'.[30]

'Penryn is nothing to Adelaide'

Laurimer had also been keen to paint a picture of cosy familiarity and good-feeling between the several families from Falmouth and Penryn that had emigrated together in the *Trusty*, an embryonic Cornish community that was already making itself comfortably at home in the new colony. His letter was full of news about mutual friends and relations:

> Alice Champion is married, a very good match she has got, her husband was in the Van Diemen's Land Company's Service ... The Montgomerys are doing well, Robert will be a father before you receive this letter ... I have seen Mallett, Robins, and Organ, the latter lost his son at sea – they are all doing well. If Mrs Mallett could see her younger son, she would kiss him to death. He has grown such a nice little fellow.[31]

Alice Champion was part of an extended family of that name, rooted in Penryn and Mylor. The Montgomerys were also Mylor people. On the date of his application for free passage to South Australia (23 December 1837), Robert Montgomery – described as a kitchen gardener and agricultural labourer – was twenty-seven years old, his wife a mere nineteen. They had no children although, as Laurimer intimated, a son was born shortly after their arrival in the colony. An early example of chain emigration, where those left at home were encouraged or persuaded to follow their more intrepid kinsmen, was evident in early 1838 when two other members of the Montgomery family – eighteen-year-old Sampson, a husbandman, and sixteen-year old Mary, a mantua [dress] maker – submitted applications to join Robert and his wife in South Australia.[32]

Before the mines: Early Cornish Emigration to South Australia

The Malletts, also friends of Marmaduke Laurimer, were another Penryn family. There was twenty-year-old Henry Mallett, described as a 'butcher, shepherd and farmer', together with his twenty-five-year-old wife and their daughters, aged three and one. Additionally, there was fifteen-year-old John Mallett, another butcher, probably Henry's younger brother, the 'younger son' who, as Laurimer put it, was 'such a nice little fellow' and would be kissed 'to death' by his mother back in Cornwall, if only she could see him. There is a glimpse here, among all the positive stories, of the downside of emigration, the sense of loss and extreme distance from loved-ones and old friends. So too in the experience of the Organ family, again from Penryn. Twenty-five-year-old Benjamin Organ – a saddle and harness maker from Market Street in that town – emigrated with his wife, aged twenty-two, and their child of sixteen months. Alas, this was the son lost to the Organs during the long and (especially for infants) hazardous voyage in the *Trusty*.[33]

Loss could also turn to frustration and irritability, as in the instance of Samuel Robins, a mason from St Gluvias Street, Penryn, another of Laurimer's shipmates in the *Trusty*. Samuel Robins had left Cornwall in optimistic high spirits (family tradition insists that, in a romantic gesture, he married his sweetheart Jane Penaluna at sea, off the Lizard, on 10 December 1837, the ceremony performed by the ship's captain) but, perhaps stupidly, he had placated his anxious family by promising to return home within ten years.[34] As his sojourn in South Australia approached its tenth anniversary, his sister in Penryn reminded Robins of his pledge to come back. But South Australia had been kind to Samuel and Jane Robins, and they had prospered and purchased land in Adelaide. The prospect of returning to Cornwall, now in the grip of the potato blight and food riots (and with further emigration to South Australia in full swing), was too appalling to contemplate. 'You remind me of my promise to return in ten years', Robins replied to his sister, admitting that 'I was young and foolish when I uttered that speech, and I hope you will not expect me to leave a country like this'. Indeed, he added, 'I cannot help thinking how inconsistent you write; you give me a wretched account of things at home, and expect me to leave a country that is flourishing fast … It is a pity you make remarks about this country, when you know nothing of it'.[35]

Warming to his theme, Robins berated his sister:

> A handsome expression to tell me that I am bringing up my children unnamed savages. Penryn is nothing to Adelaide – we can buy everything we want, from a needle to an anchor, and we have schools, chapels, and other institutions that are needful – Unnamed savages!!! What next shall we hear from home? You think this place is a wilderness – you are as much mistaken as though you were to say Plymouth is in France. I am determined to stop were [sic] I am and nothing you can say will alter my mind ... the remarks in your letter about Australia, it makes the heart sick.[36]

One can only imagine the stinging impact of Robins' forceful language upon his poor sister but we do know that a copy of his letter found its way to the *South Australian News*, published in London, where it became useful publicity in the current emigration drive in Cornwall, fuelled this time by the copper bonanza that Marmaduke Laurimer had predicted so accurately some years before. We also know that, like many of South Australia's Cornish population, Samuel and Jane Robins moved to Victoria during the gold-rush years, where Samuel found work as a bricklayer in Sandhurst.[37]

'Londoners in South Australia, are already put by by Cornishmen'

Penryn and Falmouth had emerged as an important centre of emigration to South Australia during the mid and late 1830s. But this intense interest was replicated across Cornwall, as Isaac Latimer and his colleagues tirelessly pursued their recruitment campaign. As early as 1836, even before Governor Hindmarsh had made his historic proclamation of the new colony, there was a clutch of applications from the Penwith peninsula in far-western Cornwall. At St Levan, thirty-year old James Bennetts, a carpenter and wheelwright, and his wife, aged twenty-four, applied for free passage on 21 April 1836, indicating that they were also interested in purchasing land in the colony.

Indeed, James Bennetts, his wife Hannah and their four young children were very early emigrants to South Australia, arriving in December 1836 at Holdfast Bay on the *Buffalo*, the first official ship to come with passengers to the South Australian mainland (as distinct

Before the mines: Early Cornish Emigration to South Australia

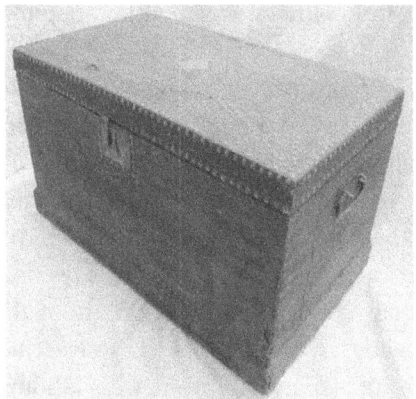

from Kangaroo Island). The ship's manifest has them as coming from Trevehar, St Levan, Cornwall, which most likely was the hamlet of Trebehor. The South Australian Migration Museum holds a trunk bearing the inscription:

> Jas Bennetts
> Trebehor Farm
> Near Adelaid
> South Austerila
> [*sic*]

It seems that James did purchase some land as intended, which he named after his place of origin in Cornwall.[38] Whether he acquired the trunk after he had come to Australia, or it was sent to him with belongings some time after his initial voyage, is not known.

At nearby Madron, James Bennetts' kinsman, Pascoe Grenfell, another wheelwright, also submitted an application. Grenfell's wife was thirty-years old, and they had three sons (aged ten, three and one) and three daughters (aged eleven, eight and six). But Grenfell himself was thirty-four, four years over the formal age limit, and anxious that he might prove ineligible, he explained that in the last resort he would be prepared to pay for his own passage. At neighbouring Sancreed, John Richards, an agricultural labourer and sheepshearer, expressed an interest in emigrating to South Australia, as did his namesake, another John Richards (a labourer) further east at Falmouth. Much further east, at Warleggan on Bodmin Moor, an application for free passage was submitted by one John Harmer – but we know that his application was either rejected or withdrawn, for we find him applying again three years later in 1839.[39]

By 1837 this trickle of Cornish applicants had turned to a constant stream, some ninety-seven being received during the year from adult males (usually in their capacities as heads of households), with another twenty-three from single or widowed women (married women were included on their husbands' applications, and were not recorded separately). Penryn and Falmouth, as we have seen, featured prominently in these applications. But now information about the new colony was spreading far and wide, from Stithians in the west to Lewannick in the east. The largest group of male applicants were labourers, and they came from across Cornwall – Richard Cornelius at Redruth Highway, Zacharias Gray from Holmbush, St Austell, William Hoskyn from Penquite, St Breward, Thomas Sleep from Linkinhorne … But many sported crafts and trades, important skills badly needed in infant South Australia, and their applications were usually looked upon favourably. There was William Carne, for example, a carpenter and joiner from Penryn, J. Paul, a boot and shoemaker from Bodinnick-by-Fowey, and William Scown, a bricklayer and mason from Launceston. Most of these 1837 applicants were accepted, those not sailing in *Trusty* emigrating in the *Emma*, *Red Admiral* and *Katherine Stewart Forbes*.[40]

In 1838 the stream became a flood, the number of applications for free passage expanding to 170. Again, they are marked by their geographical diversity – from Torpoint and Tresmeer, Altarnun and St Blazey and St Ewe, Perranarworthal and Wendron and Towednack. There was a maltster from Ruan High Lanes, a blacksmith from St Dominick, a thatcher from Hayle Foundry, a harness maker from Calstock, and very many more. The following year, 1839, the total applications more than doubled, reaching 360. This time, forty-five were miners – ten from the parish of Gwennap (the heartland of Cornish copper), and others ranged across a variety of mining parishes, such as Marazion, Redruth, Illogan, Perranzabuloe, St Austell and St Blazey. This may have reflected the interest provoked by early indications of South Australia's potential mineral wealth, such as that intimated by Marmaduke Laurimer. But it is at least equally likely that, in aspiring to emigrate, miners and their families wished to leave their arduous, dangerous lives behind them,

Before the mines: Early Cornish Emigration to South Australia

hoping to find new prosperity overseas as farmers or trades people, acquiring property into the bargain. Alongside the miners, there were applications from agricultural districts across Cornwall, such as St Goran and Gerrans on the Roseland peninsula, and Landrake and North Petherwin (the latter then still formally part of Devon, despite being west of the Tamar) in the east. There was a dairymaid from North Hill, another from St Clether, and no fewer than four from Bodmin. There were bonnet-makers from Helston and Truro, seamstresses from Crowan, Lostwithiel and Penzance, and a washerwoman from Gwennap. Again, many of these 1839 applicants were accepted, voyaging in the *Somersetshire*, *Cleveland*, *Recovery*, and the ill-fated *Java* in which a number of passengers, Cornish among them, died during a long and disease-ridden journey to Port Adelaide.[41]

In 1840 the number of Cornish applicants declined slightly, to just over 300, although in the copper heartlands of Camborne, Illogan, Redruth, Gwennap and surrounding parishes, the number of miner-applicants rose sharply to 132. Among their number were individuals such as Isaac Barkla of Mingoose, St Agnes, Francis Blight of Illogan Churchtown, Charles Glasson of Old Chapel Street, Camborne, William Menadue of Mithian, and John Climas from Rosewarne Downs. There were also two bal-maidens (female mine workers), Sukey and Jane Fletcher of Wheal Butson, St Agnes. However, non-miners continued to dominate the applications, as one might expect in this early period. There was, for example, forty-year-old Thomas Bonython, a shoemaker from St Columb Minor (and grandfather of John Langdon Bonython, later to become a South Australian newspaper magnate), together with John Bossnall, a tailor from St Thomas (by Launceston), Thomas Smith, a net and ropemaker from St Clement (near Truro), Mary Tregea, a domestic housekeeper from Perranporth, Mary Ann Arnall, a dressmaker from Camelford, and Jane Dunstan, a farm servant from Veryan.[42]

Those Cornish emigrants who arrived in the period 1836-40 formed an important element of Adelaide's early population, contributing to the mix of skills essential to the secure foundation of the new colony. In addition to the Bennetts family, two of the colony's earliest Cornish settlers were James and Harriett Harvey (brother and sister), who also arrived in December 1836 with Captain Hindmarsh in the *Buffalo*. They reputedly erected the colony's first limekiln, and opened a wheelwright's business in Adelaide. Charles and Mary Dunn, from Piper's Pool in the parish of Trewen, set up a blacksmith's business in Currie Street during 1839. They chose their friends from people they had known at home – Grace Sloggatt, together with Mr Dinham and Mr Harvey (both from Camelford) who together ran a drapery and grocery shop in Adelaide. Other Currie Street residents included James and Ann Verco, who hailed from Callington and arrived in South Australia in the *John Brightman* in December 1840. A mason by trade, James found work as Foreman of the Works with the colonial government. His friend, Philip Santo, from Saltash, who had also sailed in the *John Brightman,* was employed in Adelaide as a carpenter. Samuel Sanders, from Tideford in the parish of St Germans, was another early mason, arriving in the *Recovery* in 1839 and establishing a building firm in Waymouth Street, said to be responsible for several of the city's early stone buildings. Robert Dunstone, from Redruth, yet another mason, arrived in the *Java* in February 1840. Other early settlers included Joseph Allen from St Ewe, who set up a tentmaker's store in Leigh St, Adelaide, and Samuel Coombe, from Lewannick, who found work as a brickmaker.[43]

As before, many of these emigrants wrote home to Cornwall with news and impressions of the new colony. In November 1839, for example, Mrs E.J. Willoughby, originally from Newlyn, wrote to her father at St Clement, near Truro, explaining that in the twelve months she had been in South Australia, she had set up shop with a turnover of £150 per week. Glorying in her new-found prosperity, she added that she now employed a shop assistant paid £50 per annum, together with a personal maidservant on £18 a year: 'She is a Cornish girl, from near Launceston'. Her advice to friends and relations was unequivocal: they should join her in the colony, 'for if you are steady and careful, you could soon make your fortune'.[44] Likewise, in 1838, William, Joseph and James Pedler had written to their brother Thomas in Perranarworthal, their effusive letter soon finding its way into the pages of the *South Australian Record*. Labourers earned from six to seven shillings per day, they reported, while masons and carpenters could command between ten and twelve shillings. Sawyers might get as much as twenty shillings a day, they thought, while 'shoemaking' attracted £2 14s per week. As they concluded, the 'climate is excellent, especially for those of an asthmatic affection; therefore, the only thing that makes us uncomfortable is the absence of our families'.[45] The answer, of course, was for relations to join them in the colony.

William Scown, the bricklayer and mason who had emigrated from Launceston in 1837 in the *Katherine Stewart Forbes*, wrote home in similar manner, reporting that Cornish mechanics of all kinds were in great demand in the colony, and were often preferred to other workers – especially Londoners. He and his colleague had secured a lucrative government contract. 'We build as many homes as we like', he boasted, 'at such prices that we receive £1 per day by our own hands; this we have earned and received that we have worked in this colony'. Moreover, he emphasised: 'We have not only given general satisfaction, but other mechanics are surprised at these Cornish operatives. Londoners in South Australia, are already put by by Cornishmen'.[46]

'I could name many who left Cornwall, who found a grave in Australia'
Samuel Bray, from Falmouth, admitted that 'I would not persuade anyone to leave their native land, but all men are sure to do much better in this country than at home'.[47] His letter was addressed to his father but these comments were intended principally for his friends, John Peters and James Sawle. The latter, a stonemason and Methodist local preacher in Truro, took Bray's advice, and came out with his family to South Australia. However, Sawle's arrival in the colony coincided with the sudden financial crisis and economic depression of the early 1840s, after the initial land boom had spent itself. In 1838 Captain Hindmarsh had been replaced as Governor by George Gawler. Gawler was surprised by the apparent lack of progress and was disappointed that farming was still on a relatively small scale. Many of the colonists were still clustered together in Adelaide, and, Gawler believed, many preferred to speculate in land rather than actually tilling it. Accordingly, he initiated a new period of rapid expansion, and during 1839 some 170,000 acres of land were surveyed and sold. By 1841 half-a-million acres had been made available for settlement, while a number of roads and other public works were completed. Such developments were costly, and when George Grey replaced Gawler as Governor in 1841, he accused his predecessor of irresponsible over-spending.

Grey attempted to balance the Budget by adopting a severe deflationary policy. Business confidence fell to a low level, many agriculturalists found themselves in difficulties, and companies could not meet their debts. Capital and labour began to flow from the colony, one Cornish colonist later recalling that he had returned home to Saltash 'because of what he took to be the smash-up of South Australia when Governor Gawler's bills were dishonoured'.[48] James Sawle, meanwhile, had landed in a colony beset by gloom and pessimism, and was astonished by what he found, especially after all he had heard and read in Cornwall. He wrote an angry letter to his brother in Truro, railing against the colony and all its apparent failings. From the moment he had landed at Port Adelaide, he explained, he had been treated with indifference and suffered any number of humiliations and frustrations. 'After some delay and insolence of the part of the driver, you are brought into the midst of some very poor-looking wood huts', he complained, 'your luggage is taken or rather thrown down, so that your little glass, or whatever else you have, is often knocked to pieces'.[49] Worse was to come:

> After selecting what you can find of your things for the night, you ask where you are to lodge; you are directed to a wood hut, there may be a casement in the window-place, or there may not; however, there is no chimney for you to burn a little fire, and if there was it would be of no use to you for the night; you are now exhausted with hunger and fatigue, your dear children crying with hunger and cold. You now enter a place, out of which, perhaps, two or three or more of a family have been carried dead, probably some old dirty garments remain, your floor is nothing but earth and dust; the smell from the burning of the oil and other causes is almost insufferable.[50]

James Sawle claimed that fever and dysentery were rife in the colony – 'I could name many who left Cornwall, who have found a grave in Australia' – and he was scathing about its economic prospects: 'with regard to the abundance of labour, this is not true … The prospects of the Colony are getting worse every day – those who were thought the richest men in the Colony, are now proved to be worth nothing, so that trade is at a standstill'. His conclusion was emphatic: 'Do not let any of my neighbours be deceived by false representations'.[51]

Before the mines: Early Cornish Emigration to South Australia

One result of the depression was that emigration to South Australia was severely curtailed. The intake was cut back in 1841, with a mere 145 persons arriving from all parts of the United Kingdom and Europe during 1842. Yet the brake on emigration to South Australia did not last long. The bumper harvest of 1842 revealed a severe labour shortage in the colony, and to this was added the all-important development of the Glen Osmond silver-lead mines, after the discovery of Wheal Gawler in 1841 by a couple of prospectors, Hutchins and Thomas, 'we believe two emigrants from Cornwall', as the press reported.[52] This was near the spot where the 'first undoubted indication of the existence of silver-lead ore was made in 1838, on a section belonging to Mr Osmond Gilles, at the foot of the hills near Adelaide', perhaps the place where James Nicholls, Marmaduke Laurimer's shipmate, had picked up his specimens.[53] At any rate, a small company with capital of £6,000 was formed, and by April 1841 Australia's very first metalliferous mine was in production. Before long other silver-lead mines were opened in the locality – Wheal Watkins, the Glen Osmond Union, Wheal Hardy – and, as the colony's prospects began to improve, so interest in its fortunes was rekindled in Cornwall.

'some few Cornish miners ... quietly following pastoral and agricultural pursuits'

To the discovery of silver-lead was added, even more spectacularly, that of copper. In the latter part of 1842, copper was found in pastoral country at Kapunda, and by 1844, following further discoveries, a mine was in full production. Charles Bagot, co-owner of the mine, described how he and his colleague, Francis Dutton, had managed to get the venture off the ground. The 'result of our first trial was encouraging', he wrote, 'and induced us at once to prepare for opening the mine in a regular and permanent manner. To effect this I agreed with Robert Nicholls, a Cornish miner, for a twelve month to work on tribute. He forthwith began, and in a little time turned out a fine pile of good ore'.[54] Francis Dutton added his own perspective, explaining that:

> Cornish miners ... were not slow ... to resume those occupations most congenial to the pursuits they had been accustomed to in the mother country ... I may instance, in particular, two brothers of the name of

Nicholls, (I believe from the parish of Gwennap in Cornwall) who obtained the first set, for the space of twelve months at Kapunda.[55]

Acknowledging that many Cornish miners had come to South Australia to acquire land and to try their hands at farming, Dutton knew that the promise of high remuneration for their specialist skills would lure them back to their old occupation. As he put it:

> Amongst the general population of the colony were some few Cornish miners who were quietly following pastoral and agricultural pursuits; when we gave notice of intending to commence working the mine, the pickaxe was quickly resumed by them, and we gave them a liberal 'tribute' for the first year (3s 6d per £1) to set the thing going. These men were highly successful, and raised a considerable quantity of rich ore.[56]

Not surprisingly, the discovery of Kapunda turned the attention of Adelaide Hills prospectors from silver-lead to copper, with Francis Dutton opining that the development of new finds 'will undoubtedly be furthered by their engaging, as soon as possible, the assistance of practical Cornish mining captains, as the proprietors of the Kapunda mine have done'.[57] The Montacute mine, only ten miles north-east of Adelaide, was in production by early 1844, under the supervision of Captain Tyrell, a Cornishman. Abandoned temporarily in 1847, the mine was revived in 1848 under Captain Morcom, another Cousin Jack. Adjacent to the Montacute were workings of the Adelaide Mining Company, supervised by Captain Tyrell during 1848, and the North Montacute (opened in 1845), together with the Mukurta mine some three miles distant.[58] Nearby was Wheal Acraman, worked from 1848 to 1851 by Captain Long, a committee member of Adelaide's Cornwall & Devon Society.[59]

Before long, the Adelaide Hills mines had stretched further into the interior, to Tungkillo – where the Reedy Creek, Great Wheal Orford and others were worked by Cornish hands – and onwards to the tract of mineralised country running from Mount Barker through to Callington, where names such as Wheal Emma, Wheal Fanny, Wheal Harmony, Wheal Margaret, Wheal Maria, Wheal Prosper and Wheal Rose were entirely redolent of Cornwall. This, indeed, was the locality dubbed 'the Cornwall of Australia' by the *Register* newspaper, so apparent was the

Before the mines: Early Cornish Emigration to South Australia

Cornish influence in the mines themselves and in the villages, such as Kanmantoo, Callington and St Ives, that had sprung up in their midst.[60]

Conclusion

Although the resumption of emigration in 1844 precipitated a new round of arrivals from Cornwall, it was the existence of an initial reservoir of Cornish skills in South Australia, created 'before the mines', that facilitated the rapid exploitation of the colony's early mineral discoveries at Glen Osmond, Kapunda and in the Adelaide Hills. Thomas Roberts, who had worked in the small Greenwith mine near Truro in Cornwall, was one of those miners who had come out to South Australia in the early days, arriving in the colony in 1839. His experience may be taken as typical, an exemplar. Like other Cornish miners, he was persuaded to resume his former occupation when the extent of South Australia's mineral wealth became apparent. He found work at the Montacute mine in 1844, and was later engaged by the South Australian Mining Association to prospect on its behalf in the Adelaide Hills before being sent north in September 1845 to open the newly-discovered Burra Burra copper mine.[61] Thereafter, the Burra would become the principal magnet drawing Cornish emigrants to the colony, initiating a new cycle of emigration from Cornwall to South Australia. The 'Reforming Thirties' had sped Cornish settlers to the radical 'Paradise of Dissent' in pursuit of economic opportunity and social, religious and political freedoms. Now, in a change of mood and tempo, the newly self-styled 'Copper Kingdom' would draw thousands of Cornish miners and their families, anxious to escape the worst effects of the 'Hungry Forties' – not least the failure of the potato crop in the mid-1840s – and to earn a living wage in the colony's booming mining industry.

Postscript

Even James Sawle, hitherto a fierce critic of the colony, was forced to change his mind about South Australia. Writing in 1847 to his friend Thomas Crocker in Truro, he boasted that his blossoming agricultural property, purchased in the aftermath of those gloomy days when first he had arrived in the colony, was 'the richest you ever saw'. Moreover, he conceded, the colony's economic prospects were now exceptionally bright. 'I must tell you about our copper mines', he enthused: 'The Monster [Burra] Mine is the most noted ... I suppose we have enough for a world'.[62]

Notes

1. Edwin Jaggard (ed.), *Liberalism in West Cornwall: The 1868 Election Papers of A. Pendarves Vivian M.P.*, Exeter, 2000, p. xx
2. *West Briton*, 20 July 1810
3. *Royal Cornwall Gazette*, 7 April 1809, 15 September 1810, 27 October 1810; 12 October 1811
4. *West Briton*, 15 June 1832.
5. Brian Elvins, 'Cornwall's Newspaper War: The Political Rivalry between the *Royal Cornwall Gazette* and the *West Briton*, Part Two, 1832–1855', in Philip Payton (ed.), *Cornish Studies: Eleven*, Exeter, 2003, pp. 57-84
6. *Royal Cornwall Gazette*, 16 July 1841
7. Elvins, 2003, p. 73
8. Ibid., p. 78
9. A.C. Todd and David James, *Ever Westward the Land: Samuel James and his Cornish Family on the trail to Oregon and the Pacific North-West 1842–52*, Exeter, 1986, p. 9
10. The title of Douglas Pike's seminal book, *Paradise of Dissent: South Australia 1829-1857*, London, 1957
11. *West Briton*, 27 April 1838
12. *Royal Cornwall Gazette*, 29 September 1838
13. *West Briton*, 1 March 1839
14. Ibid.
15. Emigration Advertisement, c. 1839, reproduced in D. Bradford Barton, *Essays in Cornish Mining History: Volume 1*, Truro, 1968, p. 72
16. *West Briton*, 13 September 1839
17. *West Briton*, 1 March 1839
18. See note 22
19. *West Briton*, 30 August 1839
20. John Stephens, *The Land of Promise: Being an Authentic and Impartial History of the Rise and Progress of the New British Province of South Australia*, London, 1839, p. 1
21. Ibid., p. 85
22. State Library of South Australia [SLSA] D6029/21(L), Letters written Home by Cornish Folk who emigrated to Australia in the nineteenth century, collected by Dr John M. Tregenza, Poster issued by Isaac Latimer 'Free Emigration to Port Adelaide, South Australia', 4 October 1839
23. SLSA 1529, Alphabetical Index to Applications for Free Passage from the United Kingdom to South Australia 1836-40
24. *West Briton*, 13 September 1839
25. *South Australian Record*, 2 December 1839, 11 December 1839, 30 May 1840; *South Australian News*, September 1847

26 *South Australian Register*, 20 March 1847
27 SLSA PRG 174 George Fife Angas Papers, SA Colonisation Commissioners, 666, Poster issued by A.B. Duckham, 24 June 1839
28 Ibid.
29 Ibid.
30 Ibid.
31 Ibid.
32 SLSA 1529
33 Ibid.
34 Lillian Dell and Joy Menhennet, *Cornish Pioneers of Ballarat*, Ballarat, 1992, p. 39
35 *South Australian News*, July 1847
36 Ibid.
37 Dell & Menhennet, 1992, p. 39
38 The trunk was found in an 'op shop' in 2011 but fortunately someone recognised its significance and donated it to History SA (the History Trust of SA), a statutory authority, which then transferred it to the SA Migration Museum for display. The farm is no longer called Trebehor, but its location between Aldinga and McLaren Vale, south of Adelaide, is known (now 2887 Main South Road, Tatachilla).
39 SLSA 1529; see also Philip Payton, *The Cornish Farmer in Australia*, Redruth, 1987, especially Chapter 2 and pp. 118-32
40 Ibid.
41 Ibid.
42 Ibid.
43 Payton, 1987, pp. 30-1
44 *West Briton*, 24 April 1840
45 *South Australian Record*, 11 July 1838
46 *South Australian Record*, 10 October 1839
47 *South Australian Record*, 2 December 1839
48 James Penn Boucaut, *Letters to My Boys*, London, 1906, p. 118
49 SLSA PRG 174
50 Ibid.
51 Ibid.
52 *South Australian News*, August 1841
53 Edwin Hodder, *The History of South Australia from its Foundation to the Year of its Jubilee*, London, 1893, p. 187
54 SLSA A1118, published in SLSA 1348 Pioneer Association of South Australia Publications, No.9, *A Holograph Memoir of Captain Charles Bagot of the 87th Regiment*, Adelaide, n.d., pp. 34-5.
55 Francis Dutton, *South Australia and Its Mines*, London, 1846, pp. 290-300.
56 Ibid., p. 267
57 Ibid., p. 281
58 *South Australian Register*, 5 December 1846, 19 April 1848; *Mining Journal*, 2 September 1848

59 *South Australian Register*, 12 April 1848, 1 January 1851
60 *South Australian Register*, 30 April 1857
61 *South Australian Gazette and Colonial Register*, 27 September 1846
62 *South Australian News*, January 1848

Acknowledgement

The photograph of James Bennetts' trunk came from Elspeth Grant, then (2011) on the staff of the South Australian Migration Museum, part of History SA (the History Trust of South Australia). At the time, the museum was attempting to trace the provenance of the trunk, which had been donated to it.

Captains of the Kapunda Mine

GREG DREW OAM

Introduction

Cornish mine captains played a significant role in the development of the South Australian mining industry from the mid-1840s until the early 1900s. While the purser or mine accountant undertook the financial management of the mine, the mine captain or mine agent was responsible for the underground and surface operations. This included the supervision of the Cornish employment systems known as tribute and tutwork which were used in early South Australian mines. They also imposed workplace discipline and social leadership, often reinforced by their role as lay preachers in Methodist chapels.

The first metalliferous mine in Australia at Glen Osmond in the Adelaide foothills produced only a few tons of lead ore for export in 1841.[1] In late 1842, Francis Dutton discovered green copper ore in an outcrop while searching for stray sheep. He discussed the find with his neighbour, Captain Charles Bagot, who was already aware of the ore, through brightly coloured specimens collected by his son. The mineralisation was located on unsurveyed Crown land and, as required by the regulations, an 80-acre section was surveyed over the land.[2] Bagot purchased the 80-acre section around the outcrop in July 1843 and samples sent to England for assay in 1843 recorded 32% copper. The results were received in late 1843 and, on 8 January 1844, ore was raised at Australia's first commercial metal mine, then known officially as Kapunda.

Bagot travelled to Adelaide to engage miners and found that there was a considerable number of Cornish miners in the colony but most

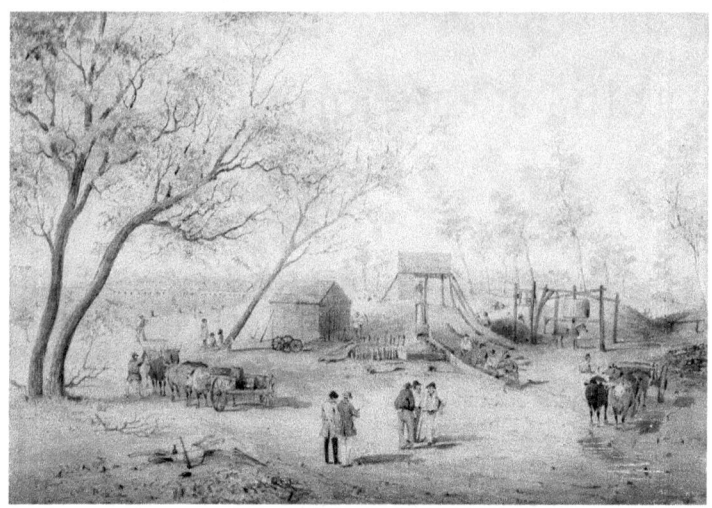

The Kapunda Mine, 1845, S.T. Gill
Note the first two rows of Mine Square cottages, left background

were uninterested as they had emigrated to South Australia to establish lives away from mining.[3] They initially demanded a high rate of tribute of 7s in the pound, which was one third of the value of the ore, but eventually he contracted several men at one-sixth tribute. The first lode opened was about 1.2 m in width and 10 tons of high ore were raised to a depth of 4 m. During 1844, an average of a dozen Cornish miners worked on tribute, and underground mining commenced. The ore needed little further dressing other than that which the pick and shovel gave and the mine produced more than 350 tons by the end of 1844, about 250 tons of which was shipped.[4]

The workings were initially shallow and conducted by a handful of Cornish miners, but by 1845 the workings reached water level and the first horse whim in the colony was erected for baling and hauling. The mine now required additional mining expertise and as a result Captain John Richards, an experienced Cornish mine captain, was appointed underground manager by Bagot in early 1846. Richards arrived at Kapunda in mid-1846 and was the first of six Cornish captains to have leading roles at the mine from 1846 until closure in 1878. Captain Thomas Roberts had been engaged to take charge of the Burra Mine in September 1845 and Captain William Jury was appointed manager at the Montacute

Mine in 1844. But Richards, who arrived in Australia in July 1846, was the first captain to be brought from overseas to manage the workings of a South Australian mine. He was the first of four Cornish underground captains throughout the life of the Kapunda mine. The other two of the six Cornish captains were a 'grass' (or surface) manager and the last general manager, Stephen Osborne. Here are their stories.

John Richards (1846–1848)

John Richards was born in Cornwall in 1796 and in July 1821 married Amy Eddy in the tin and copper mining district of St Austell on the central south coast of Cornwall. John and Amy's first child was born in St Austell but by 1825 the family had moved to Tywardreath, a prominent copper mining district just west of St Austell. The population rose rapidly there after the expansion of mining with the amalgamation of smaller mines into the large Fowey Consols Mine in 1822: by 1844, this mine employed 1700 people. Four children were born to John and Amy in Tywardreath between 1825 and 1833; by the end of this period Richards was a mine captain.

By 1838, Richards had been engaged by the Mining Company of Ireland and moved with his young family to County Wicklow, south of Dublin, where a daughter Amy was born. This company had been established in Dublin in 1824 and acquired mining leases all over Ireland, including County Wicklow and County Waterford. Richards was appointed captain of the Luganure Lead Mine about 10 km northwest of Rathdrum. The Luganure vein, which had been discovered in 1798 and first worked from 1809 to 1820, was acquired by the Mining Company of Ireland in 1824 and worked under the management of Richards from about 1838 until the mid-1840s when it was abandoned.[5] A major exploratory adit was named after Captain Richards.

So, how did a Cornish captain of the now-closed Luganure Mine in Ireland come to be engaged as underground manager of the Kapunda Mine? The answer is quite simple. On the closure of the mine, the Mining Company of Ireland recommended Richards in 1845 to Captain Bagot,[6] who presumably had links to the company. Richards arrived with his wife and eight children in South Australia on the *Medway* in July 1846 and they quickly made their way to Kapunda where a newly completed

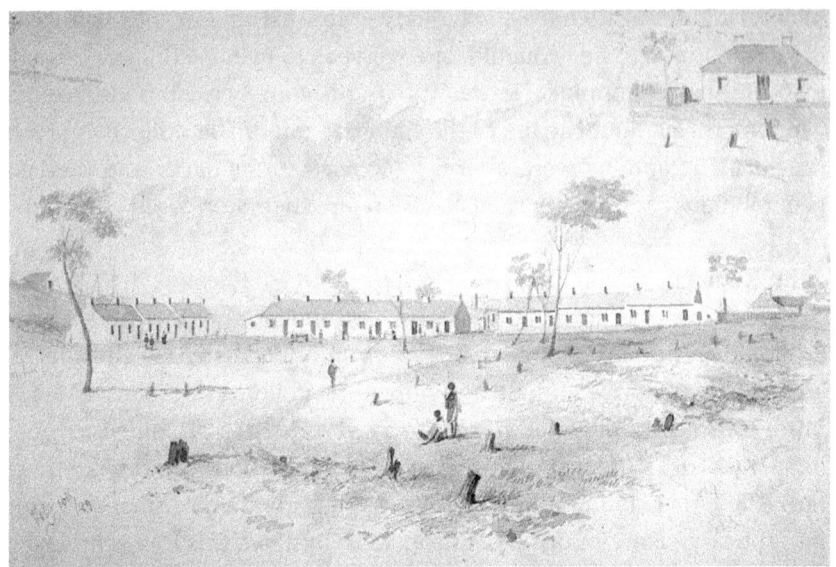
Mine Square Cottages, 1849, S.T. Gill

cottage was available for them in Mine Square. The oldest son John did not accompany the family but emigrated to South Australia in the late 1840s, married at Gawler in 1850 and travelled to Clunes, Victoria, to join the gold rush.

By 1847, a small mining village of about twenty cottages had developed on the northern part of the Kapunda Mine property and a walled quadrangle containing blacksmiths' and carpenters' workshops had been erected.[7] However, the horse whim which had kept the mine dry to the 15-fathom-level was not capable of handling the increased volume of water that would be encountered as the mine was deepened and Richards was responsible for the conversion of the mine to steam power. A second-hand, 30-inch double-acting beam rotative engine was purchased in Cornwall and arrived in 55 pieces at the mine in October 1847, where an engine-house had been built between Bagot and Old Main shafts.[8] An experienced engineer named Blackwell travelled with the engine to superintend its erection and Thomas Terrill, who had been engaged in Cornwall as the engineman to operate the engine, arrived on the *Lady McNaughton* at about the same time.[9] By April 1848, the mine advertised for a pitman and eight sump men to install and maintain the pumping equipment. Named the Draft Engine, it was the first Cornish beam engine to be erected in Australia and started pumping operations on 1 July 1848.

Captain Richards and engineer Blackwell were praised for their ability in erecting the engine and within two days the water level had been reduced by 5.5 m. Shortly after pumping operations commenced, hauling and crushing machinery were added. The Draft Engine allowed the development of lodes below the 15-fathom-level and facilitated further exploration. As a result, the 1.2 m wide 'champion' or main lode was discovered on the 15-fathom-level in September 1848. Unfortunately, Richards died suddenly aged 52 in September 1848, just as the main lode was discovered. He was buried in the original Methodist cemetery in the main street of Kapunda but his headstone was relocated to the side of the new church in 1858 where it remains to the present day.

William Tuckfield (1848–1850)

On Richards' sudden death the mine was without an underground manager at a crucial point in its development. But Bagot had a suitable replacement already working at the mine: Captain William Tuckfield. Tuckfield was born in the Cornish mining district of Gwennap in 1801 and married Constance Gillard there in April 1828. Their first four children were born in the mining village of Carharrack, just east of Redruth. Tuckfield arrived in South Australia with his heavily pregnant wife Constance and three young children in the *Royal Admiral* in January 1838 with a contingent of 112 Cornish emigrants;[10] five days after landing Constance gave birth to a son William in Adelaide. They remained in Adelaide for a time and, in May 1839, William's 22-year-old sister Mary, who had accompanied them on their voyage from Cornwall, married Richard Cornelius: he was an emigrant on the same ship and later became the captain of the Paringa Mine in the Mount Barker district. As mining had not begun in the young colony, William and family took up land in the Meadows area south of Adelaide, but by 1848 William had been engaged by Bagot.[11] On Captain Richards' death he took over as underground manager, but sadly he died less than two years later after a 'lingering illness' in June 1850, aged just 49.[12]

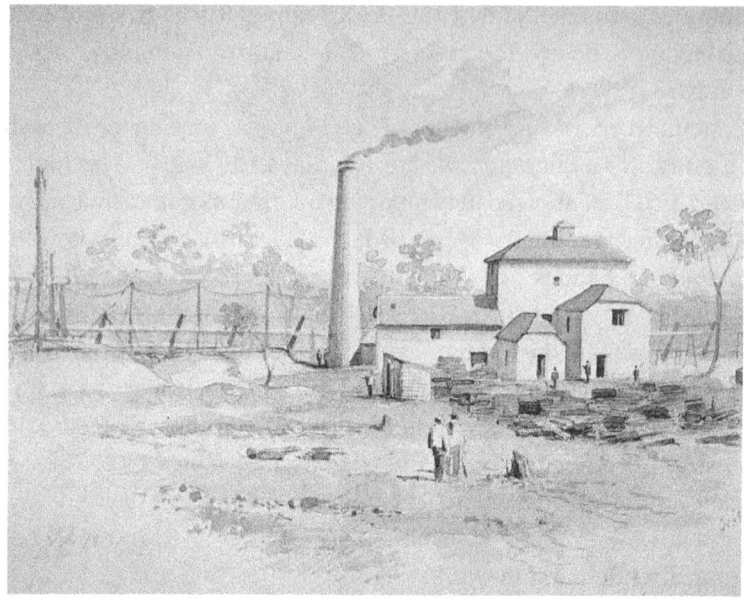

The Draft Enginehouse, 1849 S.T. Gill

William Barkla (1852–1861)

Due to the lack of miners in South Australia during the Victorian gold rush, there was no urgency to replace Captain Tuckfield and it was another one and a half years before the third underground manager, William Barkla, arrived at Kapunda. Barkla was born in the mining district of St Agnes on the central north coast of Cornwall in 1796 and married Elizabeth Prout there in 1826.[13] Their first four children were born in St Agnes between 1831 and 1835 but, by about 1836, William was contracted by the Mining Company of Ireland to manage their copper mine near Knockmahon in County Waterford on the Irish south-east coast. A major copper deposit had been discovered there in 1830 and by 1835 development work had been completed. This resulted in significant employment of Cornish miners with a workforce of about 1000 at its peak in the early 1840s. Cornish technology was imported to the area including a large Cornish engine which was erected in 1837; the area is now part of the Irish Copper Coast Geopark.

Five children were born to William and Elizabeth at Knockmahon between 1837 and 1851; in 1845 William Barkla was listed on a petition of miners whose children attended the Knockmahon school, requesting a site for a scriptural school.[14] In 1851, Barkla, now aged 55, was recommended to Bagot by the Irish company just as Captain Richards had been five years earlier. He arrived in South Australia from Liverpool with his large family in the *Waterlily* in January 1852 to take up his position as underground manager at Kapunda. A second engine had just been erected to be used exclusively for pumping and, under Barkla's management, it allowed the mine workings to be developed to the 60-fathom-level by 1860, with peak ore production having been reached in 1857. On his resignation in June 1861 to become manager of the North Rhine Mine, the miners gave him a presentation expressing their respect and admiration.[15] After his wife's death in 1863 William Barkla retired to the land at Auburn, north of Kapunda.

(John) William Perry (1861–1878)

Barkla was replaced by Captain John William Perry, who was born in 1813 in the Cornish mining district of Wendron, just north of Helston. At the time of his marriage to Betsey Thomas in 1838 he was a tin miner in the St Austell mining district. Their first two children, William and John, were born in St Austell in 1840 and 1843 but they died within three days of each other in April 1845. Perry arrived in South Australia in the *Cressy* in August 1847 with his wife and daughter Grace[16] and resided briefly at Hindmarsh where Mary was born in July 1848. About 1850, he began his career in the mine, gradually working his way up, until he was appointed underground captain when William Barkla retired in 1861. He lived in the captain's cottage in Mine Square. Perry took control of the underground workings at about the time that the mine had reached its peak in terms of ore production and employment.

Perry's first major job was to supervise the transfer of the Draft Engine to a new site in late 1861, a costly and difficult undertaking. The workings had already reached the 60-fathom-level and the losses by the company after 1863 were due to the increased costs of raising deeper ore. As a result, no further development was carried out until the mid-1870s when the workings were extended to the 70-fathom-level. When Captain Stephen Osborne was appointed superintendent of the mine in 1866, Perry retained his position as underground manager until the closure of the mine in 1878.¹⁷ During this period he had the difficult task of managing an aging and increasingly dangerous mine which saw the deaths of four miners between 1866 and 1870.

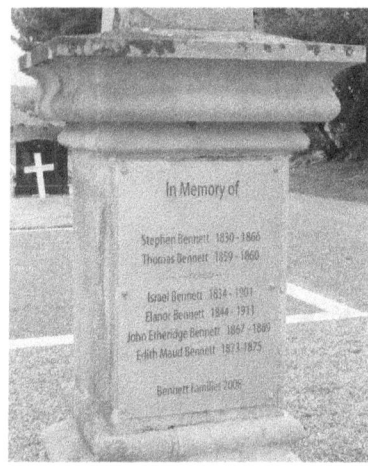

Monument near Bennett family graves, including Israel Bennett's, Kapunda General Cemetery

Israel Bennett (1863–1872)

The mine also employed Captain Israel Bennett as grass captain (surface manager) in 1862. Bennett was born in Chacewater, near Truro, in Cornwall in 1834 and by the age of eleven he was employed as a tin dresser under the supervision of his father Stephen who was a noted mining engineer.¹⁸ In 1851, he was working as an engineer at the Pentire Glaze Lead Mine, St Minver, on the north coast of Cornwall (where his father was the chief engineer) and later gained experience in Devon. By 1860, he was employed as a mining engineer in the Linares silver lead mine in Jaen, Spain, but became ill and returned to Cornwall in 1862; soon after he accepted the position to manage the surface ore dressing operations at Kapunda. About this time he married Eleanor Mitchell but no record of the marriage has been found; they lived in a Mine Square cottage where five children were born between 1864 and 1873. At Kapunda, Israel Bennett was reunited with his older brother Stephen who had settled there in 1855 and had established a business as an auctioneer. Stephen died suddenly in March 1866 and the firm of Bennett and Barton was declared insolvent several months later.[19]

After 1866 when the mine was leased, the operation of the Henderson plant was added to Bennett's duties. He resigned from the mine in 1872 to manage the Wolca, Edina and Boolboonda mines in the Mount Perry mining district about 360 km northwest of Brisbane. On his leaving Kapunda in May 1872, a large public meeting was held, at which he received several presentations, including one from two friendly societies and another from the employees of the mine. In 1874, he assumed the management of the Mount Perry Mine, a position he retained until 1890, when he was appointed a Queensland mining inspector for the Rockhampton district. On his retirement due to ill health, he returned to Adelaide. He is buried at Kapunda near the prominent sandstone memorial that was erected in 1867 over the grave of his brother Stephen by friends and brethren of the various friendly societies with which he was connected.[20]

Stephen Osborne (1866–1879)

In 1866, the mine was leased to the Kapunda Copper Company, a private company of Glasgow shareholders that was keen to treat the tailings and the near-surface low grade ore by the Henderson process.[21] This was a patented process for extracting copper from low grade ore (3 to 8% copper) using an acid leaching process, which was already in extensive operation in Britain and Spain. Cornishman Captain Stephen Osborne, who had several years of experience in managing the Alderley Edge open cut mine near Manchester which used the Henderson process, was appointed manager.[22]

Osborne was born in April 1831 in the parish of St Hilary, between Marazion and Breage in west Cornwall. Like his father, Stephen became an experienced miner in the district's tin and copper mines. In 1849, he married Arabella Wearn Pope in the nearby village of Perranuthnoe and the baptism record of his son William in September 1851 lists his occupation as 'mine captain'. There is no record of the births of his three sons between 1857 and 1864 and the family is not recorded in the 1861 census. However, Stephen was engaged as mine captain for the Alderley Edge Mining Company in early 1863 where he was responsible for the open-cut operations.[23] Osborne arrived at Kapunda with his family in

August 1866 to begin preparations for the erection of the Henderson plant. William Oldham, who had been mine manager since 1859, was retained by the new company as joint manager with Osborne, but this arrangement proved unworkable and Oldham retired in February 1867.[24]

Osborne's first duty was to direct the expenditure of about £60,000 provided for equipping the mine and construction of the treatment plant which commenced in April 1867. By the end of June 1867, the hill to the south of the mine workings had been transformed by the major elements of the Henderson plant which had been erected on three levels.[25] Low grade ore for the plant was mined from a series of shallow open cuts, which was the first use of this method in Australia. Copper-bearing material was loaded into trucks and then hauled up an inclined tramway to the treatment plant. The ore, previously estimated to contain 4% copper, proved to contain only 0.5% and the leaching process was an economic failure. By early 1878, the Kapunda Copper Company decided it could no longer continue due to the falling price of copper and closed operations: soon afterwards the Kapunda Mining Co. went into voluntary liquidation. The mine at its peak in 1862 had employed 400 people and produced about 13,000 tons of copper worth more than £1m over its 35-year life from 1844 to 1878.

Captain Osborne resigned in early 1879 but the Directors of the Kapunda Copper Company expressed their approval of his management of the mine over the previous 12 years by indicating that they would find him a senior position in one of their other mines.[26] However, Osborne had already accepted the management of the Belade nickel and copper mine in New Caledonia which he had inspected in 1876 and been offered a high salary to manage at that time. On his return to South Australia in 1882 he was engaged on a six-month contract to prospect the claims of the Mount Wells Tin Mining Company in the Northern Territory. In 1883, he took out a patent with Adelaide assayer Andrew Thomas for a process of extracting gold from pyrite using knowledge gained from the use of the Henderson process at Kapunda.[27] The Silverton boom in the Barrier ranges of New South Wales attracted him as a prospector in the mid-1880s and in 1888 he discovered mineralisation about 20 km south of Cockburn near the South Australia-New South Wales border where he was the first manager of the subsequent Mutooroo Mine. In November

1893, he travelled to the newly discovered Coolgardie goldfield in Western Australia to report on mining properties for the Neales and Osborne Prospecting Syndicate.[28] By early 1894, the syndicate had secured a claim of 30 acres at the 25 Mile line of reefs and commenced development work prior to floating the claim into a company.[29] Osborne abandoned the claim after six months and returned to Adelaide, suggesting the field was very much overrated.[30] He returned to Western Australia in 1895 as manager of the Starlight and other mines on the Kalgoorlie field, where he remained for several years. He retired in the early 1900s and died at Semaphore in 1912.

Notes

Advertiser denotes the *South Australian Advertiser* to 1889, *Advertiser* from 1889;
Chronicle means *South Australian Chronicle and Weekly Mail* to 1881, *South Australian Chronicle* from 1889 to 1895, *Chronicle* from 1895;
Kapunda Herald denotes the *Kapunda Herald and Northern Intelligencer* to 1878, *Kapunda Herald* from 1878;
Register denotes *South Australian Register;*
SA Gazette denotes *South Australian Gazette and Colonial Register* to 1839.

1 Both and Drew, 2008, p. 25
2 Drew, 2015
3 *South Australian*, 23 July 1844
4 *Register*, 14 December 1844
5 Hall, Mr and Mrs, 1843, p. 417
6 *Advertiser*, 2 August 1906
7 *South Australian*, 3 April 1846
8 Drew, 2017, p. 67
9 *Chronicle*, 1 August 1914
10 *SA Gazette*, 20 January 1838
11 *Kapunda Herald*, 8 June 1917
12 *Register*, 21 June 1850
13 https://histfam.familysearch.org//getperson.php?personID=I79475&tree=SouthAustralia
14 Power, 2014, p. 46
15 *Advertiser*, 6 June 1861
16 *Register*, 21 August 1847
17 *Kapunda Herald*, 1 December 1885
18 M.J.F.Royle, 1981, 'Mining and Mining Finance at Mount Perry 1869-1919'. In *The Journal of the Royal Historical Society of Queensland, Vol 11, 83-98*
19 *Kapunda Herald*, 3 August 1866
20 *Kapunda Herald*, 8 February 1867
21 *Register*, 13 February 1866

22 *Register*, 25 August 1866
23 *Mining Journal*, November 1863
24 *Kapunda Herald*, 15 February 1867
25 *Register*, 28 June 1867
26 *Chronicle*, 8 February 1879
27 *Register*, 9 May 1883
28 *Advertiser*, 11 November 1893
29 *Advertiser*, 8 January 1894
30 *Chronicle*, 12 May 1894

References

Both, R.A. & Drew, G.J. (2008), 'The Glen Osmond silver-lead mines, South Australia: Australia's first metalliferous mines'. *Journal of Australasian Mining History,* vol. 6, 21-45

Drew, G.J. (2015), *Discovering Historic Kapunda*. Kapunda & Light Tourism Inc.

Drew, G.J. (2017), *Captain Bagot's Mine: A History of the Kapunda Mine 1845-1912*. Drew, Belair

Hall, Mr & Mrs (1843), *Ireland: Its Scenery, Character and History, Vol 2*. How & Parsons, London

Acknowledgements

Three photographs of paintings by S.T. Gill (1818-1880) used in this paper are of originals held in the Collection: Art Gallery of South Australia, Adelaide:

The Kapunda Mine, 1845

Mine Square Cottages, 1849

The Draft Enginehouse, 1849

The photograph of the Bennett family monument was taken by the author.

Thomas Roberts: From Greenwith via Montacute to Burra

KEITH JOHNS OAM

Cornish mining in decline

Thomas Roberts (1806–1857), the author's maternal great-great-grandfather, was a Cornish miner – as were two younger brothers (Jonathon and Emmanuel); their father, also named Thomas (1776–1827), was a miner before them.

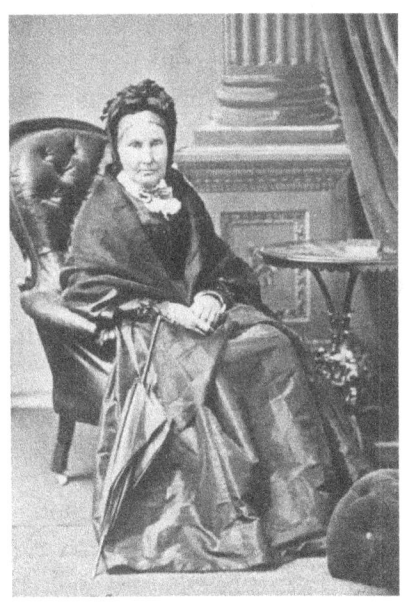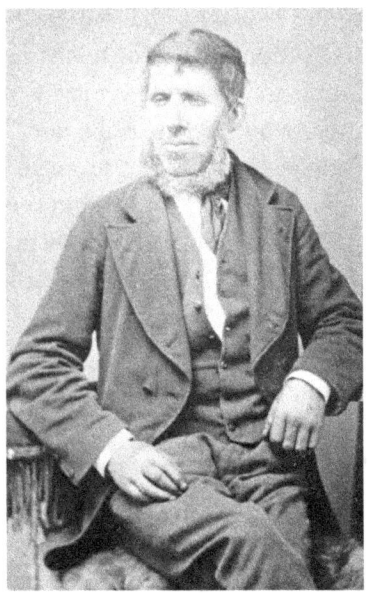

Hannah and Thomas Roberts

The Cornish copper and tin industry (which was of world-wide renown, following the advent of steam power during the period of the

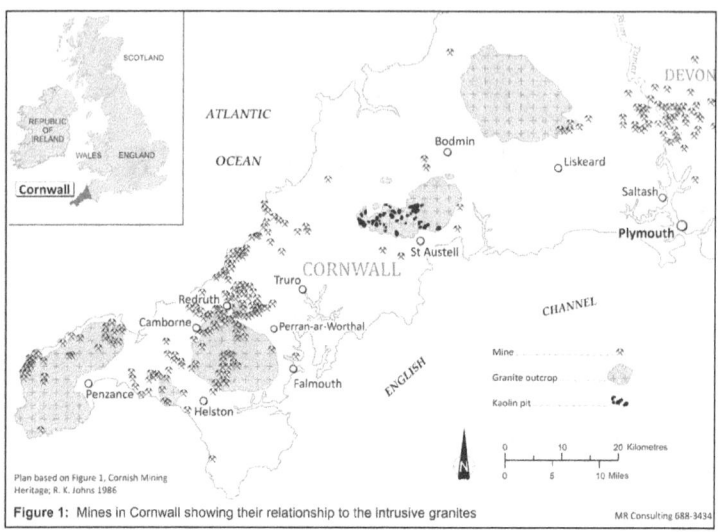

Figure 1: Mines in Cornwall showing their relationship to the intrusive granites

Industrial Revolution in Britain) was showing the first signs of decline by the 1830s. As shallow, easily-won ore had been depleted the cost of production rose as the mines were forced to extend operations to greater depths to recover lower grade mineralisation. Many Cornish miners had already taken their skills abroad to Spain, North America, Mexico and Chile, enticed by the promise of high wages, while others decided to embark on new careers and seek new opportunities elsewhere.

Thomas Roberts lived at Perran-ar-Worthal, in the parish of Gwennap, and was employed on the Greenwith Mine, five miles south of Truro. Both of these places are on the map of Cornwall's mining areas below.

Bound for South Australia

While no metals or metallic minerals had been discovered in Australia to that time, Cornish miners joined farmers and others to emigrate, particularly to South Australia. Other colonies had been founded as penal settlements, but the new Colony of South Australia (proclaimed on 28 December, 1836) was different – it would be populated by free settlers.

Those prepared to take their chances in South Australia included Thomas Roberts among large numbers emigrating in 1839. He, his wife Hannah and five children (William, John, James, Elizabeth and Harriet), were joined by his brother Jonathon, his sister-in-law Amanda and their son in boarding the emigrant sailing vessel *Sir Charles Forbes* at Penzance; they arrived in South Australia on 7 June 1839. Thomas acquired Lot 45 in Section 1, Hundred of Adelaide in George Street, Thebarton, adjoining blocks purchased by his brother. (Thebarton is shown just to the left of Adelaide on the 1845 map below.)

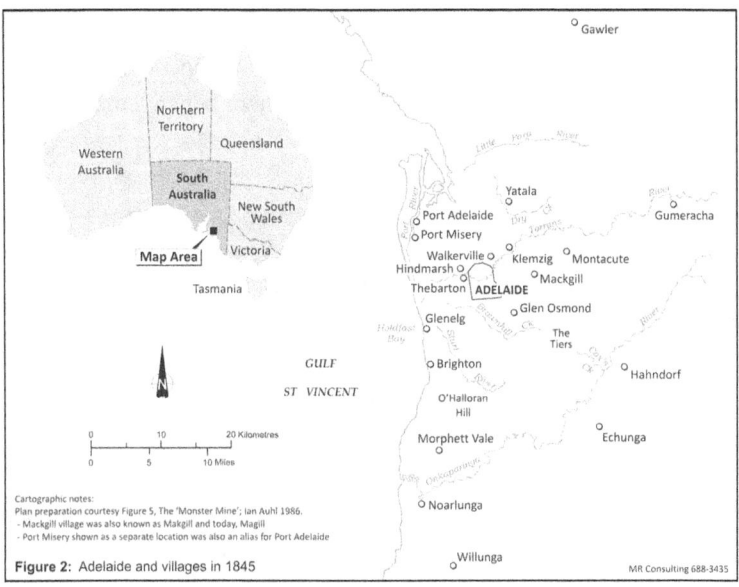

Figure 2: Adelaide and villages in 1845

Reproduced below is a letter, typical of those used by local agents to recruit suitable Cornish migrants to South Australia, sent to Cornwall by Thomas Roberts three months after he and his family reached the colony. The letter's arrival was reported in the *Royal Cornwall Gazette*, c. 1840, as was the letter itself:

> *The following letter has been sent home to his relations who reside at Perranarworthal, near Truro, Cornwall, by Thomas Roberts formerly a common miner. The letter, says the Cornwall Gazette of the 15th instant from which we extract it, is directed to Mr. W. Roberts, who will show the original to any one desirous of seeing it.*

Adelaide, September 22, 1839

Dear Mother, Brothers, – and Sisters, – We are happy to inform you that we are all in good health, and we have had no sickness since we have left home. We had a pleasant passage as Heaven could bless us with. We put in at the Cape of Good Hope. We wrote you a letter with Thos. Pedlar. We hope it found you in good health, as it is with us at present. The Cape of Good Hope is a very pleasant place; its harbour abounds with fish of various kinds. We cast anchor at Holdfast Bay on the 8th of June 1839, and at Port the 11th; landed on the 13th all in good health. There were bullock carts waiting to take our baggage to Adelaide which is about seven miles. We were put into the Government cottages. We had one week's rations served out to us. I lived there two months Jonathon [his brother] three months. I paid rent for three weeks, 12s .a week. Dear brothers, Johnathon and I have been working in a quarry ever since we have been here; we have 3s. 6d. a load; we have good masters; we receive our wages every week; we have not come under £4 a week each. William and John [two of the writer's children] work with us; they have £1 5s. a week. Dear brothers, we often think of you; we wish mother, brothers and sisters were all here; it is a pleasant country. Tradesmen are sure to do well here. Masons and sawyers are sure to do well here, and all tradesmen. We cannot recommend miners [The writer means to say he cannot recommend miners as miners; but they make the best of quarrymen, and receive excellent wages]. Dear brothers, we wish you were all here. We have bought two lots of land. 24 feet frontage each, in the city of Adelaide, for £3. We have bought one acre about half-a-mile from the city for £76; one lotment 35 feet frontage, 103 back, for £8. We have bought lotments for £3 10s. I built in the city, and Johnathon has one part. We have a fine garden planted for us of all kinds of vegetables. Johnathon is going to build next week adjoining.

Two hundred weight of best flour, £6 10s.; beef from 9d. to 1s. per lb.; best lump sugar, 8d. per lb; brown sugar from 3 ½ d. to 6d. per lb; coffee, 2s. per lb;. tea from 2s. to 5s. There is every prospect for steady men to do well. We have saved £10 a month since we have been here. Common labourers get from 6s. to 7s. a day; tradesmen get from 12s. to 14s. per day. The natives are very civil; there is nothing to harm us here. Land in the city is now selling for £1000 per acre. We have parrots very plenty – as plenty as sparrows with you.

Ian Auhl tells us in his book, *The Story of the 'Monster Mine'* (p. 29), that Thomas turned to farming after his quarry work, there being no mining activity in South Australia when he arrived. That was to change in only a few years.

The South Australian Mining Association (SAMA)
It was timely that an enterprising group of Adelaide citizens had the foresight to establish an entity (which dated from 16 April 1845) for the purchase, working or sale of the mineral lands of the colony. Its Secretary, Henry Ayers, had been instrumental in preparing the prospectus and, on 1 May 1845, he was signatory to an advertisement which appeared in the *South Australian* newspaper intimating that the Directors of SAMA were open to offers for the purchase of land containing minerals 'or to give premium for information afforded them as to the localities where minerals were to be found'.

The 88 shareholders held original scrip certificates, each of £5, totalling 2464 shares. The shareholders included: ROBERTS, Thomas – miner, of Adelaide (3 shares); ROBERTS, William – of North Adelaide, gentleman (7 shares); and ROBERTS, Jonathon – of Adelaide, miner (1 share). The company's first acquisition was of the so-called Montacute Mine, 10 miles north east of Adelaide where 20 miners were engaged under the charge of Captain Jury on sections 5536 and 5540. Records of several meetings of the Directors of SAMA mentioned the name Roberts. The record dated 5 July 1845 referred to several lodes in the locality 'adjacent to that purchased by Mr. Roberts'. Then, on 22 July 1845 it was resolved 'that Thomas Roberts and another miner [presumably brother Jonathon] be employed to open the lode in the north east corner of sec. 5536 ... it was resolved that the Secretary pay Thomas Roberts 10/- for his time and expenses attending the Directors in sec. 5536, 39 from the petty cash'. On 18 August 1845: 'Report received from Mr. Mildred that he had attended the operations of Roberts and his mate' and, on 30 August 1845, 'letter from G.A. Anstey recommending Thomas Roberts to the notice of the Directors, dated 26 August 1845 ... it was resolved to pay £12.0.0 to Thomas Roberts and his mate for four weeks work on sec. 5536'.

Copper ore at Burra

On 9 June 1845 a shepherd, William Streair, met with Henry Ayers to impart knowledge of his discovery and display specimens of copper minerals taken from a deposit, 100 miles north of Adelaide, referred to as Princess Royal; he was paid £8 by SAMA 'for showing the land, plus £1.5.0 for his expenses in Adelaide'. Shortly afterwards, another shepherd, Thomas Pickett, disclosed the discovery of another copper-bearing outcrop adjacent to the Burra Creek, eight miles to the north of the former – it was referred to as the Northern Lode. Records of the meeting of Directors of SAMA, dated 16 September 1845, referred to payment of £10.0.0 to Thomas Pickett, 'account of discovering North Lode'.

South Australia's Governor George Grey had provided for the acquisition of land, beyond surveyed counties, by means of purchase of the land defined by a special survey – a compact block whose shape was to be in the form of a parallelogram, no one side of which would be more than twice the length of any other, resulting in a rectangle measuring 8 miles by 4 miles. The purchaser would be required to lodge £20,000 for an area of 20,000 acres.

The Burra Special Survey was completed in August 1845, barely encompassing the two deposits of interest at diametrically opposite corners. In due course, rival bids were resolved as being from two groups – one representing capital and pastoral interests, including operators of the newly-opened Kapunda Copper Mine (who were referred to as the 'Nobs'), the other, representing Adelaide business identities (referred to as the 'Snobs'). By each party agreeing to contribute £10,000 they were able to satisfy the financial requirement for allotment of the single block surveyed, which would be split into two rectangular sections each of 10,000 acres.

Ownership of these sections was to be decided by ballot. The Nobs drew the Princess Royal in Section 2, which later proved to be a deposit of little consequence. At the north-western extremity of Section 1 the Northern Monster lode became the property of the South Australian Mining Association. The *South Australian* of 23 September 1845 (p. 2) reported that 'both parties seem perfectly satisfied with the decision; each affirms they have procured the half they wished for'. The article continued on to say that twenty applications had been received for the position of Captain, to commence work at the newly acquired property near Burra Creek, but that 'some of the candidates do not know B from a bull's foot'!

Thomas Roberts was appointed Captain of the Burra Burra Mines and took 10 miners with experience in Cornwall with him to Burra; they included his brother Jonathon and his son, William, the author's great-grandfather. In a letter signed by Henry Ayers, 'Sammie's' Secretary, dated 24 September 1845, detailed instructions (for which Ayers became renowned) were addressed to Roberts:

> The 10 Miners and mining smith engaged by you for one month from this date will be under your control. Your pay will be £3 per week, the pay of each man 35/- per week, the whole party finding themselves in rations and paying their travelling expenses, the luggage and stores for the men being conveyed to the mine by drays employed by the Association. A cart with 2 horses is provided for conveying the men to the mine, but as the cart will contain tools the whole of them must ride and walk in turn.
>
> On arrival of the first party at the mine, if the horses are not too much jaded by their journey, you will send on one of your party to meet the walking party in order that as little delay takes place on the road.
>
> No times must be lost on arrival to obtain ore for loading the drays which accompany the party and for any other drays that may be hereafter dispatched.
>
> You will commence the working of the mines as you think advisable not only for the purpose of raising as much ore as possible during your present engagement but with a view to future operations.
>
> As you take with you two tarpaulins for the use of the men you need not lose much time in erecting huts.
>
> You will brand the cart and horses and all other articles that you can with the brand of the Association and you will be held responsible for the safekeeping and careful management of the tools, materials etc. provided for the use of the party.
>
> You must communicate to me (for the information of the directors) all particulars with reference to your operations by every opportunity that offers and particularly to the probable quantity of ore that you could raise

within a month with your present party and if it would be desirable to put a greater number of men immediately.

I understand there is a bunch of ore superior to the ore you know of towards the south east of the great lode, and you will use every spare moment in examining the land, and if you can send me a plan of what you discover, it would be satisfactory to the directors.

The sappers and miners are now on their way out to survey more land at the north-east angle of our boundary; you will consider it part of your duty to examine this and report especially on it, sending in samples of what you find with the direction in which the lodes, if any, appear to run. I wish you to understand that on the success and good management you are able to display on this occasion will depend on some degree how far the directors will patronise you in their future operations.

Before the expiration of your engagement you will again hear from me.

Meetings of Directors of SAMA

The mine, initially called 'Great Wheal Grey', was in operation by late September 1845. Details of materials needed and steps taken to open it up are recorded in minutes of meetings of the Mining Association's Directors at the time. Here is an example:

30 September 1845

A committee appointed on 22 September 1845 reported that:

they have engaged Thomas Roberts to take charge of the miners for 1 month to be paid the usual Captain's wages of three pounds per week. They have also engaged 10 miners and a mining smith for a like period to be paid 35/- for one week each, funding themselves in rations, but being at liberty to draw £1 each in advance and to give orders on the Association for stores to the extent of about £15 which will be deducted from their wages. Their wives to be at liberty to draw 12/- a week.

Your committee found it necessary to purchase the several articles mentioned in the paper herewith annexed marked A. *The memorandum referred to in the annexed reports:*

Smith's Tools, 1 anvil, 1 pr. Bellows, 1 Forge Back, 2 Two Irons, 1 Hammer, 1 Tongs, 1 Sledgehammer, 2 Files.

Thomas Roberts: From Greenwith via Montacute to Burra

Materials, Iron bars, 200 Board Pailing, 12 lbs. Pailing Nails, 12lbs. various Nails, 32lbs. Rope, odd lots of rope, 3lbs Candles, 2 Bales Twine, 2 quires Brown Paper, 2 bars Shear Steel, 3 Blister Steel, 6 casks Blasting Powder.

Implements, 1 large Beam Scales and Chains for weighing ore, 6 ½ cwt, 1¼ cwt, 17 lb. weights, 1 Grindstone, 1 Water cask, 1 small bucket, 2 Dray Covers.

Mason's Tools, 1 Hammer, 2 Trowels.

Miners' Tools, 2 Wheelbarrows, 2 Hand Barrows, 6 Cornish Shovels, 2 Crow Bars, 1 Rammer, 7 Borers, 18 Picks, 6 Gads, 18 Wedges for Picks, 4 Large Hammers.

Other Tools etc. 5 Augurs, 6 Gimlets, 1 Hand Saw, 2 felling Axes, 1 narrow axe and handle, 1 adze, 2 Claw Hammers, 2 Pick Axes, 3 Hand Saw Files, 1 spoke shave.

Two grey horses, 2 sets of Harness and outriggers, saddle, bridle and 2 pair hobbles, 2 Tether ropes and head stalls, one cart whip and three seat straps, 1 Leather strap.

Your committee agreed with Mr. Hack [early pioneer John Barton Hack] for the cartage of the tools, stores etc to the mine to remain there for two loads of ore of about two tons each and to return with the same to Town for £16.

Your committee have since despatched eight drays belonging to different parties and have agreed to pay them at the rate of £3 per ton.

Your committee beg to refer to the letters of the Secretary addressed to Messrs. Roberts and Hack and dated respectively the 26th inst. As showing the instructions given them by the Committee.

On 24 September 1845 the first charges of gunpowder were fired to expose a large mass of rich red oxide of copper. In the course of a few hours after the arrival of the party at the site 'about 10 tons of the most splendid copper ore was placed in the dray and departed for Adelaide the following morning. A few days later, 16 more drays and their drivers were sent up to bring away their loads of ore'. It was a modest start to the Burra Burra mines that would see the population of the colony quadrupled in seven years and the value of copper exports come to exceed the value of exports of wool and grain. In 1851 Burra, with a population of 5000, was the largest inland town in Australia and was exceeded in size at the time only by Sydney, Melbourne, Hobart, Adelaide, Launceston and Geelong.

Thomas Roberts had a not insignificant role in contributing to the Colony of South Australia's development early in its history.

References

Auhl, I. (1986), *The Story of The 'Monster Mine'*. Investigator Press, Hawthorndene, South Australia

Johns, R.K. (1986), *Cornish Mining Heritage*. Special Pub. no. 5, South Australian Dept of Mines & Energy

Johns, R.K. (1993), Sir Henry Ayers, First President of the Institute and the Burra Burra Mines. Australasian Institute of Mining & Metallurgy Centenary Conference, Adelaide, pp. 31-37

Johns, R.K. (1996), The Burra Burra Mines – 150 Years On. *Australasian Institute of Mining & Metallurgy Bulletin*, February, pp. 40-41

Johns, R.K. (2006), The Cornish at Burra, South Australia. *Journal of Australasian Mining History*, vol. 4, September, pp. 166-182

Johns, R.K. (2012), *Croweaters from Cornwall of Mine*. O'Neil Historical & Editorial Services, Adelaide

Acknowledgements

Some of the material in this paper is drawn from letters and minutes pertaining to the South Australian Mining Association (SAMA) and its secretary, Sir Henry Ayers. These are held at the State Library of South Australia, Adelaide, as is the letter, written by Thomas Roberts back to his family in Cornwall (in addition, please see the list of the author's publications).

The diagrams in Figures 1 and 2 are used courtesy of the South Australian Department for Energy and Mining (known as the Department of Mines and Energy when the author was its Director-General).

The photographs of Thomas and Hannah Roberts are from the author's own collection.

'Songs of the Old Home': Cornish Carols in South Australia

KATE NEALE

Introduction

Writing in 1949 under the pen-name John Penwith, J.H. Martin, a long-time contributor to the *Cornishman* newspaper, was concerned about the state of Cornish carols. Despite the 19th century upsurge of interest in carol singing and the British folk-song revival a century later, Martin felt that Cornish carols had suffered a damaging neglect:

> It was these carols, the 'curls' composed by the miners themselves, which form a really valuable contribution to music. Unfortunately, they are seldom heard at all in Cornwall today and are more likely to be sung in Cornish centres overseas than in the county of their origin. [...] But some of the old music books may remain, and who knows what treasure may still turn up in Butte or Detroit, Johannesburg or Adelaide?[1]

Martin's mention of Adelaide here is not a coincidence; he had recently heard a BBC broadcast of Cornish carols from Maughan Church in central Adelaide and been impressed with the vitality of the singers, and consequently saddened by the carols' comparative decline in popularity in Cornwall itself. Carols were peculiarly popular with Cornish migrants of the 19th and 20th centuries, and were documented across the USA, South Africa, and of course in Australia. Indeed, Philip Payton has noted that the carolling traditions lie at the intersection of two well-established Cornish cultural signifiers: Methodism and music, thereby becoming particularly emblematic of Cornish identity overseas.[2]

This chapter focuses, therefore, on one element of my doctoral research completed at Cardiff University and the Institute of Cornish

Studies at the University of Exeter in 2019: the early history and development of Cornish carolling in the Copper Triangle (northern Yorke Peninsula, South Australia) and Adelaide.[3] I examine the emergence of the Cornish carols in South Australia, exploring their early history and uncovering some of the circumstances of their growth into a key facet of Cornish culture in that part of Australia. To this end, I first discuss the early accounts of carolling in the Copper Triangle, showing that the practice was gradually associated with Cornish migrants. I then consider the actual musical material of Cornish carols in the Copper Triangle, examining musical manuscripts, the development of printed sources, and their dissemination. I conclude by showing how the Cornish Association of South Australia, in its earliest years, contributed to the popularisation of the carols through the activities of the Cornish Musical Society.

What are Cornish carols?

Before exploring Cornish carols in South Australia, it is first necessary to give a brief overview of the musical form of the Cornish carol itself. In 1928, Dr Ralph Dunstan described the Cornish carols in a manner that was often echoed by later writers:

> [...] the chief characteristics of the tunes are (a) a more or less florid 'air' (or treble, though often sung by men) [...] (b) a good "rolling" bass; (c) a "counter-tenor" [...] (d) frequent 'points of imitation', one part after another imitating a short phrase or theme proposed by the air, counter or bass [...][4]

Dunstan's 'points of imitation' refer to the fugue, a musical structure within which different voices or parts 'enter successively in imitation of each other', creating an overlapping and interweaving of different parts.[5] Here, Cornish carols are part of a broader British genre of post-reformation fuging psalmody that dates from the eighteenth century. While the fugue has a long history in Western art music, historical musicologist Nicholas Temperley states that the first examples of fuging church music are found in printed collections in the late 1600s, with the full imitative four-part fuging style becoming popular by the 1740s.[6] Country music teachers and itinerant musicians working in parish churches adopted and developed the style during the eighteenth century, which became very popular across rural England.[7]

'Songs of the Old Home': Cornish Carols in South Australia

The style took a strong hold in Cornwall, perhaps as a result of the importance of singing in Methodist worship. This is a little ironic since John Wesley was in fact vehemently opposed to the use of the fuging forms for choral singing since it obscured the words of hymns, and made music more into a performance in its own right rather than as an aid to worship.[8] Nevertheless, the fuging style remained popular in Cornwall while its appeal declined elsewhere in the UK, and eventually became particularly associated with Christmas carols. It was used for carol texts from both local writers and well-known authors such as Nahum Tate, Isaac Watts and James Montgomery. The fuging genre is also related to 'West Gallery' music, so well described by Thomas Hardy in *Under The Greenwood Tree*.[9] Rural churches were often unable to immediately replace organs that had been removed during the Reformation. As a result, many country choirs of this period employed local musicians, who were often housed in a gallery at the western side of the church, to provide the accompaniment for singing.[10] This style persisted in many places until the 19th century. However, gradually harmoniums and organs began to displace such musical ensembles, which in some cases continued to perform their repertoire outside of churches, often incorporating house-visiting customs.[11] As such, it is this form of the Cornish carol that subsequently appears in South Australia.

Early carolling in the Copper Triangle

There is documentary evidence that carolling of this type took place in the Copper Triangle. The earliest newspaper in the area, the *Wallaroo Times and Mining Journal,* began production in 1865, and while Christmas carols may well have been sung in the area before that time, it has not yet been possible to find information before that year. As such, the earliest mention of Christmas carols in the Copper Triangle actually occurs in 1865 in reference to Wallaroo:

> That time-honored custom of ushering in the natal day of our Saviour, by singing carols, was observed for the first time in this township on Christmas Eve. Through the enthusiastic exertions of a gentleman from Kadina, an efficient body of choristers were in a short time got together, and these, on Sunday night, provided with lanterns of a unique

description, circumambulated the township, stopping at intervals to carol a quaint old hymn commemorative of the 'first Nowell that angels did say to three poor shepherds in the fields as they lay', and the timely harmony breaking through the stillness of the night aroused many pleasant memories of by-gone days, and carried the mind back to the wonderful scene attending the announcement of the birth of the Messiah.[12]

Carolling was also popular in Kadina; the following year a local writer reported that 'In passing through the mines of an evening I observe parties are already practising their Christmas carols, so that during the festive time we may expect to hear some really good singing'.[13] In Wallaroo, the carolling was maintained and expanded the following year, with the report stating that:

> One party was accompanied by a brass instrument or two, and sang a variety of anthems and sacred pieces very nicely. The others were the 'original serenaders' of last year, and they sung two ancient Christmas carols. The singing was kept up until daybreak on Christmas morning.[14]

The earliest reference to carolling in Moonta itself appears in 1868, when the *Wallaroo Times and Mining Journal* reported on the Christmas celebrations in the town. The writer remarked that 'Christmas Eve was kept up in the usual style. The pubs seemed to do a thriving trade. The bands and knots of songsters were parading the town and mine the greater part of the night, carolling forth songs commemorative of the ascension'.[15] In 1872, the *Yorke's Peninsula Advertiser* noted that:

> Christmas carols have been the 'ruling passion' of this district for the last few days and some very excellent singing has been volunteered by itinerant carol singers. We believe there are few places which can boast of the strict observance of this form of celebrating Christmas-tide as the mining townships of the Peninsula; and, we may add, of so many good singers to sing them'.[16]

Indeed, carolling seems to have been so popular that one report in 1880 stated that the town was 'overrun by carol singers good, bad, and indifferent (the former being very much in the minority) which made it impossible for any but deaf people to obtain sleep'.[17] This mix of musical

'Songs of the Old Home': Cornish Carols in South Australia

abilities was commented on a number of times, with another writer mentioning 'carol singing of every kind and degree, from the melodious music of well-trained voices to the shrieking and discordant howling of youngsters'.[18]

Gradually carolling, alongside other Christmas customs such as bringing greenery into the towns, began to be associated with Cornish inhabitants of the Copper Triangle; in 1874 a writer remarked that 'The time honored fashion of carol-singing was not discarded in our midst, our Cornish friends cling to the good old custom with tenacity'.[19] Carolling in the Copper Triangle appears to have reflected the traditional practices in Cornwall and the area had become well known for its carol singing at Christmas, apparently in contrast to neighbouring districts. In 1881, referring to Mallala (100 km away), a writer said:

> The idea of carol singing is almost unknown in the district, there being only here and there one who has been brought to it, thus one coming from the higher end of Yorke's Peninsula feels a longing to be at home once again, for the purpose of joining in the song of gratitude.[20]

Here then, carolling practices that included singing in the streets and house-visiting were clearly commonplace across the Copper Triangle towns from at least the mid-1860s.

Due to the informal nature of these public and house-visiting customs, there is little information as to what the groups actually sang. However, choirs were performing carols in the various churches of the district, and during the 1880s more formal musical groups were established that included Christmas carols in their performances. Here, reports either advertising or reporting on their programs begin to reveal the actual carol repertoire. For example, in 1886 the Moonta Philharmonic Society gave a Christmas concert which, alongside selections from Handel's *Messiah*, included carols 'Awake, Arise, Rejoice and Sing', 'Awake With Joyful Strains of Mirth' and 'Sound Sound Your Instruments of Joy'.[21] In 1888 the Moonta Band of Hope gave a Christmas entertainment, including a number of carols (see next page).[22]

By the late 19th century carolling had gained a particular association with the Copper Triangle and was particularly connected with Cornish settlers. However, apart from newspaper reports and concert programs,

> **Wesleyan Lecture Hall.**
> MOONTA.
>
> ## CHRISTMAS NIGHT ! !
>
> A GRAND
> # Entertainment
>
> *Will be given in the above Hall, by members of the Moonta Band of Hope. The Rev. T. Piper will preside*
>
> **PROGRAMME.**
>
> CAROL—"Let all adore," .... COMPANY
> PRAYER— ....
> ADDRESS— .... CHAIRMAN
> CAROL—"Sound, sound your instruments of joy." ...COMPANY
> RECITATION—"How Jane Conquest rang the Bell," MR. J. B. HARRIS
> DUET—"Flowers, Sweet Flowers," MISSES A. BREAKER & L. MICHELL
> DRAMA—"When I'm a Man," ...... BY 10 BOYS
> CAROL—"Awake, Arise," ....COMPANY
> RECITATION—"Baltimore Greys," ...... MR. W. JEFFERY
> CAROL—"Awake with Joy," ....COMPANY
> DIALOGUE—"The Two Dolls," MISSES F. RISBY & M. SEDUNARY
> SOLO—"The Lighthouse-keeper's Story," MR. J. BUTSON
> RECITATION—"Santa Claus," ...... MISS J. MARTIN
> DUET & CHORUS—"The Prodigal Coming Home," ...COMPANY
> DRAMA—"The Prodigal's Return," ...... COMPANY
> CAROL—"See the Morning fair and bright," ....COMPANY
> RECITATION—"The Hero of the Slums," ...MR. F. MARTIN
> CAROL—"Calm of the listening ear of Night." ....COMPANY
> SOLO— ....
> DRAMA—"How Tupper spent his wages," ....COMPANY
> CAROL—"Angelic Host," ...... COMPANY
>
> —**God save the Queen.**—
>
> *Doors open at 7.15 ; To commence at 7.45.*

there is little indication of what was actually performed by these groups. However, the National Trust Museum at Moonta holds a source that gives some indication today of this 19th century repertoire. It is a handwritten manuscript book of carols and other church music dated 24 December 1875. It is signed by Matthias Deacon Abbott.

Abbott, who lived from about 1846 to 1907, was a miner from Pensilva in Cornwall. He migrated to South Australia in 1865 and lived at Cross Roads, near Moonta, where he died 'in his 61st year'.[23] Abbott appears to have been a musical man since two wooden flutes that he brought

'Songs of the Old Home': Cornish Carols in South Australia

to Australia from Cornwall accompany the manuscript. Abbott's manuscript is significant since it is as yet the earliest remaining source of carol material in the Copper Triangle, and includes material that appears in local published collections. An embossed stamp inside the book reveals that the seller was 'G.N. and W.H. Birks, Booksellers etc., Adelaide, Kadina, Moonta and Wallaroo', and as such it is likely that the material within the manuscript was written in South Australia, rather than brought by Abbott from Cornwall. The variation in the handwriting and ink perhaps indicates that the music was added to the manuscript at different times. This is supported by the presence of a song titled 'Hush! Don't Wake The Baby', which is added in pencil by a child-like hand towards the back of the book.[24] The contents of the manuscript are as follows (with Abbott's spelling retained but capitalisation edited to conform to modern convention):

No.	Title	Genre	Fuging?
1	Let All Adore the Immortal King	Carol	Y (4 parts)
2	Arise and Sing and Dispele Your Fears	Carol	? (Alto & tenor missing)
3	Awake With Joy Salute The Morn	Carol	Y (4 parts)
4	The Heavenly Music	Carol	Y (2 parts)
5	The Star Of Bethlehem	Carol	N
6	Rejoice	Unknown	? (Alto & tenor missing)
7	Awake Ye Nations Of The Earth	Carol	Y (3 and 2 parts)
8	Hail Source Of Living Light Divine	Carol	Y (4 parts)
9	Awake Arise	Carol	Y (4 parts)
10	While Shepherds	Carol	Y (varied)
11	Angelic Host	Carol	Y (4 parts)
12	Mount Zion – SM	Hymn tune	N
13	Shoals – LM	Hymn tune	N
14	Windsor Chapel – CM	Hymn tune	N
15	Victor – P meter – 8 x 7 & 4	Hymn tune	N
16	Consalation 4 lines 7	Hymn tune	N
17	Invatation 10 x 11	Hymn tune	N
18	Chelsea – LM	Hymn tune	N
19	Hebron – LM	Hymn tune	N
20	Babylon – 6 lines 8	Hymn tune	N
21	Harmony 10 x 11	Hymn tune	N
22	Madrid six lines 8	Hymn tune	N
23	Hush Don't Wake The Baby	Song	NA
24	Bright and Joyful	Carol	Y (4 parts)

Table 1. Contents of the Matthias Deacon Abbott manuscript[25]

The manuscript contains 11 hymn tunes, 11 carols, one unknown piece and one song. Unfortunately, there are no words to accompany any of the carols or hymns.[26] However, there is an obvious distinction between the carols and the hymns, since with two exceptions the carols all feature the fuging structure associated with Cornish carols, whereas the hymn tunes are comparatively homophonic, with the parts moving in unison. The first exception is 'The Star of Bethlehem' (No. 5), which features the popular tune written by Samuel Stanleys for Jehodia Brewer's text 'Lo! The Eastern Sages Rise'. The other exception is 'Rejoice' (No. 6) which I have not yet managed to identify, because the alto and tenor lines are missing. On the score, the blanks in the upper lines would imply that the soprano and alto lines are missing. However, cross-referencing the carols across later publications shows Abbott placed the melody, now usually taken by the soprano part, in the tenor line. This is a reflection of older practices in country psalmody.[27]

The Abbott manuscript is very valuable as an early indicator of the carol music that was performed in the Copper Triangle, and shows that carols in the area featured the fuging structure so popular in Cornwall during the 19th century. Although it is not clear whether this manuscript book was used in a home or a church context, the carols it contains were evidently popular, since some of them went on to appear in print.

Carol publication in the Copper Triangle

The popularity of carolling in the Copper Triangle was aided enormously by the local publication of several carol books between the late 19th century and the inter-war period. The first of these was *The Christmas Welcome: A Choice Collection of Cornish Carols*. Although none of the editions is dated, initial information can be gained from their covers.

The book is a compilation of carols written by a variety of composers, principally John Henry Thomas, William Holman, James Richards, and a number of others. Adolph Grummet, a German migrant who owned a bookselling and stationer's business in Moonta, was the publisher. However, the booklet was actually printed in Leipzig, Germany, by Carl Gottlieb Röder, a specialised music printer whose firm was used by publishers worldwide during the 19th century.[28]

Some uncertainty has emerged surrounding the date of publication; in

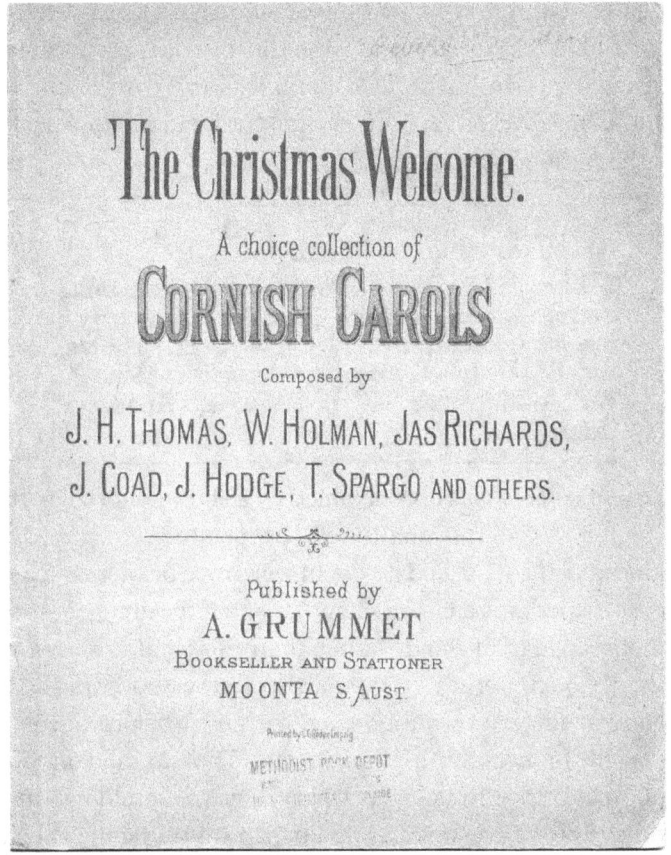

The cover of the 1909 edition of *The Christmas Welcome*

his re-publication of the book in 1984, Philip Payton takes Oswald Pryor's date of publication as circa 1893, although he acknowledges that 'it may have been compiled at a rather earlier date'.[29] Payton suggested in his re-issue that *The Christmas Welcome* can 'never have run to more than a few hundred copies'. However, investigation of historic newspaper reports has enabled me to trace the publication history of *The Christmas Welcome*, and while exact numbers are not yet known, it is clear that the book enjoyed a much longer and broader spread of popularity than previously imagined. This has only been possible because Adolph Grummet consistently advertised the booklet, forwarding copies of *The Christmas Welcome* to newspaper offices across South Australia and beyond.

Interestingly, the first known reference to *The Christmas Welcome* occurs in Burra, rather than at Moonta. Burra was established as a copper mining town in the 1840s, and was therefore home to many Cornish miners.[30] An advertisement for the volume appeared in the pages of the *Burra Record* in 1889:[31]

> JUST OUT.
>
> The "Christmas Welcome," containing twelve choice Cornish Carols, with organ accompaniment, compiled by J. H. Thomas and W. Holman, may be obtained at Mr. T. W. Wilkinson's, Market-square, Kooringa. Price, 1s.

The advertisement was accompanied by a short editorial on the same page, which praised the quality of the printing, stating that 'The compilation is well got up, and no doubt will prove of interest to all lovers of music'.[32] It is perhaps a little incongruous that the first advertisements for the book appear in Burra rather than the local *Yorke's Peninsula Advertiser*, although perhaps the publisher – or composers – wanted to gauge whether material would be well received before advertising in Moonta itself. Indeed, both Holman and Thomas had independent connections in Burra; Holman was born there to a mining family, and Thomas had lived in the town as an infant with his family shortly after their arrival from Cornwall.

It is, therefore, finally possible to date the first edition of *The Christmas Welcome* to 1889. Advertisements for the book, containing twelve carols, appear in the *Yorke's Peninsula Advertiser* from 1890, as part of Grummet's front page adverts for Christmas gifts. The adverts also indicated that individual carols could be purchased in sheet form. Unfortunately, I have not found a copy of this first edition in any museum, archive or library collections I have examined. However, Grummet's practice of forwarding the book to sellers and newspaper reviewers was evidently successful, since he repeated the process in 1895, sending the new edition (containing twenty carols) to a number of different newspaper offices. It was reviewed by a writer for the *South Australian Register*, whose report is so scathing that it is worth quoting at length:

'Songs of the Old Home': Cornish Carols in South Australia

> The publisher, Mr. A. Grummett, of Moonta, has sent a small collection of original Christmas carols composed by Messrs. J.H. Thomas, W. Holman, T. Richards, J. Coad, J. Hodge, and T. Spargo. These are written in a pleasing vocal style, much after the fashion of the 'Union Tunebook,' so popular in churches many years ago. It is unfortunate, however, that the writers did not engage the services of some competent musical man to revise and correct their harmonies, or, better still, obtain a knowledge of harmony and composition themselves, before publishing this little work, as the carols all contain serious grammatical errors which very much mar the many good qualities they possess. The writers show a strange predilection for common time in the key of F major, no less than seventeen out of the twenty carols being written in this key and time. This unfortunately gives an effect of sameness to the whole collection which might have been avoided.[33]

Despite this rather uncomplimentary report, the book was well received by other writers. The *Bunyip* in Gawler described the carols as 'pleasing and simple',[34] and the Adelaide *Advertiser* wrote that 'Cornish carols are always delightfully harmonious and at the Christmas season the Cornish music-books are resorted to largely by choristers of all churches for appropriate glees and choruses'.[35] A little local rivalry appears to be evident in the reports from the *Yorke's Peninsula Advertiser* and the *Kadina and Wallaroo Times*, with each keen to emphasise the contribution of the composers of their district. However, the latter noted that 'The work reflects credit on the enterprise of the publisher, and should command a ready sale during the Christmas season'.[36]

By examining the contents of the second (shown in Table 2), it is possible to estimate the contents of the first edition. The *Burra Record*'s 1889 report indicated that the first version contained twelve carols attributed to either Thomas or Holman. Cross-checking against the contents of the second edition shows that the additional eight carols are by other composers; James Richards, John Hodge, J. Coad, Thomas Spargo, and a version of 'While Shepherds' which is unattributed. I suggest, therefore, that the twelve carols attributed to Thomas and Holman in the second edition are likely to have constituted the original publication. Further, two of the carols in Abbott's manuscript ('Awake, Arise, Rejoice and Sing' and 'Let All Adore Immortal King') appear here attributed to John Henry Thomas.

No.	Title	Attribution
1	Sound, Sound Your Instruments of Joy	J.H. Thomas
2	Awake, Arise, Rejoice And Sing	J.H. Thomas
3	What heavenly music's this I hear?	Wm. Holman
4	The King Of Glory	Jas. Richards
5	Let All Adore Immortal King	J.H. Thomas
6	Hail, Ever Hail, The auspicious morn	Jas. Richards
7	Awake with Joyful Strains of Mirth	Wm. Holman
8	Calm on the listening ear of night	J.H. Thomas
9	The New-born King	J.H. Thomas
10	The Prince of Life	J. Coad
11	Joy To The World, The Lord Is Come	Wm. Holman
12	Mortals Awake, Why Slumber So?	J.H. Thomas
13	Behold a Lucid Light Appears	J.H. Thomas
14	Arise and Hail The Happy Day	John Hodge
15	Hark! Hark! What News The Angels Bring	Jas. Richards
16	While Shepherds Watched Their Flocks By Night	Unattributed
17	What Melody Is This I Hear	J.H. Thomas
18	Christians Awake	Jas. Richards
19	See Seraphic Throngs Descending	T. Spargo
20	Resplendent Beauty	J.H. Thomas

Table 2. Contents of *The Christmas Welcome* (Moonta: A. Grummet) 1895

The third edition of *The Christmas Welcome*, published in 1897, contained twenty-six carols, with four new additions by Joseph Glasson, and one each by Thomas Spargo and William Andrew.[37] In following years this edition was available from booksellers in Broken Hill in New South Wales and Port Pirie in South Australia, with the price increased to a shilling and sixpence.[38]

The fourth edition, published in 1902, contained thirty-one carols, with new material from Glasson, Thomas, and one unattributed carol titled 'Hark! Hark!'. Grummet had sent copies of this edition to the *Kadina and Wallaroo Times* and the *Chronicle* in Adelaide. The *Advertiser* in Adelaide also published an advertisement for the book at the Methodist Book Depot, alongside other collections of Cornish carols. Grummet sent a copy as far afield as Bendigo in Victoria, where, very incongruously, the local paper reported that the booklet is 'a choice collection of

'Songs of the Old Home': Cornish Carols in South Australia

English carols'.[39] This is doubly curious since not only is the familiar phrase 'Cornish carols' clearly visible on the cover, but also Bendigo's gold mines were well known at the time as a major destination for Cornish miners.

The fifth and final edition of *The Christmas Welcome*, published in 1909, also contained thirty-one carols but had exchanged six of its numbers for new material. It is in this edition that carols by James Leslie Davey first appear. Davey, born in Moonta, became a well-known figure in musical circles as a composer, and conducted the Moonta Harmony Choir and the Port Adelaide Orpheus Society before his early death in 1931. The edition also includes two new versions of 'Joy To the World', both in the fuging style. One was contributed by Ernest Edward Butson, who was born in Moonta and relocated to Fremantle in Western Australia, where he became well known as an organist and conductor. The other contribution was by R.H. Paull, a composer and conductor based in Kadina. Grummet forwarded copies to the *Kadina and Wallaroo Times* and the Adelaide *Evening Journal*. The Adelaide *Advertiser* and the Laura *Standard* likewise reported on the new edition.

The Christmas Welcome was clearly not only popular but also a commercial success, with five editions whose publication spanned two decades. Although no further issues of the book appear to have been published after 1909, there may also have been re-prints in between the editions, since some copies have added 'errata' notices that do not appear in others of the same edition. However, the death of lead composer John Henry Thomas in 1928 appears to have stimulated a rekindling of interest in the Cornish carols. That year Oswald Pryor wrote an article titled 'Christmas Carols – Memories of Moonta – Quaint Cornish Customs' for Adelaide's *News*, which reflected on the carolling traditions of Moonta, describing *The Christmas Welcome* as 'extensively used and eagerly sought'.[40] He painted an extremely evocative picture of Moonta as it was at the time, recalling miners singing underground, brass bands, and impromptu choirs parading through the Moonta streets during Christmas Eve.

Thomas's death appears to have highlighted the potential vulnerability of the Cornish carols to the march of time, particularly in light of the relatively recent closure of Moonta's mines. In response to this, in 1929 a new collection was published that specifically aimed to continue the legacy of the original publication. In October 1929, the *Advertiser* reported that:

> During the past few years the book of Cornish carols, 'The Christmas Welcome,' compiled by J.H. Thomas, has been unprocurable at any music store. Enquiries have come from all over Australia, but the book could not be supplied. The compositions of Mr Thomas and others in the book are too valuable to Cornishmen to be lost altogether, therefore, at the repeated requests of residents of Moonta and the district, Mr J.L. Davey has compiled a volume containing the most popular of the numbers in the Christmas Welcome,' and including others not in that book, and has arranged with Cawthornes Ltd. for its publication.[41]

Davey's publication was titled, *A Choice Collection of Cornish Carols, Including the Most Popular of 'The Christmas Welcome'*. The book contained 18 carols, including 12 originally published in *The Christmas Welcome*, and six new carols composed or arranged by Thomas and Davey. This publication appears to have been very popular, and was probably bought in bulk for use by church choirs, since a copy now in my possession was one of several owned by Sunnyvale Methodist Church choir. Davey's book was also reissued at least four times, as evident from the different covers and price changes. However, unfortunately there are no indications of dates for the first three reissues. These were published by Cawthornes in Adelaide, removing one of Thomas's carols in the second issue. Allans, another music-selling and publishing company, published the final version, which, according to the *Trove* resource at the National Library of Australia, was published in 1959.[42] Joseph Glasson, whose work had also featured in the original *Christmas Welcome*, published his own collection of twenty-six traditional and original carols through a bookseller called White's in Kadina in the same year. Thirteen of these were arranged from traditional settings, and the remainder were Glasson's original compositions. One of these, 'Cradled in a Manger Meanly' was taken from a cantata titled 'The Name of Jesus' which Glasson had composed several years before.[43]

The considerable publicity surrounding the publication of these two collections provided a significant boost to the visibility of the Cornish

'Songs of the Old Home': Cornish Carols in South Australia

carol genre in South Australia and beyond. Gus Cawthorne, proprietor of Cawthornes publishers, wrote in 1930 that his firm had sold 16,000 copies of Cornish carols in November alone.[44] Here then, while *The Christmas Welcome* may certainly be rare in the twenty-first century, this newly uncovered publication history reveals a considerably larger geographic reach and longer period of use than previously thought. In total, taking Payton's re-issue into account, the period of publication spans almost a century, from 1889 to 1984. Grummet's dissemination of copies to newspapers across South Australia and beyond also extended the popularity of the Copper Triangle's carols after their inception. Indeed, mentions of *The Christmas Welcome* being used by choirs occur across a number of states, as indicated below.[45]

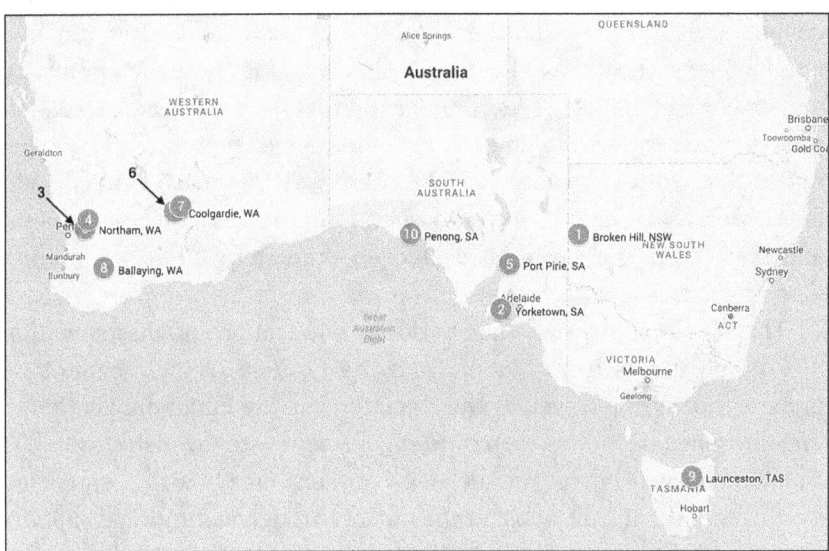

Figure 1. Spread of the use of *The Christmas Welcome* across Australia

1	18 Dec 1948	Broken Hill, NSW	6	27 Dec 1907	Coolgardie, WA
2	1 Dec 1900	Yorketown, SA	7	25 Dec 1903	Kalgoorlie, WA
3	21 Dec 1918	Northam, WA	8	25 Dec 1908	Ballaying, WA
4	21 Dec 1917	Goomalling, WA	9	27 Dec 1930	Launceston, TAS
5	21 Dec 1945	Port Pirie, SA	10	12 Jan 1906	Penong, SA

These instances demonstrate a wide geographical spread achieved by *The Christmas Welcome*, including mining centres such as Broken Hill in New South Wales, Coolgardie and Kalgoorlie in Western Australia, and also much smaller settlements such as Penong and Ballaying in South and Western Australia, respectively.

Both the Davey and Glasson collections, therefore, responded to a perceived need to preserve the carols for the future; Davey wrote in his preface that 'It would be a great pity if these Carols went out of use, and the work of Mr Thomas and others lost to the public'.[46] In turn, Glasson hoped that his contribution 'may help to a revival of Cornish carol singing'.[47] Indeed, Glasson suggested that the carols provided a social and cultural bond with Cornwall itself, stating that 'during the middle of last century many Cornish families migrated to Australia, and as new communities were formed, there also the Cornish Carol appeared as a bond between the old and the new'.[48] However, over time the popularity and long use of the local repertoire meant that the strongest association was between the carols and the communities of the Copper Triangle, rather than with Cornwall itself. Nowhere was this more evident than in the work of Oswald Pryor, who often foregrounded music in general and carols in particular in his well-loved characterisations of Moonta's 'Cousin Jacks'.

The impact of this sustained period of publication and dissemination of Cornish carols from Moonta and the Copper Triangle cannot be underestimated. However, at the same time as the initial publication of *The Christmas Welcome*, a separate engagement with Cornish carols was simultaneously occurring in Adelaide. I now examine how the genre itself was given a significant boost at the outset through institutional support from the Cornish Association of South Australia.

The Cornish Association of South Australia and the Cornish Musical Society

Formed in 1890, the Cornish Association of South Australia (henceforth referred to as CASA) was an important bastion of Cornish identity. Although a number of previous associations had aimed to bring Cornish (and Devonian) migrants together for domestic and economic purposes, CASA 'was fundamentally a socio-cultural body, with

'Songs of the Old Home': Cornish Carols in South Australia

strong romantic and nostalgic overtones'.[49] It did, however, introduce an element of cultural consciousness that had not been prioritised by previous organisations. This is demonstrated in its stated aims 'to keep alive [...] an interest in Cornish customs [...] and to gather together a library of books relating to the history of the county'.[50] The speeches of the association promoted notions of Cornish identity and difference, discussing the county's history and recounting notable achievements of Cornish people. This was particularly apparent at the inaugural banquet in February 1890, during which the Vice-President of the Association, John Langdon Bonython, argued that the Cornish had an ancient Celtic Christian past that set them racially, linguistically and culturally apart from their Anglo-Saxon neighbours.[51] Such speeches reached a much broader audience than those physically present, since they were often printed in full in the Adelaide *Advertiser* (likely due to Bonython's part-proprietorship of the newspaper at this time), and from there, reprinted by other newspapers.

Although the inaugural banquet was interspersed with musical selections and closed with a rendition of 'Trelawny', an unofficial Cornish 'national anthem', interestingly CASA did not immediately foreground music as a particularly Cornish pastime. However, in the October of 1890, a book of carols from Cornwall appeared for sale in Adelaide's Methodist Book Depot. This reached the attention of CASA, which immediately called for the formation of a musical society in order to perform them:

> The Cornish Association purposes to form a musical society to render the historic Cornish carols during Christmastide. A collection consisting of 33 carols has been recently compiled by Mr. R.H. Heath, a well-known musician residing in Redruth, Cornwall, and from this selections will be made on the formation of the society. A meeting of those interested will be held this evening in the Y.M.C.A. boardroom.[52]

Heath's collection (1889) appeared in South Australia very swiftly after its publication, indicating that there was an awareness of a market for such music in South Australia. Indeed, in his preface Heath mentions explicitly an awareness of the overseas demand for such a publication, stating that 'for some considerable time our Cornish friends at home and in the Colonies have been clamouring for a collection of Cornish Carols'.[53]

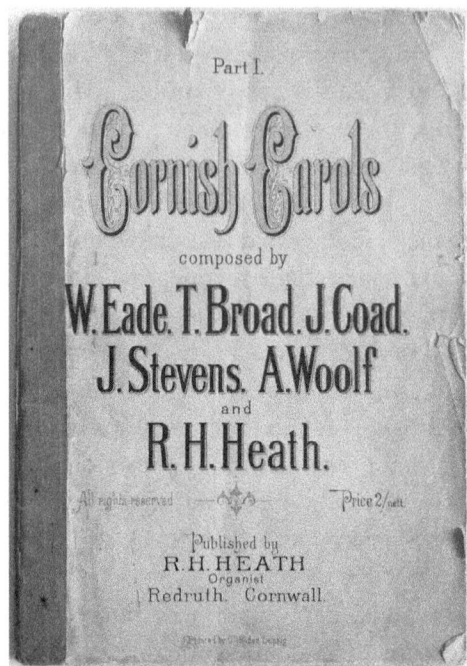

Following the call for the formation of the Cornish Musical Society, an article likely to have been authored by Bonython appeared in the *Advertiser* which described the carols as 'indigenous' and 'native' to Cornwall, and asserted that the 'carols that were sung over a thousand years ago are to be heard there yet in much of their original form'.[54] Although clearly a hyperbolic claim, Heath certainly drew on the work of earlier carol composers in his publications. His two collections, which were first published in 1889, included both his own compositions and 'old favourites' which presumably he had arranged or transcribed from other sources.[55]

Interest in the formation of a Cornish Musical Society was evidently high, with the *Advertiser,* among others, reporting that the musical society had been formed with 'unanimous and enthusiastic resolution' and that a number of prospective singers had indicated their interest, including 'several ladies'.[56] The Cornish Musical Society subsequently gave its first performances: a carol service on Christmas morning, and a concert at the YMCA hall in Gawler Place in Adelaide on 30 December

1890. An orchestra accompanied the mixed group of singers, and the carols were interspersed with other numbers from both male and female soloists.[57] The program also included 'Cornish readings', which were presumably dialect rhymes and stories that were popular at this time.

However, it was the carols that drew the most attention, with numerous reports commenting on the popularity of the 'quaint but tuneful Cornish carols and songs'.[58] The carols, repeatedly advertised as 'old' or 'ancient', were musically distinct enough to be significantly novel for Adelaide audiences; they were 'not the ordinary Christmas carols sung in Churches generally'.[59] The concert was clearly well received since the singers repeated the performance in Port Adelaide Town Hall a week later.[60] They especially captured the imagination of their Cornish listeners, in a way that other Christmas music did not. The Port Adelaide concert was chaired by Mr J. Cleave, a member of the Cornish Association, who said in his speech that

> 'Curr'l' singing would remind many others, as it did him, of the old home in Cornwall, and many of the carols to be sung by the Society that evening were the same as used to be sung when they were children, and he was sure they would all be glad of the opportunity afforded of listening to them again.[61]

The carols were a profound reminder of the lives that Cornish migrants had left behind. Yet the attraction of Cornish carols also extended to the descendants of migrants, with one report stating 'Although many of the vocalists were born Australians they seem to be imbued with the spirit which must have animated their elders who listened with rapture to the well-known songs of the old home'.[62]

It would seem that CASA saw an opportunity in this evident popularity, since the following Christmas the organisation put on a far larger, and more prominently advertised, carol concert titled the 'Grand Cornish Musical Festival'. This involved a morning carol service and an evening concert of sacred music.[63]

The program was considerably expanded from the previous year, and included excerpts from Handel's *Messiah* and Mendelssohn's oratorios. Cross-checking the numbers of the carols given in the program shows that the carols sung were again drawn from Heath's first collection of Cornish carols. Again, as Vice-President of CASA, John Langdon Bonython chaired the concert. His speech regarding the Cornish carols foregrounded Cornish identity and difference, this time with specific reference to the carol genre:

> [...] it was a long retrospect to look through nineteen centuries back to the time when the first Christmas carol was heard on the plains of Bethlehem. But Cornish people should never forget that a hundred years had not elapsed before carols celebrating the Nativity were being sung in Cornwall and that they had been sung there forever since. Passed down from generation to generation, the strains of these carols linked the present with the past and united the Cornish of today with the Cornish of the first century. It was no wonder that the people of Cornwall were carol singers, and that wherever they might be found they still sang at Christmastide the sweet songs of the old home.[64]

Bonython clearly positions the carols as a musical link between Cornwall as the homeland and Australia as the 'adopted home'. However, for Bonython, the carols not only linked distant peoples, but also the distant past. Positioning the carols as an ancient cultural inheritance buttressed the Celtic Christian Cornish identity he had outlined at the formation of CASA, thus supporting a Cornish identity that was distinct from the English.

It is curious that CASA did not include any carols from *The Christmas Welcome* in these early concerts, although this may be explained by the fact that the book does not appear to have been available for purchase in Adelaide until its second edition in 1895. However, there was a link between the Cornish Musical Society and the Copper Triangle towns; the conductor of the society in 1891 was none other than Joseph Glasson, one of the later contributors to *The Christmas Welcome*. Glasson had moved to Adelaide from Kadina with his wife and was at that time raising a family and running a music shop. A professional composer, conductor and teacher, Glasson conducted the society's Cornish carol services in the early 1890s to much acclaim, with reports stating that 'Mr. Glasson, the conductor, may well feel that his vocalists and instrumentalists did very much to maintain the old love for the motherland by reviving memories of the happy days of yore'.[65] He also conducted classical musical concerts with the Cornish Musical Society, which under his leadership gave Adelaide's first performance of Handel's oratorio 'Joshua'.[66] As Copper Triangle residents retired and moved into Adelaide, their carols came with them, as evidenced in the eventual formation of the Adelaide-based Moonta Harmony Choir in 1926.

Although the Cornish Musical Society was fairly short-lived (by 1897 it was dormant), I suggest that its early activities helped develop an awareness of and audience for Cornish carols that had not been strong beforehand. This can be gauged through an examination of the mentions of the phrase 'Cornish carols' in South Australian newspapers, which peaked in 1890, 1897 and 1929 – coinciding with publication of editions of books of carols. (Both Davey's and Glasson's books were released in 1929.) While carols adhering to the Cornish type were known and performed in the predominantly Cornish communities of the Copper Triangle prior to 1890, the incidence of references in South Australian newspapers generally indicates that Cornish carols were not at all well known as a named genre before the publication of *The Christmas Welcome* and the carol concerts promoted by CASA. Specifically, Cornish music was not publicly promoted and performed in South Australia before the formation of the Cornish Musical Society. After 1890, however, advertisements for concerts featuring specifically Cornish carols became more and more common across South Australia and beyond.

The efforts of the Cornish Musical Society, and the support offered by CASA, were key in bringing Cornish carols to a wider audience. The formation of the Cornish Musical Society had been prompted by the recent and enthusiastic formation of CASA itself, with its resultant promotion of a distinct Cornish identity. This identity found further musical expression with the arrival in the colony of Heath's collections of Cornish carols. Their popularity worked on two fronts: their archaic style was not only a tangible reminder of home for Cornish migrants, but also novel and therefore attractive to new audiences. Here the opinion and media influence of John Langdon Bonython was key. His rhetoric concerning the antiquity of Cornish carols, combined with his vehement promotion of the Cornish as a distinct element within the British colonial project, formed an evocative link between the music and the people. Further, his position within the *Advertiser* in Adelaide ensured that this strong assertion of

Cornish identity and its link with carols reached a wide audience. From this secure foundation, over the following decades, the Cornish carol became synonymous with Cornish culture in South Australia.

Conclusion

To conclude, John Penwith's hunch – that musical treasures might be found in Cornish communities overseas – was correct. The conjunction of the publication of *The Christmas Welcome* and the performance and promotion of Heath's Cornish carols by CASA is certainly curious; any specific link bringing the two together is not immediately obvious, nor is any broader event that would have spurred the simultaneous publication of Cornish Christmas carols on opposite sides of the world. However, despite this coincidence, it is clear that South Australia's own experience was distinctive. Indeed, as this chapter has shown, with its detailed reading and mapping of newspaper reports, manuscript sources and published music collections, the Cornish carol in South Australia developed on two clear fronts in the 19th century. Firstly, the performers, publishers and writers of the Copper Triangle enjoyed a key position in promoting the carols. While carolling traditions and repertoire were present in the Copper Triangle communities prior to 1890, the remarkably lively period of local publication developed and nurtured a specifically Australian branch of the genre, and facilitated the dissemination of that repertoire beyond the immediate area. Secondly, the tradition's broader visibility was given a significant boost by the attention of the Cornish Association of South Australia, bringing the genre firmly into the public eye through the Cornish Musical Society's performances of Heath's carols. This exposure cannot have failed to benefit the Copper Triangle's own publications. Indeed, in the end, it is the local carols of Thomas, Davey and Glasson, rather than Heath, that have endured as the Cornish carols of South Australia.

References

Dunstan, R. (1928), 'Cornish Christmas Carols', *Tre, Pol and Pen: The Cornish Annual* 1928, pp. 87–91. J.B. Dodsworth, Truro

Hardy, T. (1872), *Under The Greenwood Tree*. Tinsley Brothers, London

Hyatt King, A., 'C.G. Röder's Music-Printing Business in 1885', *Fontes Artis Musicae*, Vol. 13, No. 1, pp. 53–59

McKinney, G. (2001), *When Miners Sang.* Comstock Bonanza Press, Comstock

Neale, E.K. (2019), 'Cornish Carols: Heritage in California and South Australia', PhD thesis, Cardiff University and the University of Exeter

Payton, P. (1984), *The Cornish Miner in Australia: Cousin Jack Down Under.* Dyllansow Truran, Redruth

(2007), *Making Moonta: The Invention of Australia's Little Cornwall.* University of Exeter Press, Exeter

(2020), *The Cornish Overseas: A History of Cornwall's Great Emigration.* new edition. University of Exeter Press, Exeter

Penwith, J. (1949), 'Cornwall's Gift to Christmas', in *Leaves from a Cornish Notebook.* The Cornish Library, Penzance

Shaw, T. (1967), *A History of Cornish Methodism.* D. Bradford Barton Ltd, Truro

Temperley, N. (1979), *The Music of the English Parish Church*, Vol. 1. Cambridge University Press, Cambridge

Temperley, N. and Stephen Banfield, eds (2010), *Music and the Wesleys.* University of Illinois Press, Urbana, Chicago and Springfield

Temperley, N. and Charles G. Manns (1983), *Fuging Tunes in the Eighteenth Century.* Information Coordinators Inc., Detroit

'The Origins of the Fuging Tune', *Royal Musical Association Research Chronicle*, No. 17, 1981, pp. 1–32

Woodhouse, H. (1997), *Face The Music: Church and Chapel Bands in Cornwall.* Cornish Hillside Publications, St Austell

Musical publications

Davey, J.L. (compiler) (1929), *A Collection of Cornish Carols, Including the Most Popular Carols of 'The Christmas Welcome'.* Cawthornes Ltd, Adelaide

Glasson, J. (1929), *Twenty-Six Celebrated Cornish Carols.* W.J. White, Kadina

Heath, Robert H. (1889), *Cornish Carols*, (Parts 1 and 2), R.H. Heath, Redruth, Cornwall

Payton, Philip (1984), *Cornish Carols From Australia.* Dyllansow Truran, Redruth, Cornwall

Thomas, J.H. (ed.) (1889, 1895, 1897, 1902, 1909), *The Christmas Welcome: A Choice Collection of Cornish Carols.* Grummet, Moonta

Archival resources

National Trust Museum, Moonta

Online sources

A Choice Collection of Cornish Carols, Including the Most Popular of 'The Christmas Welcome' (Allan & Co., Melbourne) 1959 URL: http://nla.gov.au/nla.obj-169892676/view Accessed: 03/04/2017, 15:52

Kennedy, H., 'Hush! Don't Wake the Baby' (T.B. Harms & Co. New York) 1888 URL: http://levysheetmusic.mse.jhu.edu/catalog/levy:105.073 Accessed: 3/4/2017, 15:48

The Oxford Dictionary of Music, 2nd ed. rev. Ed. Michael Kennedy. Oxford Music Online. Oxford University Press 2006 URL: http://www.oxfordmusiconline.com/subscriber/article/opr/t237/e4041 Accessed: 3/4/2017, 16:50

West Gallery Forum, West Gallery Music Association URL: http://disc.yourwebapps.com/discussion.cgi?disc=221195;article=476 Accessed: 3/4/2017, 15:50

Newspaper sources (taken from *Trove*: www.trove.nla.gov.au)

Advertiser (Adelaide, SA: 1889–1931)
Evening Journal (Adelaide, SA: 1869–1912)
Barrier Miner (Broken Hill, NSW: 1888–1954)
The Bendigo Advertiser (Vic.: 1855–1918)
Bunyip (Gawler, SA: 1863–1954)
Burra Record (SA: 1878–1954)
Kadina and Wallaroo Times (SA: 1888–1954)
News (Adelaide, SA: 1923–1954)
Port Adelaide News and Lefevre's Peninsula Advertiser (SA: 1883–1897)
South Australian Register (Adelaide, SA: 1839–1900)
Yorke's Peninsular Advertiser (SA: 1878–1922)
Yorke's Peninsula Advertiser and Miners' News (SA: 1872–1874)
The Wallaroo Times and Mining Journal (Port Wallaroo, SA: 1865–1881)

Notes

1. John Penwith, 'Cornwall's Gift to Christmas', in *Leaves from a Cornish Notebook* (Penzance: The Cornish Library) 1949, pp. 61–64, pp. 63–64
2. Philip Payton, *The Cornish Overseas: A History of Cornwall's Great Emigration*, (Exeter: University of Exeter Press) 2005 p. 307; Philip Payton, *Cornish Carols From Australia* (Redruth: Dyllansow Truran) 1984, p. vi; Philip Payton, Foreword, Gage McKinney, *When Miners Sang* (Comstock: Comstock Bonanza Press) 2001, p. xii
3. Elizabeth K. Neale, 'Cornish Carols: Heritage in California and South Australia', PhD thesis, Cardiff University and the University of Exeter, 2019
4. Ralph Dunstan, 'Cornish Christmas Carols', *Tre, Pol and Pen: The Cornish Annual* 1928 (Truro: J.B. Dodsworth) 1928, pp. 87–91, p. 88
5. 'Fugue', *The Oxford Dictionary of Music*, 2nd ed. rev. Ed. Michael Kennedy. Oxford Music Online. Oxford University Press. http://www.oxfordmusiconline.com/subscriber/article/opr/t237/e4041 [Accessed: 3/4/2017, 16:40]
6. Nicholas Temperley and Charles G. Manns, *Fuging Tunes in the Eighteenth Century* (Detroit: Information Coordinators, Inc) 1983, p. 7; Nicholas Temperley, 'The Origins of the Fuging Tune', Royal Musical Association Research Chronicle, No. 17 (1981), pp. 1–32
7. Temperley and Manns, *Fuging Tunes in the Eighteenth Century*, pp. 4–5
8. Nicholas Temperley, *The Music of the English Parish Church*, Vol. 1 (Cambridge: Cambridge University Press) 1979, p. 176. See also Carlton R. Young, 'The Musical Settings of Charles Wesley's Hymns', in Nicholas

'Songs of the Old Home': Cornish Carols in South Australia

Temperley and Stephen Banfield, eds, *Music and the Wesleys*, (Urbana, Chicago and Springfield: University of Illinois Press) 2010, pp. 103–118 p. 109
9 Thomas Hardy, *Under The Greenwood Tree* (London: Tinsley Brothers) 1872
10 Harry Woodhouse, *Face The Music: Church and Chapel Bands in Cornwall* (St Austell: Cornish Hillside Publications) 1997, p. 3
11 Thomas Shaw, *A History of Cornish Methodism* (Truro: D. Bradford Barton Ltd) 1967, p. 102
12 Editorial, *Wallaroo Times and Mining Journal*, 27/12/1865, p. 2
13 'Kadina', *Wallaroo Times and Mining Journal*, 21/11/1866, p. 3
14 'Wallaroo', *Wallaroo Times and Mining Journal*, 26/12/1866, p. 4
15 'Moonta', *Wallaroo Times and Mining Journal*, 26/12/1868, p. 5
16 No title, *Yorke's Peninsula Advertiser and Miners' News*, 27/12/1872, p. 2
17 'Christmas Eve in Moonta', *Yorke's Peninsula Advertiser*, 29/12/1880, p. 3
18 'Halvans, Dredge and Bests', *Yorke's Peninsula Advertiser* 26/12/1889, p. 2
19 'Kadina Jottings', *Yorke's Peninsula Advertiser and Miners' News*, 29/12/1874, p. 2
20 'Mallala', *Yorke's Peninsula Advertiser*, 14/1/1881, p. 3
21 Advertising, *Yorke's Peninsula Advertiser*, 31/12/1886, p. 3
22 Advertising, *Yorke's Peninsula Advertiser*, 21/12/1888, p. 2
23 'Demise', *Yorke's Peninsula Advertiser*, 15/11/1907, p. 2
24 This was written and copyrighted by the American composer Harry Kennedy in 1888. Musical material and text for 'Hush! Don't Wake the Baby' available from John Hopkins University, http://levysheetmusic.mse.jhu.edu/catalog/levy:105.073 [Accessed: 3/4/2017, 15:48]
25 Any description within the title alongside the name (for example, indication of meter) has been included in the table. The abbreviations and numbers appended to the hymn tune titles refer to the syllabic content or meter of the relevant tune. CM = common meter; SM = short meter; LM = long meter; P meter = peculiar meter.
26 Since my interest is primarily in the carols, I have not yet identified the origins of the hymn tunes aside from 'Madrid' which was composed by William Matthews in the early 19th century, and a variant of which appears to be published in *The Canadian Church Harmonist* in 1864. Credit must go to West Gallery Music scholar Chris Brown for spotting this. See http://disc.yourwebapps.com/discussion.cgi?disc=221195;article=476 [Accessed: 3/4/2017, 15:50]
27 Temperley, *Music of the English Parish Church, Vol.* 1, pp. 184–188
28 A. Hyatt King, 'C.G. Röder's Music-Printing Business in 1885', *Fontes Artis Musicae*, Vol. 13, No. 1, pp. 53–59
29 Payton, *Cornish Carols From Australia*, p. v-vi
30 Payton, *The Cornish Overseas*, pp. 185–91.
31 Advertising, *Burra Record*, 20/12/1889, p. 2
32 'Current Topics', *Burra Record*, 20/12/1889, p. 2
33 'New Music', *South Australian Register*, 2/12/1895, p. 3
34 'Christmas Music', *Bunyip*, 20/12/1895, p. 2
35 'A Book of Cornish Carols', *Advertiser*, 27/11/1895, p. 6

36 'Christmas Carols', *Kadina and Wallaroo Times*, 23/11/1895, p. 2
37 'Cornish Carols', *Kadina and Wallaroo Times*, 29/9/1897, p. 2
38 Advertising, *Barrier Miner* (Broken Hill), 20/11/1900, p. 3
39 'New Music', *Bendigo Advertiser*, 10/10/1902, p. 3
40 'Christmas Carols – Memories of Moonta – Quaint Cornish Customs', Oswald Pryor, *News*, 20/12/1928, p. 9
41 'Cornish Carols', *Advertiser*, 26/10/1929, p. 9
42 Allans' version available at http://nla.gov.au/nla.obj-169892676/view [Accessed: 03/04/2017, 15:52]
43 'Cornish Carols: Two New Collections', *News*, 11/11/1929, p. 5
44 Carol Singing Dates Back to Dawn of History – Revival in Adelaide – Cornish Songs Make Most Appeal', *News*, 22/12/1930, p. 17
45 This only includes reports that specifically mention *The Christmas Welcome* by name. Many further likely instances can be found through searching for concordances with the actual contents of the book. This map was created using 'My Map' function in Google maps. Map data: Google.
46 James Leslie Davey, Foreword, *A Choice Collection of Cornish Carols, Including the Most Popular Carols of 'The Christmas Welcome'* (Adelaide: Cawthornes Limited) 1929, p. 1
47 Joseph Glasson, Editorial, *Twenty-Six Celebrated Cornish Carols* (England: W.J. White, Kadina) 1929, p. 2
48 Joseph Glasson, Editorial, *Twenty-Six Celebrated Cornish Carols* (England: W.J. White, Kadina) 1929, p. 2
49 Philip Payton, *The Cornish Miner in Australia: Cousin Jack Down Under* (Redruth: Dyllansow Truran) 1984, p. 69
50 No title, *Advertiser*, 5/6/1890, p. 4. For a discussion of previous societies bringing together Cornish migrants in South Australia, see Payton, *The Cornish Overseas*, pp. 188–89, and Payton, *Making Moonta*, p. 44
51 'The Cornish Association – The Inaugural Banquet – An Enthusiastic Gathering', *Advertiser*, 22/2/1890, p. 5
52 Editorial, *Advertiser*, 31/10/1890, p. 4
53 Robert Hainsworth Heath, *Cornish Carols Part 1* (Redruth: R.H. Heath) 1889, preface
54 'Cornish Christmas Carols', *Advertiser*, 1/11/1890, p. 5
55 Robert Hainsworth Heath, *Cornish Carols, Part 1* and *Part 2* (Redruth: R.H. Heath) 1889
56 'Cornish Christmas Carols', *Advertiser*, 1/11/1890, p. 5
57 'Cornish Carols', *Evening Journal*, 6/1/1891, p. 4
58 'Cornish Musical Society', *Advertiser*, 31/12/1890, p. 4
59 'The Cornish Association', *South Australian Register*, Wednesday 31/12/1890, p. 7
60 'Cornish Carols', *Port Adelaide News and Lefevre's Peninsula Advertiser*, 2/1/1891, p. 3
61 'Cornish Musical Society', *Port Adelaide News and Lefevre's Peninsula Advertiser*, 9/1/1891, p. 3
62 'The Cornish Association', *South Australian Register*, 31/12/1890, p. 7

63 Advertising, *Advertiser*, 24/12/1891, p. 2
64 'Cornish Musical Society: Christmas Carols', *The Advertiser*, 28/12/1891, p. 6
65 'Christmas Carols', *South Australian Register*, 17/12/1892, p. 6
66 'Adelaide Cornish Musical Society', *Evening Journal*, 15/11/1892, p. 3

Acknowledgements

I would not have been able to complete this research without the help of a number of institutions and individuals whom I acknowledge and thank. I first thank the bodies that have funded my research, primarily the UK Arts and Humanities Research Council through the South West and Wales Doctoral Training Partnership, and also Cardiff University, the Cornwall Heritage Trust and the Q Fund for supporting my PhD research. In South Australia, thanks are due to the Cornish Association of South Australia, in particular Noel Carthew, who first sent me copies of Cornish carol books in 2012. In Moonta, I must thank Stephen Stock, Peter Ferguson and Linda Thatcher at the National Trust for letting me have access to materials and photographs in the museum. I also thank the many, many people I have met in the course of my research who have helped me in the form of interviews, introductions, technical assistance, generous hospitality and much more.

Thomas Ninnes of Clare

MOIRA DREW

Introduction

Thomas Ninnes of Towednack, Cornwall, arrived in Australia with his family in November 1848. After a short time in Victoria and then in Burra in South Australia, the family travelled overland to the Victorian goldfields in early February 1852. Soon after their arrival on the goldfields, Thomas's wife Maria and the two youngest children died, a baby having been born on the journey; they are buried in a 'lone grave' on the outskirts of Bendigo.

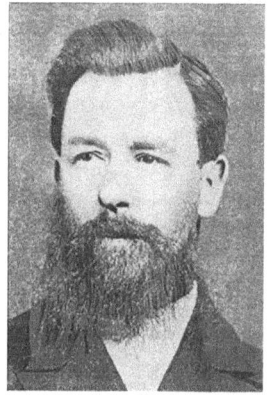

Thomas Ninnes

After approximately 18 months on the goldfields, Thomas Ninnes and his two surviving daughters returned to South Australia and settled at Spring Farm near Clare. He became active in the community as a Councillor and Justice of the Peace and was instrumental in the establishment of several churches in the area. In the early 1860s he was part of a group who 'blazed a track' from Clare to Kadina to provide an easier route to the rapidly developing markets in the area.

There are several references to Thomas in local, church and municipal history sources and newspaper reports. A report of his memorial service published in the *Northern Argus* on 14 December 1894 describes his considerable contribution to the community in detail. Another source of information – of a more personal nature – is a notebook he kept, now held in the State Library of South Australia. It was while researching the circumstances of the death of Maria Ninnes and the two children that I first studied the notebook. His 'first-hand' account clarifies much of the story as it had been repeated over time and was therefore especially significant with regard to the grave. The additional detail relating to other aspects of his life, and in particular the Clare area, were clearly of interest more widely; another family member and I therefore set about photographing and transcribing the notebook so that this information would be more easily accessible.

The notebook contents cover the various periods of his life, some day-by-day recording and some written in retrospect. There are, for example, summaries of his life in Cornwall, coming to the colony, going to the 'diggins' and the death of his wife and daughters. One section provides a record of visits and visitors – families they visited and who visited them over a 13-year period between 1870 and 1883. There is also a list of events which appear to be related to his role as a Justice of the Peace, details of his role on the Clare municipal council and offices he held in the church. In many instances, names of friends and members of the community are mentioned and that is another reason the notebook is likely to be of great value to family and social historians with an interest in the Clare and surrounding areas.

It is clear that Thomas Ninnes was an excellent record keeper and it is easy to visualise him keeping a similar diary or notebook prior to this. Although some of the entries have clearly been written in retrospect, the nature of them seems to indicate that he was taking information from his own 'primary sources'. I am pleased to be able to share some of the content of his notebook, which provides much of the detail for this paper and adds substance to the story of his life. The story is supplemented by material from other sources, including local and church histories, newspapers and resources obtained courtesy of the Clare Regional History Group.

The Thomas Ninnes notebook
Thomas's notebook is a foolscap size folio book with a black cover – clearly well used, with the remnants of sheets of newspaper and sheet music stuck to both the front and back covers. There is a small label on the front on which is written in red biro: 'Notes from Pen of Clare Pioneer,

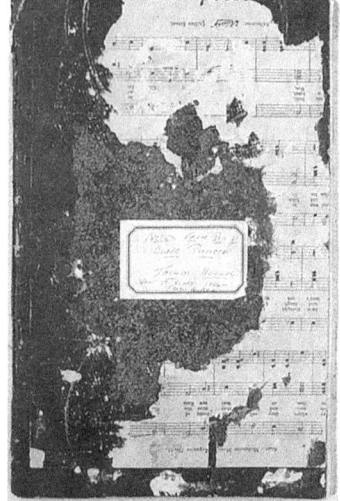

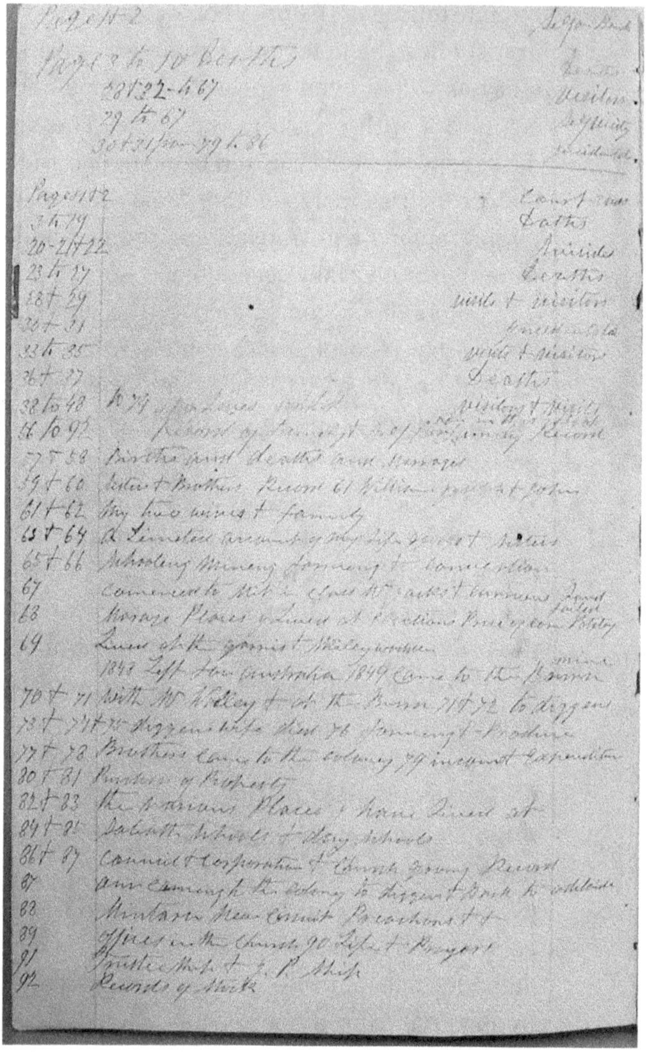

The cover and index page of Thomas Ninnes' notebook

Thomas Ninnes – went to Clare 1854 from Burra'. This appears to have been added by a third party at a later date.

The pages are numbered in his own hand, and ruled up with a top margin underneath the page heading and a side margin used primarily for dates. On numerous openings, the entries go across both pages, for example where he records visitors – visitors accommodated are listed on the left and those he and the family visited on the right. Family records too are recorded in this way, with births on the left and deaths on the right. In other sections, the dates run in sequence down each page. There are 164 handwritten pages, including an index.

There are three sections, with some overlap of page numbers between the three, from which it seems they were separate volumes at some stage. In fact at one point he records 'Record of Family and self – now in this book'. It appears that sections have been added over time. The main sections are:
- day-to-day recording of court cases, deaths (including suicides and murders) – from 1884 to 1889 – approximately 29 pages;
- visits and visitors – 1870 to 1883 – approximately 36 pages;
- meetings and incidentals – 1857 to 1888 – approximately 9 pages (this includes a wide range of subjects from family illness to notes on forming a square, with a diagram);
- summaries of the various aspects of his life in Cornwall and Australia – approximately 30 pages. As well as the summaries, this includes several pages recording income and expenditure, farm production, and property purchases and sales, and so on.

Thomas Ninnes – his early life
Thomas describes his grandfather, also Thomas Ninnes, as being of an 'original Towednack Parish family' which claimed several farms as leasehold property. His father George and mother Mary were 'honest, hardworking people' and by the time Thomas was six years old, his father had taken a lease ('3 lives or 99 years') on a small field and built a substantial stone house on it. He describes the leasehold system and how it affected the family, the changes wrought by the war between Britain and France (especially relating to higher rents and lower prices for produce), and the circumstances and work of family members.

Thomas attended 'an old grannys day school, an old woman teaching a few children there letters to ern a bit of bread to keep themselves from charity'. He did not like the 'confinement of school' and was allowed to leave when he was about nine years old, after which he was employed at home collecting fuel, potato tilling and digging and in his spare time learning the tailoring business which his sisters Mary and Dorcas had been involved in since they were 'very young'. However, Thomas 'did not like the confinement so I did not learn the trade'. Instead he went to night school and 'learnt through the various rules simple and compound to practise which I have always been able to do my own business'. He often worked with his uncles on the farm and 'liked it in preference to anything else'.

At 17 Thomas was 'a big strong boy weighing 8 stone 12 pounds' and began work at the St Ives Consols Mine to 'weel stuf from a Pare of men at 30/- per month'. The next month one of the men took a new underground pitch and invited Thomas to join the Pare. The first month he was in debt, but the second month took home £7-8-0 and described it as a 'grand afair'. He continued mining and farming for some years, initially on his father's farm and subsequently on leaseholds with his brothers. Details of prices and returns are given for several years in the lead up to the 'fearful loss' of the 'great potatoey deseas' in 1845 and 1846, after which he gave up the lease on 20 acres of land at Busalow in the parish of Madron and returned to mining.

According to Thomas, his uncles were 'strict Church of England going men but their children went to the church and the Wesleyans worship' – his parents likewise, but the children more frequent Wesleyans. When Thomas was 20 he became converted at a village prayer meeting. He 'experienced a wonderful change', began attending scripture classes and joined the (Bible) Society, after which he became an 'abstainer', although it was 'little known in those days!' 'There was a great turnabout sum of our worst men became total abstainers.'

The family of Thomas and Maria Ninnes

Thomas married Maria Nicholls in 1838 and they lived first at Skillywadden and later at Busalow. Following the potato blight they moved to live with Maria's mother Grace Nicholls at Garras. Their first child Martha Maria, born in July 1839, died in 1842. Other children were Mary Pearce (1841), another Martha Maria (1843), Thomas (April 1845), Grace (1846) and Dorcas (1848). Their son Thomas died in March 1848 not long before his third birthday.

In 1848 Thomas applied for passage for the family to Australia along with his brother Joseph, sister Mary Thomas and her family and brother Joseph's parents-in-law, Thomas and Mary Roach and their large family. (Thomas's daughter Mary was later to marry one of the younger Roach sons.) The group left Plymouth in July 1848, the Roach family obtaining a passage to Adelaide, but the others to Port Phillip *'as there was not another* ship going to Adelaide for some time'. His daughter Dorcas died on the voyage to Australia and was buried at sea, and a niece, Mary Jane Thomas, died on arrival at Port Adelaide, aged approximately 13 years. Grace died at Burra in 1849, aged 2 years 10 months, shortly after the family's arrival in South Australia. A second daughter called Grace Nicholls was born at Burra in June 1850.

Beginning life in Australia

On arrival in Port Phillip, Thomas was engaged to work for Alexander Irvine, an early settler in the Pyrenees Ranges near today's Amphitheatre. This lasted only a few months as Maria did not like it there and found it difficult to look after her own family. They returned to Geelong and Thomas found work as a stone man, which he 'liked well enogh'. In April 1849 Thomas and Maria joined his brother Joseph and sister Mary Thomas and her family who were leaving for Adelaide and then going direct to Burra.

Thomas's resourcefulness seems to have come to the fore in Burra and he describes having 'done pretty well' there. Initially he and Joseph worked 'at grass' (above ground) and Thomas rented a room in what we believe was one of the first row of Paxton Square cottages. He describes the other families, each living in one room, and the conditions: 'Roofed with shingles no sealing [ceiling] and not plastered. Fearful for dust and wind. Hundred living in huts dug out in the banks of the Burra creek'. In February 1850 he and Joseph got work in the Burra mine and worked there for two years and nine months – Thomas earning $279/4/11 in total! At the same time, he leased an allotment and built a cottage, and he and Joseph another cottage, which they rented out. When they left for the goldfields they stored their belongings in one house and let the other. Early in their time at Burra, Thomas had bought a mare, together with five or six cows which they milked, selling the milk.

To the goldfields

Their journey to the Victorian goldfields was approached in a methodical and practical manner. Thomas and Joseph bought two horses and a dray for the journey and travelled again with the Thomas family (their sister Mary) who had a Hasset bullock dray and a second bullock dray in which Thomas Ninnes and his family travelled. He describes a 'splendid tent on our dray of close tick. All our bedding in fact it was as comfortable as a bedroome'. At the hind part of the dray they had a coop of fowls which they fed and watered in a trough outside of the bars. They also took their cat with them from Burra but lost her somewhere near Tilley's Flat, thought to have been killed by wild dogs.

After rounding the Pyrenees ranges and not much further from Irvine's station where they had worked for a short time after their arrival at Point Henry, Maria gave birth on 30 March to baby Jane. It was an easy birth but the following night Maria caught a chill and became unwell and they stopped for a week. They moved on to 'Bullock Creek' in mid-April and Thomas and others 'had two good holes in Long Gully'. However by May the weather had become very wet and Maria's condition deteriorated further, and the children's health also suffered.

The child Grace died in late May of diarrhoea and on the same day baby Jane died from 'want of brest nursing'. When Thomas made the coffins for the two girls, Maria asked him to make one for her also – 'It was a severe trial to me but I managed to make it. Bound it with white cloth. It appeared very nice.' Maria died at 3.30 on 7 July, three months and seven days after her confinement. Thomas recorded in the notebook the dates and names of the doctors he called, and the total cost for doctoring and medical comforts as a little over £30/0/0 – the amount of capital he left Cornwall with in 1848.

As Thomas observed solemnly: 'John Thomas and sons dug the grave. Nicholas Trehair read the burial service. So ends the history of a good clean careful affectionate wife. Myself with Mary and Martha was left to mourn our loss.' Thomas built a stone wall around the graves and cut the names in a large tree at the head of the graves. He remained on the goldfields until November 1853, mining with some success. He notes in his summary of this time of his life that he had (since) made contact with the owner of the land and knew that 'care is taken of the spot'. This perhaps describes as well as anything else, the nature of Thomas Ninnes. In late 1853, he sold various items at the diggings, went to Adelaide to dispose of his gold sent via the South Australian Gold Escort, and returned to Burra to sell more of his possessions.

Settling at Clare

Thomas next purchased Section 107 (the usual 80-acre block) of the Hundred of Clare, with improvements, from Walter Treleaven, another Cornishman. He also purchased two teams of bullocks, ewes and calves, pigs, corn and hay for around £500. At the end of December he returned to Melbourne and married Charlotte Wallis, a widow, and she and her two sons accompanied him and his daughters Mary and Martha to Adelaide, staying at the Temperance House 'Morcoms' in Hindley Street. He took possession of the property, called Meadow Farm, in February and moved the family there. Thomas mentions that John Thomas and his brother Thomas, and the Chapman, Bray, Dunstone and Moyses families, were settled in the locality and this was an inducement for him to do so too.

Thomas's farming experience and his business knowledge from night school in Cornwall clearly served him well. Each year thereafter, he recorded some detail about seasons, crop yields, prices, improvements, purchases and borrowings and his 'result' for the year. In 1863 he let the land to his stepsons John and Thomas Wallis. Meanwhile, he continued purchasing, letting and selling land and property, often in partnership with his brother Joseph and others. In 1868 he took over Isaac Roach's grocery and drapery business in Clare when Isaac became insolvent.

From details of his landholdings, it seems that, as farming became more successful, he invested in land and property. This also coincides with a time when he was becoming less actively involved in farming. The Wallis connection with Meadow Farm continued until around 1970, when the property was sold following the death of Charlotte's great-grandson Geoffrey Ashton in 1967. He had lived there all his life and his widow was able to stay there with the help of a manager for 'several years' after his death, according to a family member. Maintaining the sense of community, the two Wallis boys had married two Moyses sisters.

Thomas's own children, Mary and Martha, the only two surviving of the eight children born to him and his first wife Maria, grew up at

Meadow Farm. Mary married Jacob Roach of Moonta in 1862 and Martha married William Chapman in 1867. There appears to have been regular contact with their father throughout their lives, and the names of their husbands also feature regularly in his notebook.

Recollections of a granddaughter

Among papers relating to research into the lone Ninnes grave in Victoria are some letters written by Ada Hancock (née Roach), a daughter of Mary and Jacob Roach, giving her own recollections of the story. She was in her 90s by that time, but when she was young she used to stay with Thomas in Clare and was able to share some of her memories. According to her, following his time on the goldfields:

> He married again a Mrs Wallace who had two sons and he got some land, built a house and planted a number of fruit trees. He also bought some pigs. He had two men working for him and they grew wheat etc. and anything else they could sell until the fruit trees began to bear. Then he bought two big vans and they toured the country twice a year with hams, bacon etc, fruit, vegetables, eggs, poultry etc. They used to come to Moonta where my mother lived and as a little child I can remember jam being made in the big copper …
>
> Eventually his second wife died and he built a home in Clare and let the two boys manage the property. He sent to Cornwall and got a niece out to look after him.

Visitors and visiting

A section of Thomas Ninnes's notebook is devoted to a record of visitors entertained and visits made by the family, which provides an overview of daily activities. Many visits are family oriented, but also include events such as trips to Clare or other centres for various reasons, for example:

1876:
- Jan 4   Self, Bessie & children to Hall
- Mar 4   Self to Clare with Chapman bot [bought] waggonette £66
-        7   Self & Bessie to Hall
-    26 & 27 Self, Bessie & children to Hall Anniversary

…..

Overnight, or longer, stays are also recorded and there is a high proportion of Cornish names among the visitors or people visited. In some instances it is possible to track illnesses of family members through visits of doctors and ministers, and several baptisms are also mentioned.

Thomas's public life
The church
The Methodist church was clearly an important aspect of Thomas Ninnes's life, from the time of his 'conversion' as a young man in Cornwall and continuing in the Clare area. He was appointed a Trustee of several Methodist churches, including Spring Farm Chapel, Clare, Penwortham, White Hut, Stanley Flat, and so on – and he laid the cornerstone of the Mintaro church.

He was involved in the administration of Spring Farm Chapel and in the establishment of a Sabbath school, of which he was treasurer, and in the formation of other churches in the circuit. He taught in the Sabbath School until 1877 and retired as Circuit Steward after 15 years, at that time describing himself as 'invalided'.

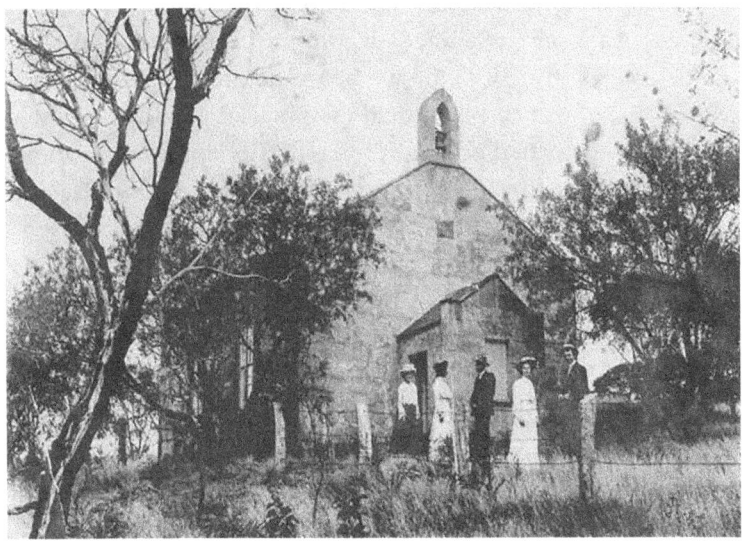

Spring Farm Chapel, Clare

Civic service

Thomas Ninnes was elected to the Clare District Council in 1856 and again in 1860, on that occasion becoming Chairman for four years. He was elected for a third term in 1868, serving 14 years in all. In 1879 he was elected a Member of the Corporation of Clare and served for nine years, retiring in 1888. In these roles he oversaw a range of development projects. It was during his second term, when he was Chairman of the District Council, that one of his projects was the opening up of a route to Kadina and the coast – for better access to the growing markets in that area, as mentioned earlier. One of a series of articles under the title 'Old Time Memories', by Thomas Dunstone and published in the *Northern Argus*, gives a description of what this involved and the circumstances behind it.

The Dunstone name is mentioned regularly by Thomas, in particular among the list of families already settled in the Spring Farm area in 1854, and in fact a niece, a daughter of his sister Dorcas, had married a Dunstone. There is 'Thos Dunstone' mentioned in the notebook as having visited the Ninnes household on 30 April 1883, and another entry on the 'who they visited' list for the same day: 'Chapman & Martha (son in law and daughter) went to Blyth with Thos. Dunstone'.

It is reasonable to assume that Thomas Dunstone had first-hand experience of the circumstances leading to the building of the Clare to Kadina track and may well have heard details of the journey direct from those involved. In the article (summarised below) he mentions that Thomas Ninnes had brought the first stripper into the Spring Farm neighbourhood for the 1855-56 harvest and 'in addition to gathering his own crop, found plenty of employment in reaping those of his neighbours.' In the late 1850s farming in the Clare area was increasing and the main market up to that time was at Burra, especially for farm produce. But with the beginnings of copper mining in the Kadina, Wallaroo and Moonta area and the sudden increase in population, a ready market was available there too. However, the two existing routes 'were circuitous and tedious', the roads bad and there was little water:

'A scheme was formulated and a party formed to blaze a track through to Kadina' and Thomas Ninnes, as Chairman of the District Council, led the group of seven (Ninnes, Hannaford, Wright, Archer a surveyor, Lloyd dray driver, Cummins dray driver, plus two axe-men). The surveyor was to direct the route and the axe-men would cut the roughest timber so the bullocks could get through 'hauling the drays after them, across the front of which was lashed a big piece of mallee'. The route taken – from Clare through Armagh to the hill they named Hannaford's Hill just to the west and where they took bearings to the Hummocks near Lochiel, then called Salt Lake. This far was not so difficult because there was an existing track but from Lochiel on, there was no water and 20 miles of predominantly dense mallee scrub. Areas of plain along the way where they were able to rest for a time were named after members of the party – hence Wright's Plain, and Ninnes Plain. After a few days' rest they returned the way they had come, clearing obstacles and, in time, with a few deviations around sand dunes, and so on, it became the 'highway' from Clare to Kadina. A dam was constructed on Ninnes Plain. Dunstone concludes his account by remarking how different the country is (in 1923) – 'in those early days had anyone hinted that wheat might be grown in that scrub he would have been looked upon as a fit subject for the lunatic asylum'!

Justice of the Peace
The first section of the notebook begins with a series of entries relating to Thomas's role as a Justice of the Peace (JP) from 1884. In fact the first entry on page 1, dated December 10 1884, is – 'Self sworn in to act as a Justice of the Peace for the province of South Australia by T F Reynolds, Clerk of Court.' Presumably related to this role, he kept a record of court cases. He records details of cases and sentences, deaths (including suicides and murders), as well as accidents and insurance matters. In many cases names are mentioned. In most instances the name of a second JP hearing each case is included. Towards the end of his notes regarding his role as a JP, he notes that he was 'satisfied justice had been done to all parties, except for one case', which had something to do with well sinking at Blyth.

Deaths
In another section deaths are recorded, beginning in 1863. This begins with family and extended family and friends, but by the time Thomas has become a JP the contents seem to be broader and include results

of accidents and notable world events such as the death of the Czar of Russia. For many of them he records the person's age and/or details such as their illness or type of accident.

Incidentals
There is also a section for incidentals such as attendances at meetings, illnesses of family members, fires or floods in the area, a shower of frogs on the Penola road, and notes on forming a triangle, complete with a diagram. Even the number of divorced persons in Germany in 1871 is recorded!

Memorial to Thomas Ninnes
Following his death in 1894, the death notice and obituary published in the local press give an overview of his life:

- Trustee of nearly all the Methodist churches in this circuit
- For years a circuit steward – financial abilities were such as to thoroughly qualify him for that important position
- Municipal Councillor – rendered yeoman service to the town
- As a Justice of the Peace – his judicial intellect was keen and shrewd, and being most conscious in all his duties
- Justly held in the highest esteem

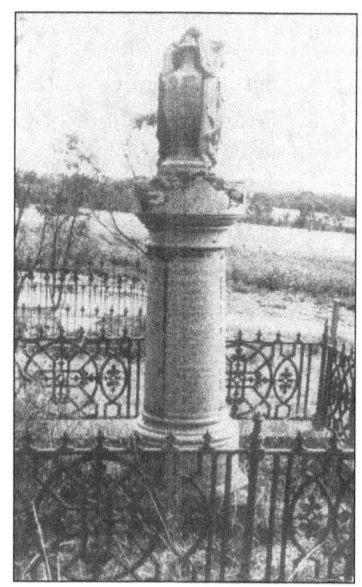

He is buried in a family plot in the Spring Farm cemetery, surrounded by the graves of those from other families who were farming pioneers in the Spring Farm area – Thomas, Roach, Chapman, Bray, Treleaven, Pryor, Buzacott, Moyses and others. The cemetery is no longer used but from time to time efforts are made to care for the graves and keep the area tidy.

The column is engraved:

In loving memory of
Thomas Ninnes
who peacefully exchanged mortality for life
at Clare

on Sunday Dec 2nd, 1894. Aged 81 years, 8 months.
Also Maria, beloved wife of the above who departed this life
July 7th, 1852.
Aged 33 years
Also Charlotte, beloved second wife of the above who departed this life
Sept 9th, 1870. Aged 63 years.
He giveth His beloved sleep
Also Bessie, long devoted niece
Erected by sorrowing daughters Mary Roach and Martha Chapman

The memorial includes the name of his first wife Maria, although clearly she is not buried there. In 1998, as part of a Roach and Ninnes family reunion, a plaque to commemorate the 150th anniversary of their arrival in South Australia was unveiled in the grounds of St Marks Church, Penwortham.

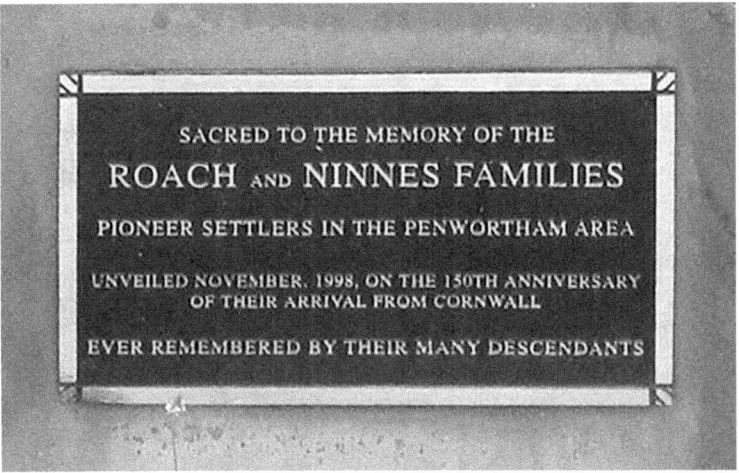

Today, some 210 years after his birth, we have the opportunity to celebrate the life of Thomas Ninnes – not remembered or memorialised in any high profile or public manner perhaps, but certainly a remarkable one.

References

Dunstone, Thomas, 'Old Time Memories, No. 3 – Drought', published in the *Northern Argus*, 2 March 1923, p. 4

Ninnes, Thomas, Notebook, deposited in the State Library of South Australia, Ref D 7054(L)

Acknowledgements

Sources of photographs:

> Spring Farm Chapel, courtesy of the Clare Regional History Group
> Ninnes Grave, photo taken by Edith Lunn, 1967 (included with her papers now held by me for the Friends of the Ninnes Grave).

The other photographs are my own or belong to my family. Thanks to Ninnes descendant Mark Roach for the photograph of Thomas Ninnes.

Information provided to various members of the Ninnes family by the Clare Regional History Group has been of great assistance in the preparation of this paper.

Fire and Grain: Stephen and Elizabeth Goldsworthy, Farming Pioneers

KERRYN GOLDSWORTHY

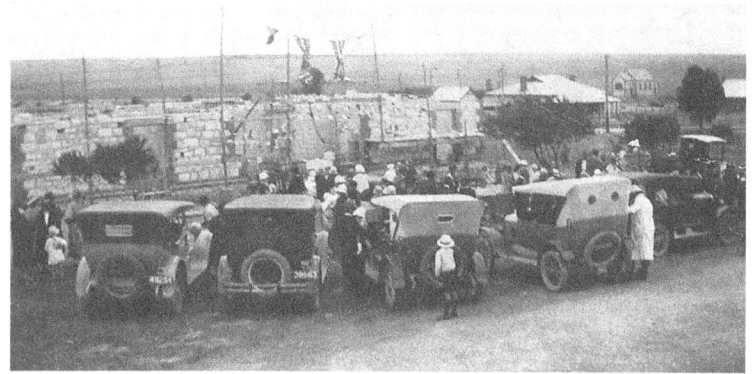

Laying the foundation stone of Curramulka Hospital, 1927

I was born in 1953 in the Curramulka Hospital, a place built in 1927 on land that had been donated for the purpose by my great-grandmother, Florence Jane Goldsworthy née Quigg, who laid the foundation stone with a silver trowel. I know this detail about the silver trowel because of *Trove*, which is the National Library's online resource by which you can search the now-vast archive of digitised newspapers from all around the country, going back to the earliest days of European settlement. The resources provided by *Trove* not only give investigators the facts and figures, but also afford humanising glimpses of the person one is researching – glimpses that work like a kind of thread stitching the facts together into a whole person. One of the most intriguing and inspiring things to me about this story, apart from the silver trowel, is that a 65-year-old woman in 1927 held land of her own; and, owning it, had seen fit to give it away.[1]

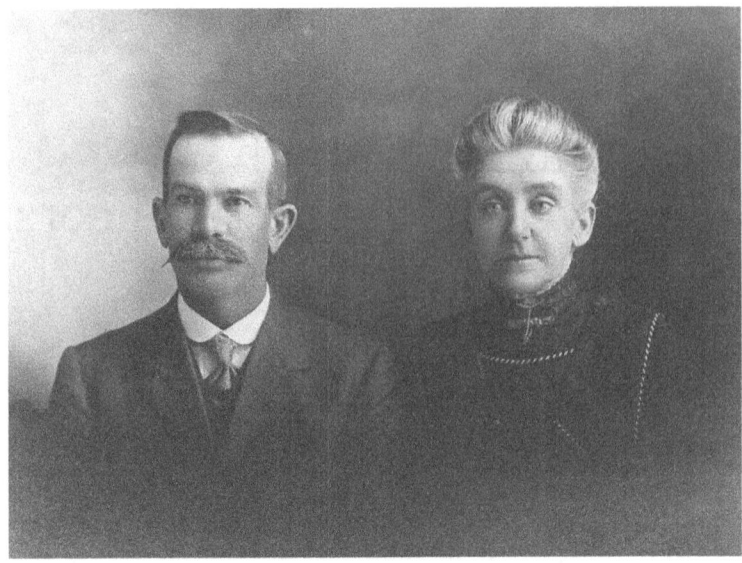

Henry and Florence Goldsworthy, c. 1905

The origins of this great-grandmother were not Cornish but Irish; she was born in South Australia of two emigrants from Kilkenny. But her husband Henry (they were known to friends and family as Harry and Florrie) was the youngest son of my Cornish great-great-grandparents; he was born fifteen years after they arrived in the colony.

Great-great-grandfather Stephen Goldsworthy was born in the parish of Sithney in Cornwall in January 1826, and arrived in Adelaide aboard the *Princess Royal* with his wife Elizabeth in March 1847. I already knew some facts about him, including the story of what must have been the most traumatic and tragic episode of his life, from the painstaking research that his grandson Leslie Goldsworthy – my grandfather – did in the State Library in the 1950s, and from other family memories that he had recorded. But since I discovered *Trove*, I have found out a lot more about Stephen, including some intriguing glimpses of his life and personality. He was not only a sheep farmer and a wheat grower; he was also a sailing-master and a prospector for gold. In his son-in-law's obituary, Stephen is described as 'one of the earliest pioneers of Yorke Peninsula',[2] and on 9 April 1887 (p. 13), the *South Australian Weekly Chronicle* reports on a banquet held at the Curramulka Hotel in honour of the newly-elected local Member of Parliament, one Mr Bartlett: 'Mr E.F. Wilson presided, and was supported on his right by the guest of the evening, and on his left by Mr. S. Goldsworthy, one of the oldest residents on the Peninsula.'

I know very little of Stephen's early life in Cornwall; the occupation of his father Thomas is given as 'husbandman', that is, a small tenant farmer who works with animals and is not very high up on Britain's 19th century social totem pole. Elizabeth was born in Lanlivery in Cornwall in 1822 to a farmer named Samuel Higgs and his wife Maria. Stephen and Elizabeth, along with his brother William and William's family, sailed for Australia together in 1846, which pre-dates some of the biggest waves of the Cornish diaspora. Stephen also bucks the predominant trend of Cornish immigration to South Australia in being neither a miner nor a Methodist, but rather a Baptist farmer. It was the mid-century decline of the mining industry in Cornwall that saw a substantial increase in the rate of emigration, but perhaps Stephen and Elizabeth saw that new wave and decided to catch it, on the chance of making for themselves a new and better life away from the rigours of the 'Hungry Forties'.

When they set sail for Australia, Stephen was 20 and Elizabeth 24. Their first child John was born three months after they arrived, which means that Elizabeth was probably about eight weeks pregnant when they left Plymouth; one hopes that she did not suffer a combination of morning sickness and sea sickness, as so many women must have done. I cannnot find any records of their marriage, or of banns being read, in the 1840s in Cornwall or anywhere else. It sounds to me as though they got a premature start in family life together and may have decided that their best bet was to run away to Australia; as we know from reading Charles Dickens, they would not have been the first, and they were certainly not the last.

When Stephen died in 1897 an obituary appeared that gives an overview of his eventful and occasionally hair-raising life.[3] The obituary reads as follows:

> Mr Stephen Goldsworthy ... died at his residence, Golden Grove, Curramulka, on September 6, at the age of 71 years. For several years after his arrival he was employed by the South Australian Company, with

whom he remained until the discovery of the Victorian gold diggings. He went to the diggings on three occasions, finally taking up land at Black Point, Yorke's Peninsula, and starting sheep farming. Some time after settling there he purchased the cutter *Xanthe*, which won many prizes in the Port Adelaide regattas. During the time he lived at Black Point he sustained a serious loss through a fire breaking out on the run, destroying 1,750 sheep, together with the shepherd and the shepherd's son, who perished in the flames, and Mr Goldsworthy and his son only escaped with their lives by jumping from a cliff 16 ft. high into the sea. At the time of the land boom he left Black Point and took up a large area of land at Curramulka, 12 miles inland from Black Point, and there carried on wheat farming until the time of his death. He leaves a widow, five sons, and one daughter.

Stephen's widow Elizabeth died six years later, and her obituary in the *Advertiser* on 23 June 1903 (p. 6) adds a couple of more personal glimpses of their life on the Peninsula:

Mrs. Goldsworthy, senior, died recently at the age of 79. She arrived in the State with her husband in 1847, and resided for some years at Port Adelaide, afterwards settling at Black Point on the Peninsula for 20 years, finally coming to Curramulka, where she resided up to the time of her death. She was held in high esteem. The homestead at Black Point was a favorite place of call to all travelling over the southern portion of the Peninsula. Mrs. Goldsworthy has left a family of five sons and one daughter ... There are also 24 grandchildren.

It was eight years between their arrival in Port Adelaide from Cornwall and their move to Yorke Peninsula to take up farming. During that time Stephen worked for the South Australian Company, which had been formed in London before emigration began and even before Colonel William Light was despatched to South Australia as its first Surveyor-General. The South Australian Company was responsible for establishing the infrastructure of the colony: building roads, bridges, mills and warehouses, establishing industries, and starting mineral exploration.

History does not record in what capacity Stephen worked for the South Australian Company, or if it does then I have not been able to find it. But whatever it was, it seems to have given him a fairly good understanding of the way that land was being allocated to settlers. When he moved across the Gulf to Black Point he was not yet 30 and was able within a couple of years to secure the tenure of a large tract of land for sheep farming. Nearly 20 years later, in December 1874, the Governor of South Australia proclaimed the Hundred of Curramulka: 'this administrative action formally signified the end of the pastoral era and the beginning of closer settlement.' By that time, 19 years after first settling on the Peninsula, Stephen had six children and extensive lease-holdings: he

> held country extending from north of Port Julia through the eastern half of the future Hundred of Curramulka to Port Vincent, all in one lease. Under separate lease he held country extending north of this along the coast to Black Point and inland along the northern part of the Hundred of Curramulka to within 4 miles of Mount Rat.[4]

He also held a lease on Wardang Island from 1870, which he handed over to the Point Pearce Aboriginal Mission in 1884. He was, incidentally, a friend of the Mission, swapping meat for eggs and vegetables, and sending his oldest son John – by then virtually grown up – to be properly taught to read and write by the Moravian pastor Julius Kühn, in classes with the Narungga children of the Mission.[5]

Like other early farming pioneers in the district, he received notice of resumption on his land leases in June 1874; the land was to be surveyed into sections for sale to farmers. He was one of the first selectors when land in the newly created Hundred of Curramulka was first offered in 1876; the limit that any one selector could purchase was 640 acres, at one pound per acre, and he bought the full allowance. By then his main concern was wheat growing; he had had an appalling experience as a sheep farmer nine years earlier when the major bushfire mentioned in his obituary swept through a large part of the Peninsula a few days before Christmas 1869, endangering his life and that of his oldest son, and destroying almost 1800 of his sheep. The worst of this disaster, however, was the death of his shepherd, Augustus Craigie, and the shepherd's ten-year-old son, who were both killed in the fire and are buried together in the Port Vincent Cemetery, where my father Colin and his cousin Nita have maintained their grave.

It is hard to imagine, given the denuded Yorke Peninsula landscape of the second half of the 20th century, what could have fed so ferocious a fire, but one old-timer, reminiscing in the *Advertiser* over 60 years later, gives us a clue:

> I remember hearing all about [the fire], and the mallee leaves falling at the Semaphore. I often had reason [after we moved to the Peninsula] to complain of its results. The dead red mallee timber even up to 1883 was very hard, and, although we had 12 strong bullocks on the roller it often pulled the team up, and we had to use the axe and chop the dead tree out before we could get on with the job. That fire travelled through the thick green scrub, taking all before it for more than 40 miles in six hours. We had many smaller scrub fires during the seventies, but nothing so widespread and disastrous.[6]

Stephen may have decided in the wake of these events that wheat farming might be preferable, or perhaps there were other factors that induced him to take up land near the planned town of Curramulka. But whatever the reason, he seems by 1879 to have been concentrating on wheat rather than sheep. He also seems to have been closely in touch with farming methods and improvements not only in Australia but overseas, for in December 1879 there appears a detailed report of his experiments with a new strain of wheat and his apparent familiarity with the South Australian politicians of the day. Something called 'Mold's Ennobled Wheat', also known as 'English creeping wheat', had been winning prizes at agricultural exhibitions both local and international, and Stephen had 20 pounds of the seed grain imported to try it for himself, as the *South Australian Register* reports in a tortuous late-Victorian opening sentence:

> On the arrival of the English creeping wheat, grown by Mr. W.H. Mold at Ashford, Kent, and known as ennobled wheat, which was sent out to the colony from the Paris Exhibition by Mr. J. Boothby, C.M.G. (U.S.), the Hon. W.H. Bundey, Attorney-General, at the request of Mr. Stephen Goldsworthy, of near Curramulka, Southern Yorke's Peninsula, obtained for him 20 lb., which he sowed this season.[7]

This article goes on to explain why it is called 'creeping wheat',

Fire and Grain: Stephen and Elizabeth Goldsworthy

although I have not been able to find the precise meaning of the word 'ennobled' as it applies to wheat:

> Mr. Goldsworthy's first impressions were unfavourable to the grain in consequence of the stalks running along the ground, or creeping, instead of standing up, and until the last few weeks he thought it would not be at all a desirable species to acclimatise. However, later experience proved him to have been mistaken, for the wheat not only sprung upwards, but has produced some of the finest wheat that is to be seen on the Peninsula.

Having persuaded the Attorney-General to procure the seed grain for him, Stephen then invited him to come and have a look at the results; the fact that he also invited the manager of the Commercial Bank suggests to me considerable canniness and foresight. And so these two sailed across the Gulf from Adelaide to check the crop for themselves:

> On Saturday, on the invitation of Mr. Goldsworthy, the Attorney-General and Mr. O'Halloran, the Manager of the Commercial Bank, accompanied by a young yachtsman, went over in the Zephyr to inspect the crops. They were met on arrival at Port Vincent by Mr. Goldsworthy, who drove them to Curramulka. ... Mr. Goldsworthy himself has been extremely fortunate in his selection, the soil being eminently adapted to the purpose to which it has been put. He has 1,000 acres under crop, a patch of which is planted with the English wheat referred to above, and Mr. Bundey will not be surprised if he obtains 20,000 bushels from it. ... The area under cultivation which he saw on the Peninsula astonished Mr. Bundey, and from what he could gather the crops all the way to the North from Port Vincent to the head of the Gulf were equally excellent.

As we have seen, Stephen was a highly respected local citizen by the time of his death in 1897. Almost 30 years earlier, the newspaper reports on the bushfire had given a glimpse of the kind of person he was. 'Mr Goldsworthy has been a heavy loser by the fire,' says one report, 'and sympathy for him is all the more felt from the fact that he is a comparatively small stockholder, and a hardworking persevering man.'[8] When Elizabeth died six years later, three of their sons were still living and farming near Curramulka, including my great-grandfather Henry, and I grew up there with the descendants of his brother William.

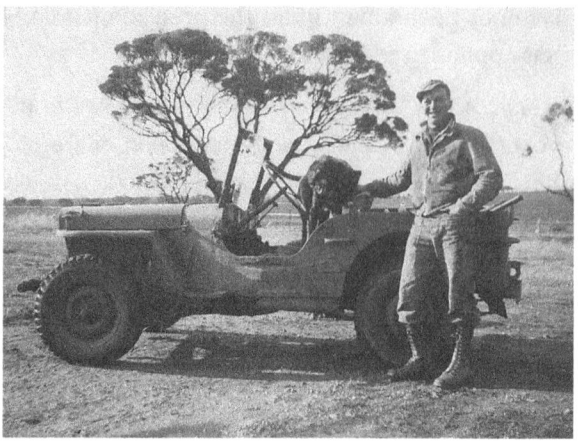

Colin Goldsworthy on the farm near Curramulka, 1949

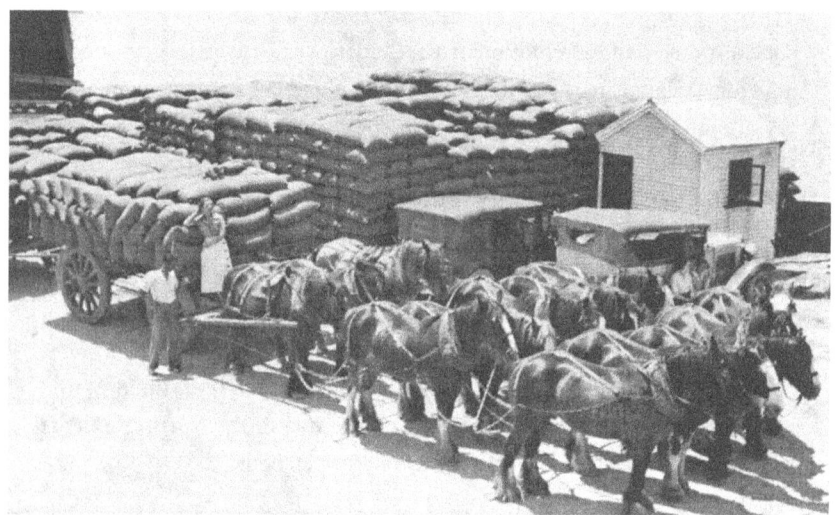

Ross Goldsworthy with Clydesdale team ready to set out for Port Julia, early 1930s

Henry's sons Leslie and Ross and his daughter Olive inherited the land and continued to farm it, as did my father Colin when Leslie retired to the city in the 1950s.

The newspapers of the era feature all of the family as active members of what was then a thriving community, back when wheat and wool were still the staples of the Australian economy. There seems to have been a family ethos of service in public and community life: Henry's wife Florence, as we have seen, donated the land for the building of the town hospital. Their son Leslie, my grandfather, spent three years during the First World War surviving in the trenches and getting promoted in the field, and was an office-bearer in the RSL and other community groups and charities after he returned home to the farm and indeed for the rest of his life. His wife Ethel, my Scottish grandmother, was President of the local Red Cross and a tireless fundraiser throughout the Second World War.

One humble but enterprising young Cornish couple in the 1840s had not only been founding pioneers of the district, but had made a lasting contribution to its development and history as a farming community, both in their own lives and through their children.

Notes
1 'Curramulka Hospital', *Register* (Adelaide), Saturday 12 March 1927, p. 14
2 Obituary: Mr John Gregor, *Advertiser*, Tuesday 16 October 1928, p. 17
3 'The Late Mr. S. Goldsworthy', *The Advertiser*, Thursday 21 October, 1897, p. 5
4 *Curramulka, 1876–1975*. Alan Jones. Published by the author, Adelaide, 1975
5 *A Journey Through Narungga History*. Skye Krichauff, for Narungga Aboriginal Progress Association Inc., Wakefield Press, Kent Town, SA, 2011
6 'Memories of Black Point', *Advertiser*, Friday 26 October 1934, p. 27
7 'Yorke's Peninsula Crops', *South Australian Register*, Wednesday 17 December 1879, p. 4
8 'The Fatal Bush Fire: Inquest on the Bodies', *South Australian Register*, Monday January 3 1870, p. 5

Acknowledgements
All photographs are the property of my family. The one of the laying of the Foundation Stone at the Curramulka Hospital was most likely taken by my great-grandfather Henry Goldsworthy.

William Abraham (1847-1922): A mine inspector's response to industrial disaster

CHERYL HAYDEN

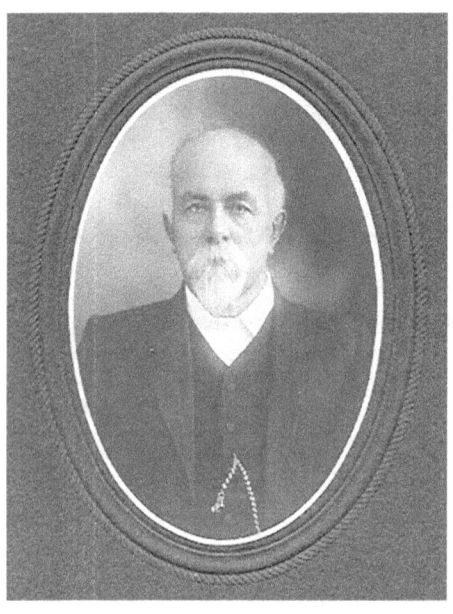

Introduction

Let me introduce my great-great-grandfather, William Abraham. He was born in Ashburton, in Devon, in 1847 and from the age of 10 years had worked in the Dartmoor mines. In 1866, at the age of nineteen, and having failed to persuade his nurseryman father that leaving England for South Australia was a worthy enterprise, he set sail for the copper mines of Moonta. He ended his career at the age of 64, as a prosperous Inspector of Mines in the Victorian district of Bendigo and enjoyed eleven years of retirement before dying in 1922 at the age of 75. For a miner, he seems to have lived an extraordinarily fortunate life: 54 years apparently without any serious illness or injury.

Why, the reader might ask, is a Devon-born miner included in a volume dedicated to the Cornish? This is an area of contested thought and before examining William's life, it is worth considering this conundrum. Here in Australia today, as we celebrate our heritage in the colonial mining landscape, those of Cornish descent have generously included the west

William Abraham (1847-1922): A mine inspector's response

Devonshire miner as 'one of us'; a sort of honorary Cornishman. There are pragmatic reasons for this. In nineteenth-century Australia, mining was in many areas dominated by the Cornish and their technology. This was particularly so in areas such as Bendigo where the mines were deep, the shafts narrow and the rock hard and difficult to mine.

As we will see, William Abraham, the west Devon miner, fitted neatly into the world of Cornish mining as it played out in the Australian colonies. I therefore gratefully acknowledge, on his behalf, the opportunity offered to him to appear in this volume because, over 100 years after his death, it has led me down a most rewarding journey of discovery. But did he identify as Cornish? Of course not. As historian Mark Stoyle has noted, people from west Devon have always been aware that on the other side of the Tamar River lies a foreign country.[1] The astonishing thing is that we can still read about what William Abraham had to say about his relationship to Cornwall because in 1913, about eighteen months after he retired, he was interviewed for the *Bendigo Independent* newspaper. The journalist noted as follows:

> Though [Abraham] vows that he never saw Cornwall in his life, he [lives] next door to a Cornishman. 'What! [the reporter quotes himself] Never from a hill-top in Devonshire looked over into the Cornishmen's land?' 'No, never! [William Abraham replied] There were no hill-tops in our part of Devonshire. We were out Dartmoor way. But there was tin-mining where we were, and that's how I started in life as a miner.'[2]

This conversation is illuminating. Firstly, the journalist seems to be acutely aware of a discrete Cornish identity among the 'English-born population' of Bendigo, and is perhaps feigning some surprise that a man from west Devon was not interested in his homeland neighbours. Secondly, Abraham's response is almost a brush-off. He had simply seen no reason to bother with Cornwall and considered the mining instruction he received from a middle-aged work mate in the Dartmoor mines to have been as good as he could have had. In Abraham's words:

> That man was a born teacher of men – an educationalist in the best sense of the word, one who teaches another to think for himself [...] The turn which he gave to my mind, I think, has never departed from it.[3]

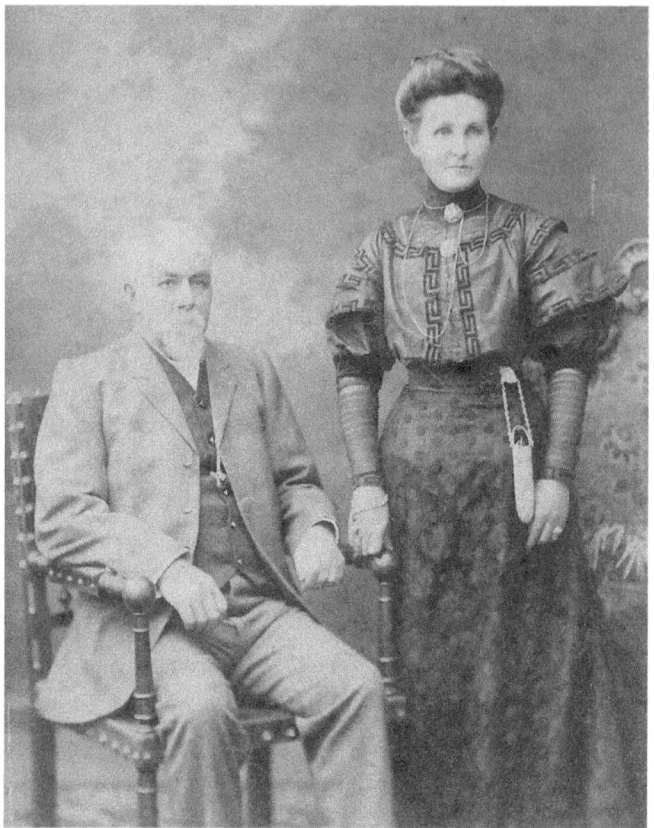

William and Mary Abraham

As a Bendigo miner, Abraham was surrounded by Cornishness, and probably the only thing that differentiated him from it was the line on the homeland map formed by the Tamar River. I will add here that Abraham's wife, Mary White, was entirely of Cornish stock, and during their life in Bendigo she ran a massive household comprised mostly of their eleven children and also, for a time, her little grand-daughter, who was to become my grandmother. I believe I can thank Mary for the tradition of Cornish pasties that has run down through the generations in my family.

Today, however, we look at William Abraham's career in terms of his contribution to the health and wellbeing of the mining community of Bendigo during a period of chronic and lethal workplace illness; a

William Abraham (1847-1922): A mine inspector's response

period that has been described as one of Australia's greatest industrial disasters. We look at it in the context of a town in which 46 per cent of all the 'English-born' fathers had been born in Cornwall.[4]

Early career

William arrived in Adelaide in 1866, and spent his first year mining at Moonta in South Australia. Here, he married, but his young bride died shortly thereafter, and so in 1867, like many South Australian miners before him, he left for Ballarat, where he worked in several mines before landing at the deep, damp alluvial Ballarat Freehold. It was in this mine that he experienced the terror of being underground when things went wrong. The description he later gave to the *Bendigo Independent* is powerful:

> The ground all about had been taken out. There was a full acre of ground standing up, held upon props. All of it was rocking and swaying, ready to crash down at any time. There were forty of us men, nevertheless, working under it. One day it began to roar – to roar like ten thousand thunderstorms ... We rushed for the levels. Our candles were all blown out by the wind that charged along behind us. Men dashed themselves against logs and beams in the darkness. The noise of the falling ground, the crashing of the timber as the weight above overwhelmed it, the violence of the wind along the levels and up the shaft, the cries and calls of the men – it was something which I can never forget ...[5]

Miraculously, no one was killed in this incident, but afterwards Abraham left Ballarat to try his luck elsewhere. He was, after all, a young widower with no children, and could do what he wanted. He returned briefly to Moonta, went back to Ballarat, then sailed across to Tasmania, where he worked near Launceston – perhaps in the mines near the infamous Beaconsfield. He returned to Victoria and by 1870 was in Bendigo. It was here, still in his mid-20s, that Abraham obtained a contract to sink the shafts of the New Chum and Victoria Quartz mines. This was nothing like the damp, alluvial mining he knew from Ballarat. Bendigo's gold was tightly bound up in quartz, in veins that meandered all over the place. To mine it, deep shafts were necessary. So, too, were the new pneumatic drills that bore through the quartz and filled the drives and the miners' lungs with silica dust. Abraham's contract at New Chum and Victoria Quartz placed him at the very beginning of an enterprise that would create two of Victoria's deepest mines – in fact, they would become among the deepest in the world. It should be noted here that this was an era during which 'there was widespread disregard for proper ventilation.'[6] The driving of a shaft dedicated to provide an 'upcast' of dust-laden air out of the mine was deemed either too expensive or unnecessary.

After the shaft at Victoria Quartz was sunk, Abraham became a shift boss, at the same time studying surveying, mechanics and mine management at the Bendigo School of Mines. On Christmas Day 1872, he married 17-year-old Mary White, and they set up home in the Ironbark area of Bendigo, right opposite the mine. But Abraham was clearly a man on the move and at some point became manager of the Confidence Extended.

The 1870s was a prosperous decade for mining in Bendigo, but this prosperity came at a price. Wages and conditions were the most hotly contested issues, with the appalling incidence of miners' disease emerging as of utmost concern in the community. Friction between miners and the mining companies grew and in 1873 the Victorian Government passed legislation to provide for oversight of working conditions in mines. Yet despite predictions that the incidence of tuberculosis on the goldfields would rise, the Act scarcely mentioned ventilation.[7] Over the final three decades of the nineteenth century, the mines became deeper and deeper. Historian Charles Fahey tells us that by the early twentieth century, they were being sunk to more than 3000 feet.[8] In fact, as we will see, they would go to more than 4000 feet before the cost of production made them unviable and forced their closure. At such depths, ventilation was a critical concern. The increasing use of pneumatic rock drills meant miners were exposed to large quantities of silica dust being released into their work areas, and there were no 'upcast' shafts to draw it out of the mine. Unsurprisingly, Bendigo began recording the highest incidence of dust- and fibre-related lung disease in Australia.[9] Among those to die of miners' disease in Bendigo was another of my great-great-grandfathers, Cornish-born Thomas Harvey from St Just-in-Penwith, who died at Golden Gully in 1883, aged fifty.

William Abraham (1847-1922): A mine inspector's response

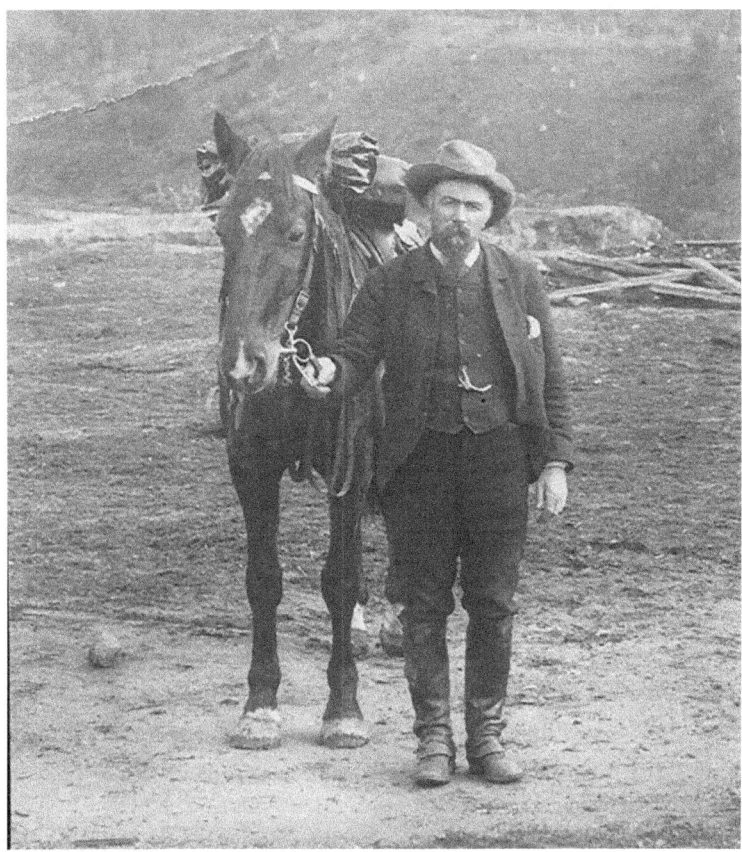

William Abraham in Omeo, north-east Victoria

While poor Thomas Harvey succumbed, Bendigo continued to treat William Abraham well. In 1890, he was appointed Government mining inspector for north-east Victoria. By this time, he and Mary had had nine of their eleven children, so it may have been with a small sense of relief that Abraham mounted his horse and headed off to Victoria's north-east. In this photograph we find him in Omeo, in the State's remote high country – a very long way from home.

Inspector of Mines, Bendigo District

William Abraham's entrée into mine inspection, in 1890, seems to have been timed to perfection. By the time he returned to Bendigo in about

1895, the disastrous combination of deep shafts, poor ventilation, pneumatic drilling and silica dust had created a health crisis for miners and a social catastrophe for the community. Also, silica dust had been officially recognised in Victoria as the cause of lung disease afflicting miners.[10] Exacerbating the matter was the propensity of a lung scarred by silica dust to become vulnerable to 'miners' disease', a catch-all for serious and highly infectious diseases such as tuberculosis.[11] Therefore, the industrial disease affecting miners had the potential to take root in the non-mining community, affecting the miners' wives, children and others.

The lure of gold was turning Bendigo into a vortex of intractable health and social problems. However, notwithstanding the creation of a position of Chief Ventilation Inspector in 1900, there was still no inspector with any power to compel mine owners to comply with their obligations.[12] Despite this, some commentators have described mine inspectors as an extension of the legislators and policy makers and, therefore, part of the problem.[13] William Abraham, himself, was singled out as 'ineffectual' on the basis of a report in which he claimed that the ventilation in a particular mine he had inspected was 'as good as you could expect.'[14] The question I ask here is what exactly did William Abraham mean? Such a comment might just as well have been an expression of his exasperation at the lack of legislated power mine inspectors actually had to enforce what was already becoming accepted as best practice in the mines; that is, the sinking of a fourth 'upcast' ventilation shaft that would draw silica dust out of the mine. But was this a fair assessment of his attitude towards his job, or of the sum total of his career?

For a more informed assessment of William Abraham's approach to his duties, I turned to the reports he submitted annually to the Minister for Mining and Water Supply. For the purposes of this chapter, I have chosen to focus on how he reported on the critical matter of ventilation in the mines of Bendigo. Was he an advocate for reform, or was he really just part of the problem?

I found that as early as 1895, when he started as an inspector in Bendigo, William Abraham began calling for reform regarding ventilation. During his years in the north-west of Victoria, he had regularly described the mines as being 'well ventilated'. In his first report from Bendigo, he noted the depth of the mines and called for the driving of winzes and the interconnecting of mines to improve air-flow.[15] However, it was not until seven years later, in 1903, that a serious public campaign began, which included a series of articles in the *Bendigo Advertiser* on the extent of miners' phthisis in the community.[16] In that year, William Abraham noted in his report to the Minister that:

> Some of our northern mines have recently started shafts from the surface, and have made a great mistake in not sinking shafts with four compartments, one to be used for an upcast. Some of them can see it now, and this should be made part of the Mines Act.[17]

Here, Abraham is lending his voice and whatever influence he had to the public campaign. It was a direct appeal to the Minister to legislate for reform. Supporting him was the Senior Inspector Mines for Melbourne, Mr Meekison, who reported that two ventilation inspectors had been traversing the State to improve conditions in this regard. Meekison said the greatest challenge was the narrow nature of deep shafts that only had three compartments.[18] The year 1903, therefore, reveals the start of a five-year campaign for the inspectors to be given powers to enforce ventilation requirements.[19] Already, William Abraham's voice was part of this movement.

During the following year – 1904 – the argument heated up. The Minister for Mines fought back, claiming it would be unfair to the mining companies if inspectors were given the power to compel them to spend thousands of pounds on ventilation. He also engaged in a discourse in which miners were blamed for their own misfortune, because they were disinclined to adhere to the proper application of water sprays as they drilled. [20] At the end of the year, however, William Abraham continued his reporting on ventilation, saying that the matter was receiving 'special attention' and that many companies were undertaking significant work to form underground connections with adjoining mines. He referred to regulations pertaining to air quality but his use of the words 'where practical' in matters of enforcement may allude to the fact that he had no power to enforce a recommendation.[21] In 1905, his advocacy continued:

> I strongly advise that all companies sinking main engine shafts below 2000 feet should be compelled to take down [i.e.: open up] the fourth compartment for ventilation purposes.[22]

In 1906, Abraham reported that ventilation in Bendigo's mines was improving. The New Chum and Victoria Company had both installed fourth compartments to depths of just over 3000 feet. He reported a significant reduction in the temperatures taken in the mine and an increase in the use of water jets to reduce dust.[23] Even in the absence of legislated power, William Abraham reported seeing improvements in mining ventilation and a reduction in the miners' exposure to excessive heat and dust. This report coincided with the publication of the first of two reports by Dr Walter Summons, which provided 'incontrovertible evidence that fine quartz dust from mining with rock drills, when inhaled, causes extensive damage to the lungs.'[24]

The second of Summons' papers was published in 1907, by which time Victoria had a new chief mining inspector, A.H. Merrin. At the end of this year, Merrin reported on the recently passed *Amending Mines Act* and in doing so, provided an insight into the particular difficulties being faced at Bendigo. Merrin stated:

> the rock temperature increases at the rate of one degree F [Fahrenheit] for, say, every 75 feet in depth below the zone of invariable temperature, and at 4000 feet the temperature due to [the] heat of the rocks at this depth is 114 degrees F.[25]

Merrin explained that the heat in Bendigo's mines was exacerbated by high humidity in the workings, making ventilation critically important. The temperatures of numerous mines were recorded, the coolest measurement taken being at Hustler's Reef, where the platform temperature at 1429 feet was 61 degrees. The highest temperatures were recorded at the New Chum Railway mine. Here, much deeper recordings were taken. At 4284 feet, it was 90.5 degrees at the platform. At the rockface, it was 95 degrees and the temperature of the water inside the rock was 114 degrees. Hot and humid, indeed. It should be noted that these temperatures would have been taken and recorded by William Abraham – that was part of his job.

For his part, also in 1907, William Abraham reported on a visit to the Victoria Quartz mine. This particular report has been a poignant research find for me because we have always treasured a photograph of William taken at 4156 feet below the surface of the Victoria Quartz mine. This report explains why he was there. On 13 January 1908, he was checking the temperature and airflow. His report describes the Victoria Quartz as a 'down cast' operation: that is, it did not have an upcast shaft that would take the air back to the surface. He notes platform temperatures – that is, temperatures at the shaft, where the ladders, winze and air-flow were – of 78 and 77 degrees Fahrenheit at two levels well below 4000 feet. Away from the shaft, at 210 feet distance, he recorded a temperature of 87 degrees in the workings. This was eight degrees cooler than the New Chum Railway mine, at the same depth. He went on to inform the Minister that it was unreasonable for anyone to suggest that any attempts to improve mine ventilation would 'hamper mining'. On the contrary, he said, it would be 'of equal advantage to the miner and the mine owner'. [26] Once again, we hear William Abraham advocating for reform.

The legislation passed on 23 December 1907 was a turning point for mine inspectors. They now had the power 'to compel mine owners to observe their legal obligations regarding ventilation.'[27] And, as though to signal his intent, Abraham commented that the companies which had

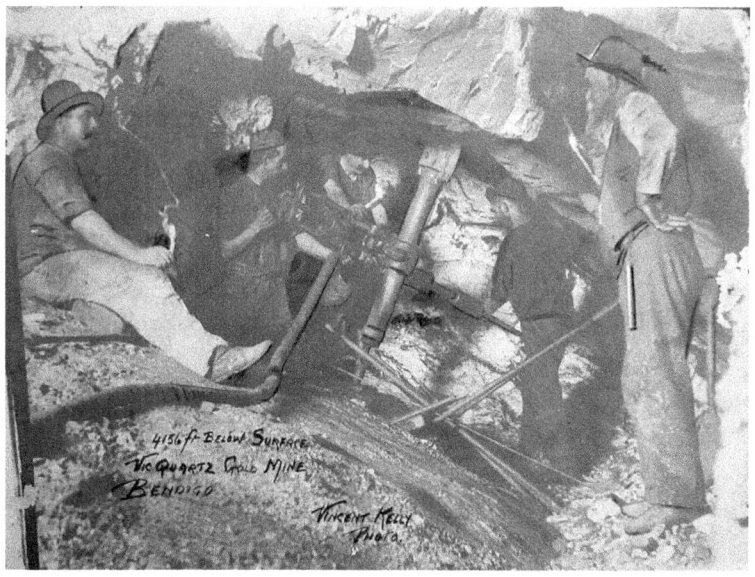

A rare photo of of miners under ground: '4,156 feet below the surface in the Bendigo quartz gold mine'. Abraham is at far right.

installed the four-compartment shaft, including the 'up cast' shaft for ventilation, were pleased with the results. He noted also that water jets were being introduced, the purpose of which was to significantly reduce the amount of silica dust being produced by the drilling process. Now, after years of asserting his opinion, temperature and airflow were to be quantified, recorded and monitored, and action could be taken against mining companies which failed to abide by the new measures. One course of action an inspector could take if the 'air in any working place is not maintained at the standard herein', was to reduce shifts from eight to six consecutive hours. Merrin noted that such a reduction in hours had already been introduced at some of the deep mines in Bendigo and Ballarat.[28]

By 1908, William Abraham was able to report to the Minister that 'the companies are now all falling into line' with their four compartment shafts.[29] In this year, the Labor Member of Parliament for Bendigo West tried to legislate for compensation for miners' phthisis. Sadly for the predominantly Cornish miners of Bendigo, the vote in the Legislative Assembly was lost.[30] Meanwhile, the Victoria Quartz became the world's deepest mine at 4478 feet.[31]

In 1909, Abraham reported that the ventilation requirements of the new Act had improved conditions in the mines, and noted its provisions pertaining to the use of water jets or sprays to reduce dust were commonly complied with. He noted also in this report that the Victoria Quartz Company had been granted $10,000 to sink a main engine shaft to below 4250 feet and described the technology as 'the most up-to-date winding plant in this State'. Most tellingly, perhaps, is his comment that several of the deep mines had closed.[32] Already, the cost of installing the compulsory fourth shaft for upcast ventilation was having an adverse impact on production costs.

William Abraham's report for 1910 was the last before his retirement. On the subject of ventilation he said:

> Ventilation in a great number of mines has been improved. Several of the deep mines on the New Chum line have stopped work. Water jets or sprays are now provided. This portion of the Act is being strictly enforced where rock drills are in use.

William Abraham (1847-1922): A mine inspector's response

He also appears to have been moved by the closure in December 1910 of the Victoria Quartz mine, noting that all the tools had been left under the water and that the shaft had reached a depth of 4614 feet.[33] It seems that even a £10,000 grant had been insufficient to keep the world's deepest gold mine viable.

I have focused here on ventilation as a critical issue in William Abraham's work as an inspector of mines because in Bendigo, during the time he was in this position, it was not merely the most critical aspect of miners' health, it had become a social and economic catastrophe. Bendigo was the town in which he had chosen to settle. His eleven children – all of whom survived to adulthood – went to school there, and every one of them would have known other children whose fathers were sick, dying or dead; his own friends and associates belonged to the Bendigo mining community. He cannot have been immune to the horror, grief and poverty being caused by the disease that was pervading the industry he was so passionate about.

Ventilation, of course, was not the only thing he had to consider when inspecting mines. The state of boilers, machinery and equipment such as the elevator cages the miners used to travel up and down the shafts, were all matters for scrutiny, as was sanitation. The mines were also the sites of terrible accidents, many of which were fatal. William Abraham was frequently required to testify in the Coroner's court, particularly when issues of negligence or culpability needed to be determined. Always, his opinions were strong and clear; he was not a man to suffer fools, nor to be taken lightly. He had made his way solo in a difficult world, and done extraordinarily well. I would like to believe that he did what he could with the power he had to help the Cornish mining community of Bendigo.

Conclusion

William Abraham was involved in mining for 54 years. He began as a small child in the mines of Dartmoor, but forged a career among Victoria's Cornish mining community as a fearless expert and advocate who did not shy away from giving his opinion. He was also a life-time learner, and I think it's fair to say he probably knew as much about gold mining in Victoria at that time as anyone could.

For 20 years, he was a mine inspector and, of these, 15 were spent in one of the most challenging industrial environments in the world. The wealth generated by Bendigo's goldfields is still there for all to see – not only in Bendigo's public buildings, but also in Melbourne's. The pursuit of gold, however, came at an enormous cost for the thousands of Cornish miners who, ironically, had come to Australia for a better life. I would like to think that at the height of Bendigo's great health crisis, my great-great-grandfather made a contribution to reform in his field of expertise, for I believe that the evidence shows that his intention was to do as much good as possible.

Notes

1. Mark Stoyle, *West Britons: Cornish Identities and the Early Modern British State*, University of Exeter Press, 2002, 1
2. 'Pioneers and All', *Bendigo Independent*, Thursday 12 June 1913, p. 6. National Library of Australia, http://nla.gov.au/nla.news-article227866641
3. Ibid.
4. Yolande Collins and Sandra Kippen, 'A Social Disease with medical aspects: Miners' phthisis and the politics of occupational health in Bendigo, 1880s–1910', *Journal of Australasian Mining History*, 6, Sept. 2008, 70–89 (70 &72)
5. 'Pioneers and All', op. cit.
6. Beris Penrose, 'The State and Gold Miners' Health in Victoria, 1870–1910', *Labour History*, 101, Nov. 2011, 35–53 (37)
7. Penrose, 38–39
8. Charles Fahey, 'Labour and Trade Unionism' in *Gold: Forgotten Histories and Lost Objects of Australia* (Eds: Iain McCalman, Alexander Cook and Andrew Reeves), Cambridge University Press, 2001, 69
9. Collins and Kippen, 71
10. Penrose, 40; this recognition was the result of the 1888 report of the Mines Ventilation Board.
11. Ibid, 38
12. Ibid, 43
13. Collins and Kippen, 70
14. Collins and Kippen, 76
15. William Abraham, Inspector of Mines, Bendigo. *Annual Report of the Ministry of Mines and Water Supply for the year 1895.* State of Victoria 1896, 33
16. Collins and Kippen, 83
17. William Abraham, Inspector of Mines, Bendigo. *Annual Report of the Ministry of Mines and Water Supply for the year 1903.* State of Victoria 1904, 63 https://www.parliament.vic.gov.au/papers/govpub/VPARL1904No14.pdf
18. E.R. Meekison, Senior Inspector of Mines. *Annual Report of the Ministry of Mines and Water Supply for the year 1903,* State of Victoria 1904, 59 https://www.parliament.vic.gov.au/papers/govpub/VPARL1904No14.pdf
19. Penrose, 36
20. Penrose, 46

21 William Abraham, Inspector of Mines, Bendigo District, *Annual Report of the Minister of Mining and Water Supply for the year 1904.* State of Victoria, 1905, 60 https://viewer.slv.vic.gov.au/?entity=IE8412240&file=FL19717117&mode=browse

22 William Abraham , Inspector of Mines, Bendigo District, *Annual Report of the Minister of Mining and Water Supply for the year 1905.* State of Victoria, 1906, 91 https://viewer.slv.vic.gov.au/?entity=IE8415807&file=FL19719497&mode=browse

23 Abraham reported that the temperature at the platform at 3157 feet had been 90 degrees F, but that following the opening of the fourth compartment, it was 82 degrees at 3357 feet and 84 degrees at the bottom of the shaft. William Abraham, Inspector of Mines, Bendigo District, *Annual Report of the Minister of Mining and Water Supply for the year 1906.* State of Victoria, 1907, 101 https://viewer.slv.vic.gov.au/?entity=IE8409859&mode=browse

24 Collins and Kippen, 73

25 Chief Inspector of Mines, *Annual Report of the Minister of Mining and Water Supply for the year 1907,* State of Victoria, 1908, 119–121 https://www.parliament.vic.gov.au/papers/govpub/VPARL1908No14p101-140.pdf

26 William Abraham, Inspector of Mines, Bendigo District, *Annual Report of the Minister of Mining and Water Supply for the year 1907.* State of Victoria, 1908, 127 https://www.parliament.vic.gov.au/papers/govpub/VPARL1908No14p101-140.pdf

27 Penrose, 43

28 A.H. Merrin, Chief Mining Inspector, *Annual Report of the Minister of Mining and Water Supply for the year 1907.* State of Victoria, 1908, 119–121 https://www.parliament.vic.gov.au/papers/govpub/VPARL1908No14p101-140.pdf

29 William Abraham, Inspector of Mines, Bendigo District, *Annual Report of the Minister of Mining and Water Supply for the Year 1908.* State of Victoria 1909, 111. https://viewer.slv.vic.gov.au/?entity=IE8414560&mode=browse

30 Collins and Kippen, 77

31 https://www.goldfieldsguide.com.au/explore-location/400/victoria-hill-mining-reserve

32 William Abraham, Inspector of Mines, Bendigo District, *Annual Report of the Minister of Mining and Water Supply for the Year 1909.* State of Victoria, 1910, 119–120 https://viewer.slv.vic.gov.au/?entity=IE8413494&mode=browse

33 William Abraham, Inspector of Mines, Bendigo District, *Annual Report of the Minister of Mining and Water Supply for the Year 1910.* State of Victoria 1911, 113–115 https://viewer.slv.vic.gov.au/?entity=IE8442046&file=FL19714094&mode=browse

Acknowledgements

All photographs included in this paper are from my family's collection.

The photograph underground in the Victoria and Quartz mine was taken by Vincent Kelly.

The Cornish Influence on Music in Broken Hill

ROBYNNE SANDERSON

The world's richest lode of silver, lead and zinc was discovered in Broken Hill in 1883. Before long, many Cornish people moved to Broken Hill from Cornish mining towns in nearby South Australia and also from the Victorian goldfields. Broken Hill may have been 'in the middle of nowhere', but by the 1890s it was already developing a vibrant musical culture, thanks in no small part to the ongoing influence of Cornish musicians who were often the backbone of brass bands, orchestras and choirs. This chapter describes the musical influence of some of those Cornish people and organisations.

The early days

Mining leases were first pegged in Broken Hill on 5 September 1883, but it was not until 1885 that miners started to arrive in large numbers and the township began to take shape. Many people instead went to the nearby mining town of Silverton, which already had a population of around 3000 by 1885. Silverton's *Silver Age* newspaper reported that because of a lack of employment at Moonta and Wallaroo, many miners were leaving those centres for Silverton. Conditions were often harsh, but music was already becoming established in Silverton. The Silverton Brass Band had been formed in November 1884 and by August 1885 Mr E. Bone, who moved from Moonta, was providing music lessons for both singers and instrumentalists. By the end of 1885 the Broken Hill mines were becoming profitable. People started moving from Silverton and beyond into Broken Hill where shops, tents and huts began to spring up.

In June of that year, Rev. Paynter of the Bible Christian Methodists conducted the first religious service in Broken Hill. That occasion was possibly the first *organised* choral singing in the township, but not the first music to be heard, because the Cornish people loved to improvise harmony parts for their hymns. Rev. Paynter had already opened a Bible Christian church in Silverton, where music was an important part of the worship. The Bible Christians had also organised a concert of vocal and violin items to raise money to buy an organ.

Surprisingly, the church had arrived in Broken Hill before the publicans – the first hotel began trading in July 1885, optimistically named the Bonanza Hotel. The Silver King Hotel opened not long after. By this stage, Broken Hill was a village of a few hundred residents. The year 1886 was a time of rapid expansion for Broken Hill – with the opening of a post office, police station, schools, temporary hospital, shops, more hotels and four churches. By the end of the year the population would reach 3,000. Because so many people came to Broken Hill from South Australia, including a large number of the Cornish who were predominantly Methodist, the first church to be established was a Bible Christian Methodist church. By the end of 1886 there were two Bible Christian churches and a Wesleyan church. The Methodists had a strong tradition of hymn singing, particularly among the Cornish people arriving from Moonta and also from the goldfields of Victoria. Before the end of the year there was already a Methodist choir in Broken Hill, comprising mainly people who had come from Moonta.

Despite the sober habits of the largely Methodist population, there were now eight hotels in Broken Hill, including one named the Duke of Cornwall. Interestingly, Broken Hill had fewer hotels per adult male than Moonta did at that time. In the very early days there was little organised entertainment in the town, so the hotels were popular meeting places. A variety of entertainment did soon emerge. The *Silver Age* newspaper reported that a recently formed brass band had given a creditable performance at their first concert on Saturday 5 March 1887. The musicians were not named, but in view of the fact that many of them were already quite proficient, it is likely that they had previously been members of a brass band in Moonta. During the same year, a Dramatic and Musical Society appeared, as did sporting clubs for cricket and football.

The Primitive Methodists also fostered music – by 1888 their choir was accompanied by an organ, cello, violin, flutes, clarinet and cornet. Their popular preacher, Rev. Jacob Burrows, was also a Cornish wrestling champion. Cornish wrestling was popular in Broken Hill in the early days, so Rev. Burrows had an interesting but effective outreach to those who did not attend church. One measure of Rev. Burrows' success is that his Blende Street church had to be extended in July 1888 to accommodate 450 people.

The year 1888 was a significant one in the development of Broken Hill. At the start of the year the population was around 5,000 but by the end it had doubled. The increase in population brought with it both problems and opportunities. There were many health issues – diet was usually poor due to a lack of fruit and vegetables, and sanitation was haphazard. There was also a lack of water – a problem which would have been all too familiar to those who had come from Moonta. A severe drought exacerbated the situation. Due to these conditions, there were many deaths from typhoid and other diseases. Typhoid claimed 123 lives during an epidemic in 1888. It did not help that Doctor Sutherland at the makeshift hospital was rarely sober!

Rather than feeling sorry for themselves, the people were mobilised into action. There were public meetings about the water problem and fundraising activities to raise money for health care and those in dire circumstances. Bands and choirs began to feature prominently at these activities. For example, the Broken Hill Brass Band gave a concert which raised over five pounds for the hospital in April 1888. Concerts were also held to assist the families of men who had been killed or incapacitated on the mines. Cornishmen like William Bartley would go on to raise thousands of pounds for charity. The community spirit which embodied the Cornish motto 'One and All' would be an enduring characteristic of bands and other music groups. Musical performances for worthy causes is a proud tradition which has continued in Broken Hill to this day.

William Bartley and Bartley's Barrier Brass Band

William Bartley was one of the most colourful and influential Cornish musicians in the early days of Broken Hill. He emigrated to South Australia from Cornwall, then in 1874 in Moonta he met and married

Elizabeth Nancarrow, a Cornish immigrant from Redruth. While in Moonta, William played clarinet in the Moonta Town Band. In 1888, when William and Elizabeth decided to move to Broken Hill with their young family, Elizabeth was pregnant. However, due to the drought and typhoid epidemic in Broken Hill at that time, it was considered too risky for Elizabeth to have her baby in Broken Hill, so she returned to Moonta to give birth to their son Frank. The need for reliable health care may have made a lasting impression on William Bartley and motivated him in his ongoing charitable efforts to raise money for the local hospital.

In that same year, 1888, William Bartley founded the Broken Hill Band, which came to be known as 'Bartley's Barrier Brass Band'. Bartley's Band was soon doing the rounds of hotels and breweries to raise money for instruments and uniforms. At the opposite end of the spectrum was the Temperance Band, a fife and drum band which grew out of the Methodist church in opposition to the drinking of alcohol. Bartley had his work cut out for him as bandmaster, because many of the players in his band had little or no musical training. However, he was a good teacher and within a short time the band developed a solid reputation for its musical skill. William Bartley would go on to work with over 300 musicians and also help other bands to become established. He was one of several influential Cornish music teachers who contributed much to the standard of music in Broken Hill.

The first public performance of Bartley's Band was on the back of a brewery company horse-drawn trolley. The band played a lively selection of music as it made its way along the main thoroughfare, Argent Street, to the Globe Hotel where they enjoyed a supper provided by the band's patrons, Messrs Knight and Cosgrove. Bartley's Band gained the irreverent nickname, 'Bartley's Booze and Bastards Band'. However, the band was extremely popular, not only for its high standard of playing, but also for its tireless commitment to play at charitable performances.

In July 1892 the miners at the Proprietary Mine voted to go on strike and Bartley's Band took on a different role, that of leading processions of striking miners. It was a time of great unrest and bitterness in the town, but there was widespread support for the striking miners, with regular processions involving up to 5,000 people. When the striking unionists marched to the picket lines with their banners, crowds of onlookers cheered them on. The processions sometimes featured four or five different bands – not only Bartley's Band, but also Andrews' Broken Hill Brass Band, Bargwanna's Band, the Salvation Army Band and the newly formed Silverton Tramway Band. The strike finally ended in October 1892, but the bands of Broken Hill were to play a similar role during the 1909 lockout. (The Silverton Tramway, opened in January 1888, provided a private rail link between the South Australian border and Broken Hill, 50 km east of the border. A railway line from Adelaide to Cockburn on the SA/NSW border was completed by the South Australian government in January 1887 but the New South Wales government had refused to finance a rail link from the border to Broken Hill).

The Silverton Tramway Band was one of the bands which William Bartley helped to nurture. At the first public concert of the Tramway Band (as it was commonly known) on 21 December 1894, it was augmented by players from Bartley's Band and William Bartley conducted the combined band. In April 1895, the Tramway Band again combined with Bartley's Band to lead a grand procession in aid of the local hospital. In December 1895 the two bands again combined to present a twilight concert at the Central Reserve to raise money for the Barrier Ranges

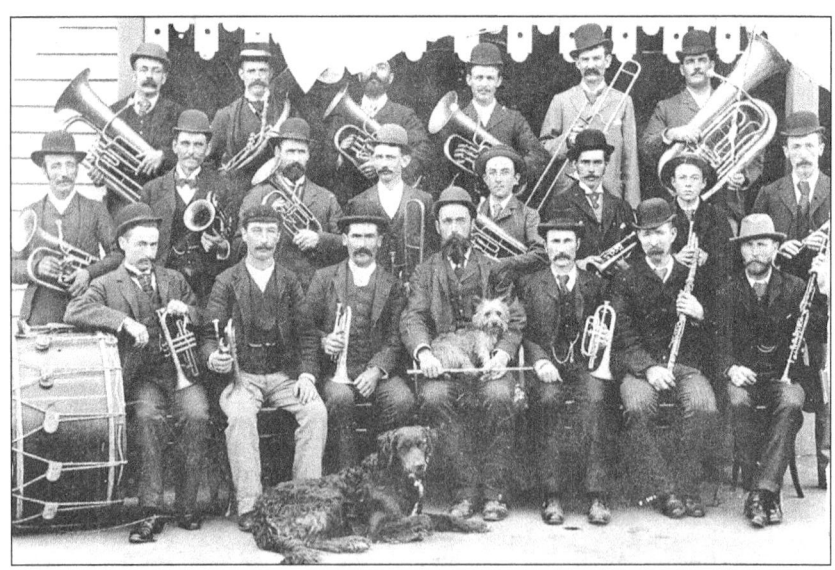

The Tramway Band in front of the Rising Sun Hotel, 1895

Cricket Association. As the Tramway Band became more established, Mr S. Gregg took over as conductor and the band continued to follow the example of Bartley's Band, playing at charitable and community events. For example, in 1896 the Tramway Band held a 'grand concert' to raise funds for the Barrier Ranges Football Association.

Bartley's Band was tireless in offering its services for social events and charitable causes. Examples include the South Broken Hill Pony Races in January 1892; the St Patrick's Day procession in 1893; the Fruiterers' Gala in November 1893 (where Bartley's Band were conveyed at the head of the procession on a four-horse drag and further back in the procession, Bartley's No. 2 Band headed the four-horse trollies); the Fruiterers' and Butchers' procession in October 1894; and many concerts in the Central Reserve to raise money for destitute families. There was an especially poignant benefit concert in May 1899 to assist a widow with six small children who were in dire circumstances after the death of her husband. J.H. Nancarrow, the man who died, had been a member of Bartley's Band. While the band did much for local charities, they also took part in fund-raising concerts for outside causes such as a coal mining disaster in New Zealand in March 1896 and the Indian Famine Relief in March 1897.

William Bartley's influence was not only as a band leader and teacher. He also arranged music for his band as well as other music groups in Broken Hill and even further afield in Western Australia. His son Frank, who left school at the age of 13 to work in the mines, gave some insight into his father's musical skill and dedication as he recalled:

> My father was a great music writer. I know I used to sit down at the table and I used to learn about the minim, crotchets and quavers, semiquavers, sharps and flats and all that. He used to have an ordinary ink pen and he'd write all the music for the band. Well, he not only used to write the music for our band but he wrote it for different bands, transpose and compose manuscripts. He'd say to Mum, 'Look, I don't want any noise now. You kids get outside.' He'd have his music paper and he'd start to write ... he'd make all the different parts in one night for a full orchestra. He'd send music away over to brother Bill in Boulder or Kalgoorlie for that band over there.[1]

William Bartley had worked at the Block 14 Mine in Broken Hill, but after a big drop in metal prices he was put off from the mine. Like many others, Bartley decided to go west to the goldfields of Western Australia, although he did return to Broken Hill several years later and conducted the Alma Brass Band. When he departed in 1901, William Bartley left his band on a sound footing and he had trained countless musicians, not only brass players but also players of other instruments such as clarinet and violin. The high regard in which William Bartley was held was evident by the number of concerts and farewells given in his honour, including a combined Amalgamated Miners' Association (AMA) Band and Bartley's Band concert at the Central Reserve; a farewell dance at Hegarty's Hall in South Broken Hill; a smoke social hosted by the Barrier Bands Association; and on the evening the train was departing, a procession of bandsmen who marched from the Criterion Hotel to the railway station to farewell their much-loved bandmaster.

Described as a tireless worker for bands in Broken Hill, William Bartley had never received monetary payment for his service to music in the town, but Bartley's Barrier Brass Band had raised over £3,000 for charity during his twelve years of leadership. He had also played a pivotal role in the formation of the Barrier Bands Association in 1899 and he was the first chairman of that organisation. Interestingly, this man who did so much for brass bands in Broken Hill was first and foremost a clarinet player.

Cornish choirs and carols
The Cornish influence on music in Broken Hill has come not only from Cornish *people*, but also Cornish *music*, especially 'curls' (carols). Cornish culture was evident in a number of ways in Broken Hill in the early days, including not only music but also mining traditions, Cornish wrestling and Cornish food – pasties were a popular item in miners' crib tins (lunchboxes) and are still very popular today.

Inspired by the formation of a Cornish Association in Adelaide in February 1890, a man using the pen name 'Cornishman' wrote a letter to the editor of the *Barrier Miner,* printed on 15 March 1890, suggesting that a Cornish Association be formed in Broken Hill. In support, he stated, 'I believe Cornwall is well represented at the present time on the Barrier among both the intellectual and craft classes'.[2] Two days later a second letter appeared in the same paper, written by 'Another Cornishman', encouraging 'Cornishman' to call a public meeting and commenting, 'I fancy he will have a larger following than even he anticipates'.[3] A meeting was eventually held in November 1891 endorsing the formation of an association, to be called 'The Barrier Ranges Cornish Association'.

This was an era when many non-Indigenous Australians were either immigrants themselves or the children of immigrants, and still felt a strong bond with their original homeland. Life could be harsh in the early days of Broken Hill, so people banded together to support and encourage each other. As well as the Cornish Association, there was a Caledonian Society (Scottish), Hibernian Society (Irish), the Deutscher Verein (German Club) and a Welsh Citizens' Committee. The motto of the Hibernian Society summed up the sentiment of these groups: 'Faithful to the Old Land, True unto the New'.

The first formal meeting of the Cornish Association took place on 14 December 1891. After a break during a very hot summer, another meeting was held in March 1892. It began with music by Brokenshire's String Band and then, after some short speeches and general business discussion, the rest of the evening was devoted to a program of musical entertainment involving both men and women, plus some recitations from members of the Dunstan family. With the Cornish love of music, it was not surprising that a choir soon emerged. The Choral Society of the Cornish Association, after practising regularly, sang Christmas carols at concerts on Christmas Day in 1892 and New Year's Day in 1893, accompanied by William Williams and conducted by Jacob Burrows. The New Year's Day concert, a fundraiser for the hospital, was held at the Town Hall, which was packed to capacity by a very appreciative and enthusiastic audience.

Over the years, other Cornish choirs appeared, such as the Cornish Glee Club in 1900 and the Alma Cornish Choir, which was reported in the *Barrier Miner* of 5 May 1910 as giving a 'benefit concert' in aid of the Wheatley family to a large audience at the Wilson Street Baptist church.[4] Some of the members of this choir were also in the Central Street Methodist choir; for example, members of the Roberts family, Miss Tonkin, the Parrott sisters, Mrs Clark, Mr Kelly and Mrs Kelly (nee Pascoe).

After a few years the first Cornish Association lapsed, but another arose in its place following a meeting on 22 Sep 1910. At this meeting, Mr William Gummow related the history of previous Cornish Associations in the Barrier district and then W.H. Thomas moved a motion to form the new Cornish Association. Less than two months after the formation of the association, a mixed-voice Cornish Association Carol Choir began, with Mr W. May as conductor and Mr William Wearne as pianist. The choir's first concert, at the Town Hall on Christmas night 1910, was so popular that hundreds of people had to be turned away. The choir continued to rehearse during the following year and by November 1911 about 70 singers were attending the weekly practice. For Christmas in 1911 the choir presented two concerts at the Town Hall, with proceeds going to several local charities. By November 1912 H. Nankivell was the conductor and the choir continued its regular Sunday afternoon practices leading up to Christmas.

Cornish carols have always been a popular feature of Christmas in Broken Hill. The tradition of singing Cornish carols at Christmas time was strong in Moonta and the tradition was carried on in Broken Hill. In Moonta, Mr J.H. 'Johnnie' Thomas gathered together and edited a collection of Cornish carols which had been sung for many years, including some he had written. He published the collection as *The Christmas Welcome* in 1893, making them accessible to the wider public. A sense of the great popularity of the Cornish carols in Broken Hill can be gained from this 1898 newspaper report:

> The Town Hall was not large enough to hold the immense crowd desirous of hearing the old Cornish carols rendered on Christmas night by a strong choir of about 40 voices, consisting of the Concord Society assisted by others. The choir was assisted by an efficient orchestra, and was conducted by Mr. Thomas, of the Concord Society.[5]

In December 1899, the Concord Society gave two concerts of Cornish carols, to packed audiences each time. The choir was accompanied by an orchestra and conducted by Mr W.E. Thomas. In 1902 Cornish carol singing was again featured in Broken Hill's Christmas celebrations. From 1906 to 1910 there was even a Cornish Carol Association in Broken Hill, but long after the demise of that association, Cornish carols remained popular. On Christmas night in 1928 a crowd of about one thousand people attended a Cornish Carol Concert at the Hillside Reserve in Railwaytown. On that occasion the music was provided by a massed choir comprising singers from Mica Street Methodist, Gypsum Street Baptist and Nicholls Street Methodist churches, accompanied by the Railwaytown Salvation Army Band and conducted by George Bargwanna.

Several years later in Broken Hill, S.G. Williams, grandson of George Williams, arranged some of the old Cornish carols for brass band. The Cornish carol arrangements were played in December 1942 at concerts by the Barrier Citizens Band, with Williams as conductor, at the Hillside Park in Railwaytown and Patton Street Park in South Broken Hill. In the same year, there was a concert of Cornish carols by starlight, conducted by Carl Thomas, at the Central Reserve on Christmas night. Ten years later Cornish carols were still being sung, with a combined choir conducted by Mr J. Trenerry presenting concerts at both the North Park and Sturt Park.

Apart from Cornish carols, there were other traditional Cornish songs which were sung at meetings of the Broken Hill Cornish Association, such as *Trelawny* which was often sung at the end of a meeting, as described in the following:

> The national anthem of Cornwall, 'Trelawny,' is an interesting one – a song which fills the hearts of Cornishmen with pride, for is not Trelawny Cornwall's hero? And when a body of Cornishmen, assembled together, give voice to their beloved Trelawny the atmosphere becomes so electrical that even the non-Cornishmen present become infused with the national spirit pervading the air.
>
> At the third annual banquet of the Broken Hill Cornish Association, held at the New Masonic Hall on Saturday night, over 100 Cornishmen lifted up their voices inquiring as to whether Trelawny shall die, and, judging by the fervor and feeling displayed, it was made abundantly clear that if they had any say in the matter Trelawny would never die.[6]

The newspaper report of the 1912 annual Cornish Association banquet also commented that although the spirit of Cornish nationalism ran high in Cornish people, they were enthusiastic in their patriotism to Australia and remembered the obligations they owed to the land in which they lived. It was almost as if they were responding to comments made by James Hebbard two years earlier …

The Hebbard family and James Hebbard

When the Broken Hill Cornish Association was formed in 1910, one prominent Cornishman in Broken Hill declined to join. His name was James Hebbard – an independent thinker and a man of firm beliefs. He wrote to the Cornish Association to say that while he was as keen in his interest in Cornwall and its people as any descendant of Cornish folk should be, he felt that patriotic sentiment to the nation of Australia should take precedence. This was reported in the *Barrier Miner* on 22 September 1910, when Australia as a nation was still in its infancy. Even today, these words challenge us to think about the fine balance between commitment to a common national future and appreciation of the heritage which has made us who we are.

Stepping back a few years, the parents of James Hebbard, John and Mary Ann Hebbard, had emigrated from Breage in Cornwall in 1847. John worked at the Burra Burra mine in South Australia for four years and then he and his young family moved to the goldfields in the Bendigo district. They initially lived at Epsom Downs, a Cornish settlement about four miles out of Bendigo. James and his brother Thomas were born during the family's time on the goldfields where they and their two older brothers, John and William, all began their working life as underground miners.

The Hebbards were Wesleyan Methodists, growing up with the rousing hymns of John Wesley and a love of music. Like many people of their era, John and Mary Ann Hebbard could neither read nor write but, true to their Cornish heritage, they loved to sing the familiar hymns. A delightful story was recounted about Mary Ann by one of her great-granddaughters:

> a grand old soul she was, despite the fact that she could neither read nor write … I used to take her to church and find her the hymns in her hymn book which she could not read anyway.[7]

James Hebbard, who first arrived in the Broken Hill district in 1884, is best known as a mine manager. However, his contribution to music in Broken Hill was also significant. By 1889, James was choir master at

The Cornish Influence on Music in Broken Hill

Sulphide Street Wesleyan Methodist Church and he led the choir for many years. A man of firm convictions, James Hebbard (and his choir) made the news in Adelaide:

> A CHURCH CHOIR ON STRIKE. AN OFFENDED ORGANIST.
>
> The choir of the Sulphide-street Church struck on Sunday night. The trouble arose during the progress of a Christian Endeavor service. Mr. J.H. Sinclair, of Adelaide, who was conducting the service, announced a hymn of exceptionally devout character, and exhorted everyone who could not sing the words from his or her heart to refrain from joining. The leader of the choir, a well-known mining manager, openly declined to solve the riddle of his choir's Christianity in so hasty a manner, and promptly walked out of the church, his example being followed by the majority of the choir. A volunteer from the congregation had to be found to take the place of the striking organist.[8]

James Hebbard's leadership of the Wesleyan choir and his experience playing in an orchestra would stand him in good stead to bring together local musicians for Hospital Sunday concerts. These concerts became very popular in Broken Hill in the late 1890s and early 1900s and are believed to have been instigated by James Hebbard, based on his experience of a similar concept in Bendigo. The purpose of Hospital Sundays was to raise money to help fund Broken Hill's hospital. The concerts were often preceded by a parade of brass bands, Friendly Societies and other groups, such as cadets and Boy Scouts. People would line the streets to watch the parade make its way from Argent Street to the Central Reserve, where many of the town's bands and choirs would come together for the good of the community. Thousands of people would throng to the reserve (now known as Sturt Park) where there would be collection boxes for people to donate money.

The first Hospital Sunday was held on 28 July 1895 at the newly-built rotunda in the Central Reserve. William Bartley was the bandmaster for a massed bands performance which brought together Bartley's Band, the Silverton Tramway Band and the Broken Hill Band (Andrews' Band). At that first Hospital Sunday there was also an orchestra and a massed choir of 130 voices, conducted by James Hebbard who would lead many combined music performances at Hospital Sundays in years to come.

As a result of the success of the combined Hospital Sunday choir, the Broken Hill Choral Society was formed later in 1895, with James Hebbard as the conductor. By the time the choir presented their second concert – a performance of sacred music on Christmas night in 1895 – the Choral Society consisted of a 60-voice chorus and six soloists, accompanied by the Standard Orchestra, all under the baton of James Hebbard. An advertisement in the *Barrier Miner* of 21 October 1896 for a Town Hall performance by the Choral Society supported again by the Standard Orchestra is of interest as it lists the names of the people in the orchestra, most of whom were Cornish: H.J. Williams, W. Hawke, A. Bennetts, G. Bargwanna sr, G. Bargwanna jr, W.J. Brokenshire, E. Brokenshire, J. Roberts.

In his working life, James Hebbard was a mining manager in the tradition of the Cornish captains, more respected by the unions than some other mine managers: 'His popularity was due as much to his success as a choirmaster at innumerable charity functions as to his canny and humane management of the Central Mine'.[9] When James Hebbard was chairman of the Mining Managers' Association, most mining companies increased their subsidies to help fund the local hospital. This shows the wide-reaching influence of music in the community and the influence of James Hebbard in particular. He was also a patron of the arts, giving his support to groups such as the Philharmonic Society choir founded in 1910.

One of James Hebbard's brothers, Thomas, also lived in Broken Hill and was a miner at the Central Mine. Thomas's family enjoyed visits from his mother, Mary Ann Hebbard, who would cook traditional Cornish pasties and confections which were remembered fondly by her youngest grandson, James Anthony Hebbard. Thomas's eldest son, John 'Jack' Hebbard, was a singer with a beautiful tenor voice. Although he was not a member of any choirs, he would often sing solos at family gatherings and musical evenings at Hegarty's Hall in South Broken Hill. This is just one example of a love of music which permeates many Cornish families.

Orchestras, ensembles and bands in abundance
Broken Hill's first venue for live theatre and public musical performances was the Theatre Royal hotel. The official opening in August 1888 was a

very colourful affair at which two bands played – a brass band just inside the entrance and a string band at the other end, close to the stage. The theatre was officially opened by Captain Piper, a well-respected Cornish mining manager who was Broken Hill's first mayor. There was much confusion about *what* and *when* each band was supposed to be playing. At one point the brass band had to be silenced so the ceremony could continue and 'the big drummer had to be dragged bodily into the street and jumped on'.[10]

The Theatre Royal proved to be a very popular venue for concerts, with everything from touring circuses to cathedral choirs performing there. In July 1890, when the well-known Quintrell family of musicians visited from Moonta, they performed a concert at the Theatre Royal and were assisted by the local Excelsior String Band. The venue was in regular use for concerts and other entertainment until a fire occurred in 1894. Following the fire, the Theatre Royal eventually reopened in February 1907.

By 1890 the population of Broken Hill had grown to 17,000 and the town had developed a vibrant musical culture. Many churches already had choirs, and several bands and ensembles had been established, thanks in no small part to the Cornish families in which music abounded. As Oswald Pryor observed, 'A surprising number of the miners, who had never received any tuition, could play tunes on the harmonium. Others played accordions'[11] and singing was a popular pastime. Pryor's words were spoken about Moonta, but also rang true for Broken Hill – particularly because many musical Cornish families had made their way directly from Moonta to Broken Hill.

Broken Hill's Cornish community produced many fine brass players who gained their early training in *Salvation Army Bands*. By 1913 there was a band at each local corps – Central, South, North and Railwaytown – but years later they merged into a single band. Some of the bands had not only brass, but also clarinets, violins and string bass.

George Bargwanna was born in Kapunda in 1864 and married Mahala Bottrell at Moonta in 1897. George's father (also a musician named George) had been born in Tywardreath in Cornwall in 1840. The Bargwanna name had been synonymous with music in Moonta and George Bargwanna and his family continued their involvement in music after moving to Broken Hill. *Bargwanna's Band* was an ensemble drawn from a small orchestra which often performed at entertainment venues in Broken Hill. Rather than comprising just brass instruments, it included any instrument that would allow a player to march and play at the same time, such as clarinets. George and Mahala's son, Jack, would grow up to be a very talented pianist, both as a soloist and accompanist.

Godkin's String Band was active in the 1890s, playing at events such as the Amalgamated Miners' Association (AMA) annual ball in April 1899. When William Bartley left Broken Hill in August 1901, George Godkin played a violin solo at a farewell function the night before Bartley boarded the train to head off to Western Australia. Godkin had also been the conductor of the *AMA Brass Band* since the beginning of 1897. In October 1902 the AMA Band decided to form an AMA Juvenile Band with Bandmaster Godkin to be responsible for training the young musicians. It was hoped that the youngsters would join the ranks of the senior band in years to come. Meanwhile, Godkin's String Band also continued to perform. In January 1902 they had organised to play for a dance social at Hegarty's Hall in South Broken Hill. However due to the death of Mr J. Hegarty, the event had to be postponed for a few days and the venue was changed to the Trades Hall, in the centre of town. One wonders if some of the people who lived 'out the South' might have reacted unfavourably to having to go over the hill from South Broken Hill into town for the dance.

The Brokenshires were another Cornish family who had arrived in Broken Hill in the early days and were very keen musicians. *Brokenshire's String Band* was much in demand. For example, when the YMCA held their inaugural meeting at the Theatre Royal in 1890, Brokenshire's band played and a combined church choir sang. Depending on the composition of the band, it was sometimes referred to as an orchestra. In November 1891, Mr E. Brokenshire conducted the orchestra which accompanied the Broken Hill Amateur Dramatic Club.

Brokenshire's Orchestra was linked with a dramatic performance of quite a different kind a couple of months later. The Fire Brigade had been the beneficiary of many charitable musical performances, as the threat of fire was an ever-present danger in the early days of Broken Hill and lack of water made the fire brigade's work even more challenging. Thus, when the visiting Gerald and Duff Dramatic Company organised a Fire

Brigade benefit concert in January 1892, many local musicians rallied to participate. A full orchestra plus Bartley's Band and the Broken Hill Brass Band all took part in what was a successful concert. Unfortunately, Messrs Gerald and Duff promptly disappeared without handing over the proceeds of the concert (about £30) to the Fire Brigade. They had also left their employees stranded in Broken Hill. Brokenshire's Orchestra came to the rescue and organised another benefit concert, this time for the stranded members of the Gerald and Duff Dramatic Company!

Brokenshire's String Band would sometimes play at meetings of the local Cornish Association. In March 1892 they contributed an overture as part of a musical program at a meeting of the Cornish Association which had been formed the previous year.[12] Through the years, the Brokenshires also played an active role in supporting the younger musicians of Broken Hill. When the *Barrier Boys Brigade (BBB) Orchestra* was formed in 1909, Mr Brokenshire offered to provide music and tuition, and he continued to assist the orchestra for over ten years. Two of the Brokenshires and some other adults also played in the BBB orchestra to support the younger musicians and to boost the overall sound of the orchestra. One of the lads who benefitted from this experience was Tom Nankivell, who would go on to become one of the finest musicians Broken Hill has ever produced.

Clarrie Roberts and the Quartette Club
Choral singing was influenced very strongly by the Cornish in Broken Hill. Some of the male singers in the town's church choirs of the 1890s were looking to broaden their repertoire beyond the traditional mixed-voice hymns of the church choirs. To meet this need, the Quartette Club was established in September 1895 as a four-part male choir. The Quartette Club would continue for 82 years. Men of Cornish and German origin formed the backbone of the choir in its early days, which is not surprising in view of the number of South Australian immigrants who came from Cornwall and Germany and later made their way to Broken Hill. In Broken Hill the Cornish vastly outnumbered the Germans and for the first fifty years of the choir's existence, over half of its members were drawn from the Methodist church. The only requirement for membership was the ability to sing in tune against the other vocal parts, with prospective members having to pass an audition before being accepted into the choir.

The choir's first public performance was a 'Continental Evening' at the Central Reserve on Boxing Night 1895. At this first performance the choir had fifteen choristers. Interspersed with the choir's musical items were performances from the Silverton Tramway Band and also a separate 26-piece orchestra conducted by Cornishman Ern Quintrell. The money raised by the performance was donated to the hospital. The choir's next formal concert was held in 1896 at the Town Hall, which was to become a regular concert venue for the Quartette Club. The indoor venue was much better suited to choral singing than the open air of the Central Reserve.

In the early years the choir was accompanied by an orchestra for two or three of its choruses in each concert – initially this was Ern Quintrell's orchestra and then later, the Broken Hill Symphony Orchestra. For the Quartette Club's 5th anniversary, they celebrated by having an orchestral accompaniment for *all* of the choir's choruses. Many years later, for the club's 80th anniversary in November 1975, a newly formed Broken Hill Civic Orchestra performed as guest artists, conducted by Hartley Harvy.

Clarrie Roberts, born in Spalding, South Australia, in 1882, was a naturally gifted musician who was mostly self-taught. He arrived in Broken Hill with his family just before 1900 and started working as a tram driver in 1902. Clarrie was a church organist and keen singer who gained valuable experience singing and conducting at the Blende Street Methodist Church, then later conducted the Mica Street Methodist Church Choir in Railwaytown. Clarrie was a good friend of Lloyd Trenaman, who would become another prominent conductor in Broken Hill. Clarrie had joined the Quartette Club as a singer in 1902 and then became conductor of the choir following some times of tension within the club, between previous conductor Edwin Cropley and the committee. Cropley, strongly aligned with the temperance movement, had moved a motion banning smoking and drinking at all club functions. When his motion was voted down at a committee meeting in 1913, he declined to stand as conductor for the following year and, due to the tension, other club members would not accept the position of conductor. Lloyd Trenaman then stepped in for two different periods during 1914 to 1916, when asked by the club to take on the role, but his other commitments precluded him from continuing beyond that.

The Cornish Influence on Music in Broken Hill

In these circumstances, Clarrie Roberts agreed to take on the conductor's role in 1917, but only as a temporary appointment. Thus when Edwin Cropley returned, Clarrie stood down and became Vice-Conductor. However, at the end of the year Cropley again decided not to continue in the conductor's role and Clarrie Roberts stepped into the breach once more. His first concert as conductor was in April 1918 and he conducted the choir for three more concerts, including a special performance in September 1918 to raise funds for the Red Cross. Clarrie diplomatically stood down yet again in June the following year when Edwin Cropley returned for a second time. After still more changes when Edwin Cropley resigned for the final time, Clarrie Roberts followed Tom Pyke as conductor at the beginning of 1925.

Around the same time, Clarrie Roberts stepped into the breach for another music group, agreeing to conduct the Broken Hill Symphony Orchestra after a motorcycle accident claimed the life of its talented young conductor Albert Guidi in 1925. After Lloyd Trenaman left Broken Hill in 1921, the Symphony Orchestra disbanded but it had been subsequently revived by Albert Guidi in 1923, evolving out of the BBB Orchestra which he had been conducting. After Guidi's tragic death, Clarrie Roberts conducted the orchestra from 1925 until he moved to Adelaide in 1927, following the closure of the Broken Hill tramway where he had worked until the end of 1926. The Broken Hill Symphony Orchestra would continue with a successful series of concerts until 1933.

When Clarrie Roberts left the city, it was not the end of his link with the Quartette Club. Not long after moving to Adelaide he founded a choir which would eventually become known as the Metropolitan Male Choir of South Australia (see Jan Lokan in this book). Because of Clarrie's connections with the Quartette Club, the Metropolitan Male Choir came to Broken Hill for a special concert in 1948. As well as performing their own program in the first half of the concert, they combined with the Quartette Club to form a massed male choir of 80 voices for the second half. The Quartette Club conductor, Arthur Beven, conducted some of the combined items and Clarrie Roberts conducted others. In addition, Clarrie's daughter Mavis Roberts appeared as a guest artist. Mavis, who was a gifted soprano soloist, had previously performed as a guest artist for a Quartette Club concert in November 1933. The 1948 concert was a great success and so the Quartette Club made a reciprocal visit to Adelaide in October 1949 where once more Arthur Beven and Clarrie Roberts shared the conducting of the massed choir in the second half of the program. The Metropolitan Male Choir made a return visit to Broken Hill in June 1952 for a similar style of concert, led again by 'the ageing, but irrepressible, Clarrie Roberts'.[13]

Altogether, Clarrie's time at the Quartette Club as either Conductor or Vice-Conductor spanned the periods 1914, 1917–1921, 1923 and 1925–1926. He wasn't the longest-serving conductor – that honour went to Arthur Beven who conducted the choir from 1933 until 1974 – but Clarrie stepped in to provide his expertise and lead the choir when they had been struggling during potentially disruptive times. His enthusiasm and sense of humour were much appreciated. Also, thanks to his influence, the combined concerts with the Metropolitan Male Choir were opportunities for the Quartette Club to gain valuable choral experience by singing with one of South Australia's leading choirs.

The Trenaman family and Lloyd Trenaman

Thomas Trenaman, born in 1829 in Cornwall, worked as a miner before emigrating to South Australia with his wife Mary Jane Polkinghorne and their young children. After Mary Jane died in 1861, Thomas married Elizabeth Ward. Thomas and Elizabeth's first child was Sydney Wellington Ward Trenaman, born on 5 Dec 1863 in Yankalilla. As a young man, Sydney moved to Broken Hill where he opened a men's clothing store in Argent Street. He conducted the choir at the Picton Wesleyan Methodist Church on the corner of Kaolin and Cummins Streets and was also a double bass player who played in small ensembles and orchestras in the early days of Broken Hill. In April 1891, at a Deutscher Verein (German Club) Sunday evening concert, he played double bass in a trio, together with Mr Andrew on cornet and Mr S. Gregg on trombone. Sydney was also in Sewell's Model String Band which played for the Hospital Ball in July 1895.

Sydney Trenaman conducted the Catholic cathedral choir for the opening of the cathedral in 1905 and was presented with a gold-trimmed wallet as a token of appreciation. He was still conducting the cathedral choir early in 1910 when there was dissatisfaction relating to

The Cornish Influence on Music in Broken Hill

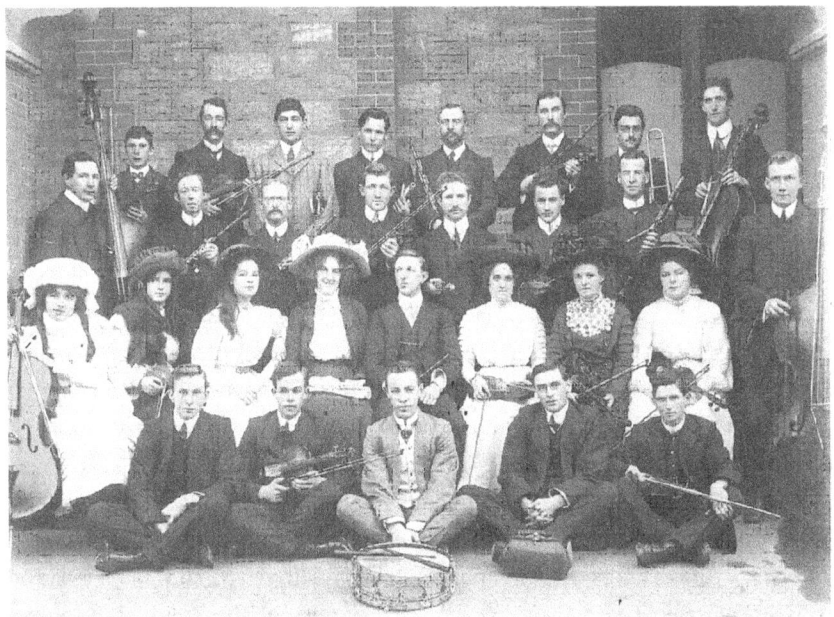

Broken Hill Symphony Orchestra, conductor S. Lloyd Trenaman, c. 1910

the appointment of an organist. This resulted in Trenaman resigning as conductor, closely followed by the resignation of the entire choir out of loyalty to their leader whom they respected and admired. After their mass exodus, the choir was looking for a new opportunity for choral singing. The following month, in March 1910, the *Broken Hill Philharmonic Society* was formed, with its chief aim being to sing in concerts to raise money for charity. Sydney Trenaman was unanimously appointed as conductor and James Hebbard was the patron.

This was the second choir in Broken Hill to be named 'the Philharmonic Society'. The first existed from 1891–1893 and was a successor to the BH Liedertafel Society (choir of the German Club); Trenaman's choir lasted from 1910–1912; and the third, which was founded in 1934, is still in existence today. Sydney's son, Sydney Lloyd Trenaman (known as Lloyd), was born in Broken Hill in 1889. He became widely known and respected in Broken Hill and beyond as a band, choir and orchestra conductor and also as a music teacher. In 1908 Lloyd Trenaman founded the *Broken Hill Symphony Orchestra* which he would lead until 1921. By the middle of 1909 the orchestra consisted of about twenty young and enthusiastic musicians. A newspaper report in that year foretold that:

> talent well directed is almost sure to bear good fruit, and the time may not be far distant when this amateur combination will be looked upon as a leading musical organisation in Broken Hill.[14]

Trenaman's orchestra soon became active in presenting concerts for charitable causes. On 7 November 1910 the Symphony Orchestra combined with the Philharmonic Society to present a concert in aid of the Children's Ward at the local hospital. The performers on that occasion comprised 100 voices and a full orchestra. In June 1920 the orchestra's concert, under Trenaman's skilful conductorship, was described as 'an all-round excellent concert and a treat for music lovers'. The orchestra also continued to give concerts for charitable causes. In February 1921 the orchestra, conducted by Lloyd Trenaman, presented a 'Grand Orchestral and Vocal Benefit Concert' at the Town Hall for the widow of the late Mr H. Mortimer.

At the age of 23, Lloyd Trenaman was appointed as conductor of the *Broken Hill City Band* in July 1912 and was fortunate to have a wealth of talent among the bandsmen. The following year, Trenaman took the City Band to the Ballarat competition, where the band's Septette came first in their section. In subsequent years, the band did very well in other competitions in Victoria and South Australia. Trenaman continued to conduct the band until 1921 and became known around Australia as a top brass band conductor.

In addition, Trenaman taught lessons in theory and practice of music. He was the local secretary of the Associated Boards of the Royal Academy of Music and the Royal College of Music (London) making it possible for local music students to be able to sit formal exams to gain qualifications in music. He was also a gifted cellist who had been a guest artist at several Quartette Club concerts between 1913 and 1919. He was already well known to the club when they offered him the position of conductor after Edwin Cropley wasn't prepared to continue in the role at the end of 1913. Lloyd Trenaman became conductor at the start of 1914 to help the choir out, but in October 1915, after almost two years as conductor, he declined to be re-nominated due to other music commitments, as mentioned earlier. Tom Pyke, a club member, agreed to take the role temporarily in the hope that Trenaman could be persuaded to resume as conductor for the start of 1916. Trenaman did return, but only for a few months. In the years that he conducted the Quartette Club, 'he was a moderating force and source of strength at a difficult time in the club's history'.[15]

As well as his many music commitments, Trenaman worked in his father's men's clothing store. However, an eighteen-month miners' strike in Broken Hill from April 1919 to November 1920, known as the 'Big Strike', put a lot of pressure on small businesses and many found it hard to remain profitable with so many mining families out of work. In April 1921 Lloyd Trenaman announced that he was closing the business in Broken Hill and leaving to work in his father's new business in Marrickville, Sydney. The Broken Hill music community was dismayed at the prospect of losing someone of such immense musical talent and called a public meeting in the Town Hall to try to find a way to enable him to remain in Broken Hill. Alas, no solution was found.

As word spread about his impending departure from Broken Hill, Lloyd Trenaman received offers to conduct leading brass bands in Adelaide and Newcastle – an indication of the high esteem in which he was held. Trenaman declined these offers due to his commitment to the family business in Sydney. Despite being so prominent in the life and music of Broken Hill, Lloyd Trenaman was a quiet person by nature, so when he left Broken Hill a couple of weeks later, he slipped away quietly without any fanfare or farewells.

The Trenerry family
The Trenerrys are another Cornish family in Broken Hill with musical involvement spanning several generations. George, Jim and John Trenerry were all involved with the Quartette Club. In December 1916, the *Barrier Miner* reported that C. Trenerry would be conducting a large orchestra for a concert at Johnson's Hillside Theatre and in the same year a Miss Trenerry had been singing in concerts and church services.

George Trenerry was a brilliant pianist from a young age and gained valuable musical experience in the Mica Street Methodist Church. He played as a soloist at several Quartette Club concerts, then at the age of 19 he became the club's accompanist. He remained in this role from 1916 to 1921, after which he went to Adelaide to further his musical career. He became an outstanding piano teacher and influenced the lives of many musicians. One of his piano students was Mavis Roberts, daughter of Clarrie Roberts. Mavis went on to become the accompanist for the Metropolitan Male Choir in Adelaide for many years. George Trenerry also taught Jack Bargwanna and Jack Williams, both of whom won scholarships to further their music studies in Adelaide and became talented and well-known pianists in Broken Hill. Many years later when Jack Bargwanna and Jack Williams met up again, they paid tribute to their former teacher. The *Barrier Daily Truth* of 23 September 1977 reported that the two 'Jacks' were both firm in their opinion that their musical career had been established by their great teacher, George Trenerry.[16]

Jim Trenerry, born in 1904, was a younger first cousin of George Trenerry. Jim gained valuable musical experience at the Nicholls Street Methodist Church, then at the Lane Street Methodist Church in North Broken Hill, where he conducted the church choir. He joined the Quartette Club in 1933, where his fine tenor voice was greatly valued for the club's vocal quartettes and he remained in the choir right up until his death in 1973. He was the club's Vice-Conductor for 17 years, from 1938 until 1954, during Arthur Beven's leadership of the choir. During these years Beven was working a roster of day, afternoon and night shifts at the mine, so he was only available for rehearsals for two out of every three weeks. It fell to the Vice-Conductor to rehearse the choir every third week. In spite of the amount of time Jim spent in this capacity, Arthur Beven would always conduct the choir for the concerts, with one exception ...

In 1954 Beven was going to be away on nine weeks' long service leave but he wanted to return to conduct the concert, even though it meant that he would have only one rehearsal with the choir before the concert. Jim felt that it was unfair for him to train the choir for two months then not be allowed to conduct the actual performance. Following a period of tension, Beven deferred to Jim's request. After 17 years as Vice-Conductor, Jim finally had the privilege of conducting the Quartette Club for a concert.

John Trenerry, who died in 2016, was very proud of his Cornish heritage. He was a son of Jim Trenerry and, like his father, was a tenor who benefited from developing his choral skills at the Methodist Church. He took over from his father as conductor of the Lane Street Methodist Church, then later in life was involved with the choir at Wesley Uniting Church. He joined the Quartette Club in 1948 and over the years featured in many of the club's ensembles. John conducted the Quartette Club for its 80th anniversary and he was the club's final conductor from 1974 until it folded in 1977. His role as Vice-Conductor for the last fourteen years of Arthur Beven's conductorship was equally important, due to the regular absences of the conductor. Later in his working life, Arthur Beven changed to working two shifts (day/afternoon) which meant that instead of missing every third practice, he would miss every second practice, until he retired from work in 1965. Following his retirement, Beven was able to attend rehearsals every week, but due to his failing eyesight and other health problems, the choir still depended significantly on the Vice-Conductor, John Trenerry. John was also a tenor in the Broken Hill Philharmonic, of which he was an assistant conductor and soloist on occasions over the years. Many of the Trenerry family have been involved in choirs at the Uniting Church and John's daughter Susan Trenerry also continued the family's music tradition, playing the flute in the Broken Hill Civic Orchestra and singing in the Philharmonic choir.

Tom Nankivell
Tom Nankivell came from an extremely talented Cornish family of musicians and was a virtuoso on the trombone – some would say that he was the most outstanding instrumentalist that Broken Hill has ever produced. He was also a brass band conductor and teacher and it is fair to say that this aspect of his contribution to music in Broken Hill was the most influential. Music was his life to such an extent that he even named two of his daughters after cornet solos by Percy Code – Zelda and Zanette.

At the age of eleven, Tom Nankivell was playing the cornet in the Salvation Army band. By the age of thirteen, he took up the trombone on which he soon excelled, thanks to a natural talent nurtured and honed by dedication – he would practise for hours each day. Tom earned seventeen gold championship medals during his playing career. His brother Richard Nankivell, known as 'Dick', was also an outstanding musician who earned many championship medals playing the euphonium.

When the Commonwealth Band passed through Broken Hill on a national tour in 1927, the band's conductor heard Tom play the trombone and signed him up for the rest of the national tour. Tom was only 22, but he had already won the South Australian trombone championship for a record three times. The Commonwealth Band tour was just the start of his professional career. When he was in Perth, Tom was hired by the Australian Broadcasting Commission (ABC). Not long after that he was hired by Perth's Capitol Theatre Orchestra. He was the solo trombonist with the Newcastle Steelworks Band for their world tour and then played with the ABC's Adelaide orchestra until 1947 when he returned to Broken Hill. Back in Broken Hill, Tom took up the conductor's baton and founded the Police Boys' Club Band in August 1947. He taught the boys from scratch and his skill and patience were such that within twelve months the band was playing at public functions.

The young musicians held Tom Nankivell in high esteem and many of the boys would go on to become members of the Barrier Industrial Unions (BIU) Band, developing a life-long love of music. Tom's total commitment to music showed itself in some interesting ways. Tom discouraged the lads from playing football, worried that they might split a lip or lose a tooth, which would affect their ability to play a brass instrument. When Dr Perkins, the ABC's Music Supervisor from Adelaide, visited Broken Hill in 1948 he was very impressed with the young band and said, as reported in the *Barrier Miner* during 1971:

> The Broken Hill Police Boys' Club Band must be one of the most outstanding in Australia. It is surprising that its standard could have developed to the extent it has in the past 15 or 16 months. This band is a great tribute to the conductor, Mr Tom Nankivell.

Tom Nankivell, who died in 1971, was described as a quiet, humble man and one of the world's true gentlemen. He was an outstanding trombone player, winning numerous championships and working as a professional musician. He was also an exceptional music teacher, imparting his love of music to others.

The Cornish Influence on Music in Broken Hill

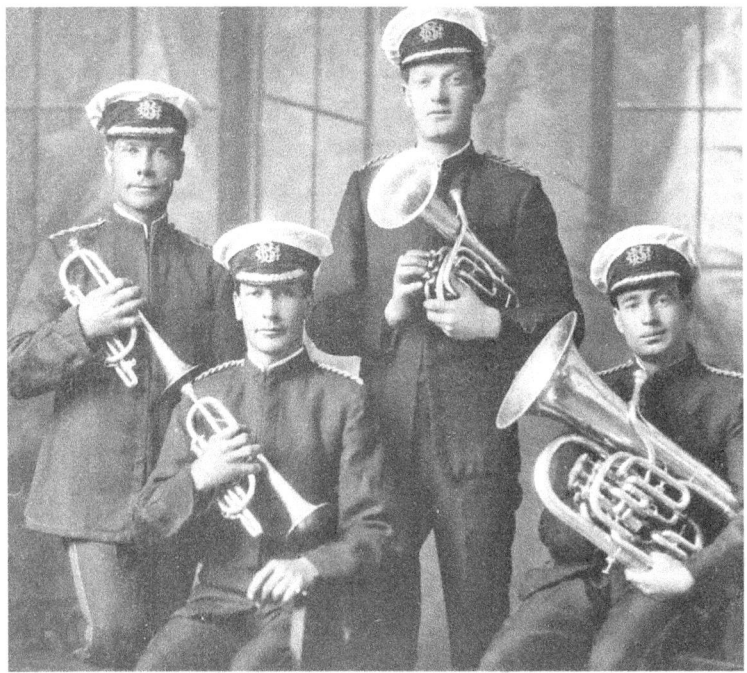

Broken Hill City Band, Silver Star Quartette, 1925
From left: J. Richards, H. Richards, T, Nankivell, D. Nankivell

The Richards family

Les, Henry and Jack Richards had a very strong musical pedigree. Their father, also named Les, played in Broken Hill's Central Salvation Army Band. Their grandfather was James 'Fiddler Jim' Richards who had been bandmaster of the Moonta Mines Brass Band and was a composer of some of the Cornish carols in *The Christmas Welcome* carol book.

The Richards brothers became outstanding brass players and, like their father, gained their early musical training in the Central Salvation Army brass band. They later joined the Broken Hill City Band, with part of Les's motivation being that he wanted to play football on Sundays and this was not allowed in the Salvation Army. As well as his musical talent, Les was also an excellent footballer.

Les Richards conducted the Broken Hill City Band from 1921 to 1935 and its successor, the BIU Band, from 1936 to 1949. At a Valedictory Dinner given in his honour after his retirement, Les was described as 'one of the finest conductors in Australia'. Under his leadership, the BIU band distinguished itself at national championships as one of the best in Australia, beating some top professional bands. In 1936 the BIU Band won the B Grade Championship, then in 1938 and 1945 they came second in the A Grade National Championship. The band would go on to win the A Grade Championship in 1961 under conductor Harold Walmsley.

Les Richards was a non-drinking, non-smoking, non-swearing man, which was somewhat unusual for a Broken Hill bandsman in those days. He was also a very patient teacher and during his 28 years as a band leader, tutored over 500 people. Not only did he give the young people of Broken Hill a strong grounding in music, but during the difficult years of the depression, he gave them something positive and enjoyable to do. In 2002, as a tribute to Les Richards' influence on music in Broken Hill, the rotunda in Sturt Park was named the 'Les Richards Band Rotunda'. The rotunda was built in 1895 when the park was known as the Central Reserve. The dedication plaque reads:

THE LES RICHARDS BAND ROTUNDA
To commemorate Broken Hill's
finest and longest serving band conductor
1921–1949

More of the Cornish diaspora in Broken Hill

Barbara Warburton's grandfather *Samuel Vine* grew up in Camborne, Cornwall, where he started his working life as a picky boy in the mines before emigrating to Australia to work on the goldfields at St Arnaud. Barbara's maternal great-grandparents, *Joseph and Alice Jennings*, also emigrated from Cornwall but had a very dramatic start to their life in Australia. Their ship, the *Marion*, was wrecked off the coast of South Australia in 1851. Samuel Vine's eldest son Herbert, father of Barbara, moved to Broken Hill where he became a fireman. He played the banjo and the guitar and would love to sit out on the verandah of their home in Broken Hill to play the guitar and sing. Barbara's nephew now has the banjo. Barbara has always had a love of music, but it wasn't until she was in her eighties that she took up the ukulele, which she thoroughly enjoys playing. Barbara also sings in a local choir.

The Cornish Influence on Music in Broken Hill

Many of the Cornish families who made their way to Broken Hill were immersed in music from an early age through involvement in the church. Hilda Ferguson, born in Burra in 1890, was one of countless Cornish people who quietly and tirelessly used their musical talents in the churches of Broken Hill. As a young girl, she attended Central Street Methodist Church. In an interview much later in life, she said,

> I played the organ for Christian Endeavour, then I became Sunday School organist and of course I joined the choir. Then I became assistant church organist and when the organist retired I took over as organist. There used to be a little church down here in McCulloch Street – it's a workshop now – and I went down there three or four years and played the organ there. I had to walk three miles to play but I did used to get a drive home. All the churches used to be full those days.

A friend then commented to the interviewer:

> 'She's really Cornish, isn't she? The way she says "did used to". She always says "did used to". Are you religious?'
>
> Hilda replied, 'Well I am Cornish. I'm pure. What about if I sang a hymn? Well, I'll have to stand up to have breath to sing it …' *Hilda then sang a couple of verses of a hymn which she had first learnt when she was six years old.'* [17]

John Bartle, who was born in Cornwall, was another person who sang in the Central Street Methodist Church Choir and had previously sung in the first Methodist church in Broken Hill. He conducted the Central Street choir for many years until ill health forced him to relinquish that role. Like many miners in the early days of Broken Hill, John Bartle contracted lead poisoning, then also had an attack of fever. He survived these illnesses, but in a weakened state. For many years he worked as a driver of a horse-drawn cab, but he was never strong enough to return to the mines or resume his leadership of the choir.

In July 1890, the well-known *Quintrell* family of musicians visited Broken Hill from Moonta for a series of concerts. They were accompanied by the 'Moonta Fisks', the choir of the Bible Christian Church, bringing the total number of performers to 23. In 1896 the Quintrell family visited Broken Hill again and performed as guest artists at a Quartette Club

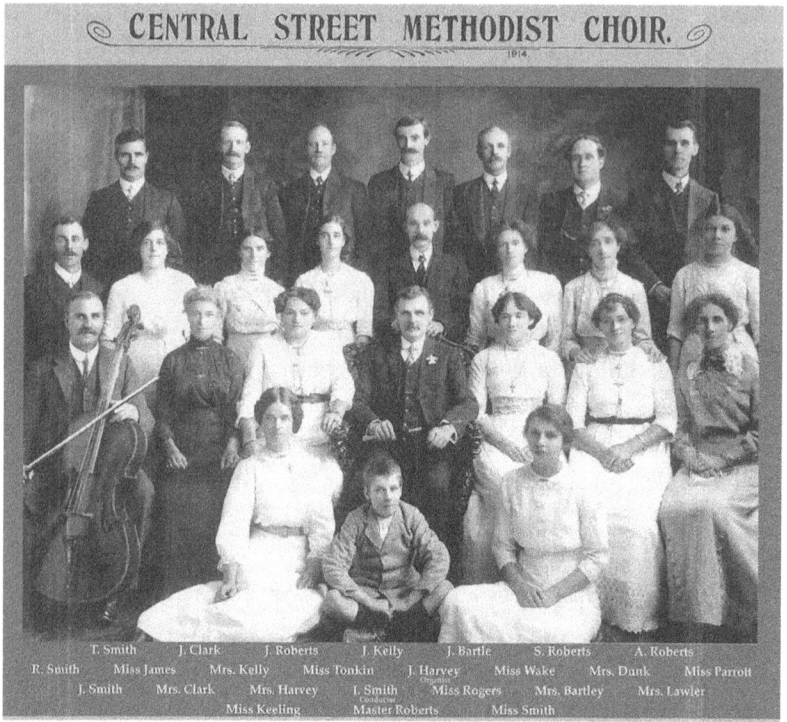

concert. Apart from visiting for concerts, the Quintrell family had other connections with Broken Hill. Mary Jane Quintrell, who emigrated to Australia as a five-year old with her parents in 1846, married Edward Paull at Kapunda then later lived at Moonta. Their son William Paull moved to Broken Hill where he married and had a family. His youngest son, Jack Paull, was a talented violin soloist who played with the Broken Hill Orchestra in the 1920s and later played in dance bands. Grace Hawes, the daughter of Jack's sister Olive, was a piano teacher and organist at St Philip's Anglican Church and sang in St Peter's church choir. In recent years Grace took up the ukulele and performed in concerts with the Village Strummers Ukulele Group in her 90s. Grace's daughter Delwyn was a violinist with the Broken Hill Civic Orchestra and now lives in Adelaide where she is a member of the South Australian Cornish Association Choir. Grace's son Donald is a talented organist. This is another example of a love of music flowing through many generations of a family with Cornish ancestry.

The Cornish Influence on Music in Broken Hill

Barnett ('Barney') W. Congdon, who had been a cornet soloist in the Kadina Brass Band, moved to Broken Hill in 1887. By 1888 roller skating was a very popular pastime in Broken Hill and Congdon was hired to lead the Skating Rink Band. Roller skating dances were particularly popular and provided regular opportunities for musicians to accompany the dancers. Roller skating to live music remained popular for many years. Barney Congdon played a key role in the formation of the Broken Hill Brass Band which evolved from the Skating Rink Band. In later years, after Congdon handed over the reins to Mr D. Andrews, the band became known as 'Andrews' Broken Hill Band'. There were other musicians in the Congdon family. A photo of the Broken Hill Banjo and Guitar Club taken in 1924 shows W Congdon playing the banjo.

Steven Semmens, who was born in St Mewan in Cornwall around 1839, emigrated to South Australia, then worked on outback mines before moving into Broken Hill where he and his family attended Central Street Wesleyan Methodist church. His youngest son, Stephen ('Ralph') William Semmens worked at the Tarrawingee Tin Mine in the Broken Hill district. As a young man, Ralph had played the trombone in the Salvation Army band. His children, Ken and Ida, sang in the Broken Hill Philharmonic Choir and church choirs. Ida, who married Tom Smith, had a rich contralto voice and was a soloist with the Philharmonic Society. She played many solo roles in musical theatre, such as the Repertory Society's performance of *South Pacific* in 1965. Ida was also a guest soloist at Quartette Club concerts on eight different occasions, spanning four decades from 1944 to 1972. She maintained her involvement in singing throughout her life and in later years was a member of the St James Singers church choir until her death in 2003.

Henry Penhall, the grandfather of one of Ken Semmens' cousins, was a Wesleyan Methodist whose parents David Penhall and Lydia Semmens had emigrated from Cornwall. When Henry married a Catholic girl in Tasmania in 1880, his Penhall family would have nothing to do with him for marrying a Roman Catholic, so he and his wife both took his mother's maiden name of Semmens. This is a reminder of the antagonism which sometimes existed between Catholics and Protestants in the 19th and early 20th centuries. Thankfully, music has a way of breaking down barriers. Musicians in Broken Hill have often played or sung in churches of many different Christian denominations regardless of their own religious affiliation and in the days of the Quartette Club, many members were proud to be able to say that they had sung in every church in Broken Hill.

The *Roberts* family were another family of Cornish heritage with a love of music. Three Roberts brothers – Alf, Jim and Samuel – all sang in the Central Street Methodist choir. The three brothers also sang in the Alma Cornish Choir. Don Mudie, grandson of Samuel Roberts and Lucy Roberts (nee Trevilyan), has a rich baritone voice and has given many fine solo performances over the years, and has been a guest artist at concerts for the Philharmonic Society and the Broken Hill Civic Orchestra. Don has also been a member of many choirs, including the Central Street Methodist Choir, the Quartette Club and the Broken Hill Philharmonic Society. He currently sings with the Broken Hill Community Voices choir. Don is one of those rare individuals who can employ either a 'choir voice' or a 'solo voice' as needed. He was also the president of the Broken Hill Civic Orchestra for several years and compered many concerts for the orchestra, as well as donating his time to compere the Broken Hill Eisteddfod.

Coda

In Moonta and other early mining towns in South Australia, the percentage of residents who had emigrated from Cornwall was very high. By the time some of these families moved to Broken Hill, the next generation was Australian-born, but many still thought of themselves as Cornish and the Cornish influence in Broken Hill's early years was strong. There was even an area in South Broken Hill known as 'Moonta Town'. It is natural to expect that, as the years roll on, the Cornish influence would diminish. However, as I gathered information for this chapter, even though we are now another couple of generations down the track, it was fascinating to see how many people still identified with their Cornish heritage. Of the people I interviewed during my research, almost every person of Cornish descent could name the town or village in Cornwall whence their ancestors had come, and some of the older generation well remember people who spoke with a 'Cornish brogue', as Don Mudie so eloquently put it.

People of Cornish ancestry continue to play an active role in music in Broken Hill and thanks to a visit by the South Australian Cornish Association Choir in 2014, there has been a resurgence of interest in Cornish music and heritage. Broken Hill Community Voices enthusiastically learnt 'Kernow bys Vyken' *(Cornwall Forever)* in Cornish and have performed it on several occasions. Later they learnt other Cornish songs, keeping alive an important aspect of Broken Hill's heritage.

Down through the years, Cornish families who came to Broken Hill have founded, led and participated in many choirs, bands and orchestras. Their community spirit and generosity has led to funds being raised for many charities and they have also been generous with their time and talents to teach hundreds of young and not so young musicians. Although some might not be aware of it, musicians in Broken Hill continue to benefit from the skill and enthusiasm of people of Cornish heritage to this day, for the good of the whole community – one and all!

References

Armstrong, Paul (2010) *Captain in industry – the story of James Hebbard*. Article in *Barrier Daily Truth*, 18 January 2010

Barrier Miner newspapers, accessed online at trove.nla.gov.au/newspaper

Barrier Daily Truth newspapers (print editions)

Curtis, Leonard (1908), *The History of Broken Hill*. Facsimile edition 1968 (reprinted 1978). Libraries Board of South Australia, Adelaide

Fiddaman, James (1983), *Hebbard Family History*. Private publication, Broken Hill

Fox (Trenerry), Jillian (2013), *125 Years of Christian Witness (1888–2013 Wesley Uniting Church Broken Hill)*; Booklet available from Wesley Uniting Church, Broken Hill.

Kearns, R.B.H. (1973), *Broken Hill Volume 1 1883–1893 Discovery and Development*. Reprinted 2013. Published by Broken Hill Historical Society, Broken Hill.

Kearns, R.B.H. (1974), *Broken Hill Volume 2 1894–1914 The Uncertain Years*. Reprinted 2013. Published by Broken Hill Historical Society, Broken Hill.

Kearns, R.B.H. (1975), *Broken Hill Volume 3 1915–1939 New Horizons*. Reprinted 2010. Published by Broken Hill Historical Society, Broken Hill.

Kennedy, Brian (1978), *Silver, Sin, and Sixpenny Ale (A Social History of Broken Hill 1883–1921)*. Melbourne University Press, Carlton, Vic.

McLennan, Don (1998), *Brothers In Song (A History of the Broken Hill Quartette Club) 1895–1977*. Self-published, Bulleen, Vic.

Pryor, Oswald (1969), *Australia's Little Cornwall*. Rigby, Adelaide

Silver Age newspapers (1885), accessed on microfiche at Outback Archives (Broken Hill City Library)

Stokes, Edward (1983), *United We Stand (Impressions of Broken Hill 1908–1910)*. The Five Mile Press, Canterbury, Vic. (photos and personal recollections of Broken Hill)

Wood, Craig (undated), *Brass Bands of the Barrier District*. Unpublished manuscript. Bound copy held by Ross Mawby, accessed November 2016

Notes

1. Stokes (1983), p. 152
2. *Barrier Miner*, 15 March 1890, p. 2
3. *Barrier Miner*, 17 March 1890, p. 2
4. *Barrier Miner*, 5 May 1910, p. 3
5. *Barrier Miner*, 27 December 1898, p. 3
6. *Barrier Miner*, 21 October 1912, p. 5
7. Fiddaman (1983), p. 3
8. *Advertiser*, 22 July 1903, p. 4
9. Kennedy (1978), p. 117
10. *Barrier Miner*, 7 February 1907, p. 2
11. Pryor (1969), p. 68
12. *Barrier Miner*, 12 March 1892, p. 2
13. McLennan (1998), p. 101
14. *Barrier Miner*, 23 August 1909, p. 3
15. McLennan (1998), p. 201
16. *Barrier Daily Truth*, 23 September 1977
17. Stokes (1983), p. 136

Acknowledgements

Images

Front cover photo: Barrier Boys Brigade Orchestra, 1920, from the Barrier Industrial Unions (BIU) Band's Collection

Tramway Band in front of Rising Sun Hotel, 1895. The original photo is owned by Ross Mawby. At the time this hotel was used as the office for the Silverton Tramway Union.

Broken Hill Symphony Orchestra, conducted by S. Lloyd Trenaman, c. 1910. Donated by Mrs H. Nankivell of Merrylands, Sydney, and held by the Outback Archives in the Broken Hill Municipal Library. Twenty of the 29 members are identified on the back of the photo. The conductor is in the second row, immediately behind the seated drummer.

Caption on back of photo:
Back row: D Doolitte, W Hawke, V Bernstein, H Spangler, ___ , A H Hunter, Thomas, B Tonkin
2nd back row: ___ , Sloan, ___ , ___ , F Burchett, R Krautz, H Dickerson, ___ , H Riggs
Ladies: Miss Fitzpatrick, Miss Fitzpatrick, Miss J Hepburn, Godden, L Trenaman (Leader), ___ , ___
Front row: ___ , A Hall, R Gummow, ___ , H Jennings

Broken Hill City 'Silver Star' Band Quartette. From BIU Band collection. Thanks to Boris Hlavica for the digital image.

Central Street Methodist Choir, 1914. Original photo owned by Don Mudie.

Interviews

My grateful thanks to those who gave their time to talk about their family history and their interest in music, bringing to life my research on the Cornish families of Broken Hill:

Mandy Edgecumbe (nee Bartley), great-great-granddaughter of William Bartley, for information about the Bartley family.

Grace Hawes, whose Cornish ancestors came from Camborne, for sharing her personal memories of the Paull and Quintrell families. Grace, aged 95, is a great-granddaughter of Mary Jane Quintrell, whom Grace remembered visiting when she was about 10 years old.

Ross Mawby, whose Cornish ancestors came from Truro (Pengelly), St Just (Phillips), and Newlyn East (Edwards), for his wealth of knowledge about local brass bands and local Cornish heritage. Ross played in the Salvation Army Band until its demise in about 1987 and he has been a member of the BIU Band since then. He also played in the Police Boys Club Band.

Don Mudie, whose Cornish ancestors were the Roberts and Trevilyan families, for information about his own family and a wealth of knowledge about local Cornish history.

Shirley Sanderson (nee Hebbard), great-granddaughter of Thomas Hebbard, who was a brother of James Hebbard. Shirley has a wealth of both family and local history knowledge and also lent me her copy of Jim Fiddaman's *Hebbard Family History.*

Ken Semmens. Ken, whose sister Ida Smith (nee Semmens) was a well-known contralto soloist in Broken Hill, shared his Cornish family history, including the fascinating story of his cousin's family who changed their name from Penhall to Semmens for religious reasons.

Scott Trenaman, great-grandson of Sydney W.W. Trenaman for information about his family.

Barbara Warburton (nee Vine), whose Cornish ancestors came from Camborne, for sharing her documented family history and personal memories. Her mother's grandfather, Joseph Jennings, was born c. 1820 in Cornwall and was well known at the Wallaroo mines in the early days.

Thanks also to Alison Wayman of *Outback Archives*, Margaret Price of *Broken Hill Historical Society* and Jenny Camilleri and her team at *Broken Hill Family History Group*, for their assistance in accessing the records of their respective organisations.

Local Cornish and their Choirs: Cornish Connections of South Australia's Metropolitan Male Choir

JAN LOKAN AND JOHN BRIMSON

As miners and others spread from Cornwall to seek better lives in other countries, particularly in the nineteenth century, they took their music traditions with them and quickly began to enjoy them in their new homes. Despite having to clear land, build dwelling places and community buildings for their new villages and towns, they found time to get together to sing, and play whatever instruments they had brought with them. Places of worship were quickly organised, even if in tents, and there was a supply of ready-made music that the immigrants would already have known, in the form of hymns.

Brass bands emerged within a year or two of settlement in Kadina in South Australia and Ballarat in Victoria, and the same was likely to have occurred in other places where a concentration of Cornish people settled. Chapels were among the earliest community buildings erected and, so the story goes, the Cornish cannot go to church or Sunday School without singing. If any impetus was needed to encourage music as a part of the new settlers' lives, the chapels would have provided it. Many of the Methodist churches established their own choirs, some of which, including the Moonta Mines church choir, were of sufficient standard to take part in competitions.

In Moonta, there was already a Glee Club in existence before the end of 1865, as shown in contributions from 'Moonta correspondent' in the *South Australian Advertiser*, who reported that the Moonta Glee Club had sung 'creditably' in the Globe Inn in November[1] and 'very satisfactorily indeed' in July 1866.[2] Hiccups occurred at other concerts in 1866 when they 'sang well' at the Moonta Mutual Improvement Society but were hampered because 'the bass singer' was 'laid up ill' (the choir must have been quite small in number at that stage);[3] and when, although the glees were 'well rendered' the songs were 'not so well, owing ... to the want of an accompaniment'.[4] ('Glees' were part songs, usually for male voices, and usually performed unaccompanied; nowadays, though, it is common to have a pianist or organist helping out.)

Along the way, there was some rather uncharitable criticism by a letter-writer to the *Wallaroo Times and Mining Journal*, who commented on the choir's poor articulation, ('turning good English into bad') and unbalanced harmony when 'the voice of the lad who took part in some of the pieces was most painfully prominent'.[5] However, the writer did conclude by saying that 'the entertainment on the whole appeared to give general satisfaction'. The criticism prompted the following rejoinder to the Editor of the same paper four days later:

> the Moonta Glee Club has induced a wish on their part that you should be put in possession of the following facts, viz :— That they wish to appear before the public in their true character, as imperfectly educated young men; and that what they have acquired has been in the intervals of hard work and little leisure. 2. That they never sang together before meeting on ship board. 3. The conductor and another at least of their number had no knowledge of music until within the last four years; and Mr Kendall often feels in his place as conductor that, having to take his part in the songs, he is not able to detect the breaches in harmony so fully as he could wish. 4. They trust to the good feeling of the public of Yorke's Peninsula not to scan too keenly their first efforts, and they on their part will do all that lies in their power to obviate the defects alluded to.[6]

In June 1867 an article referred to the 'valedictory concert' of the Glee Club because 'Mr. Nankarrow, the bass singer, has left for New Zealand'.[7] There is a reference to a Glee Club performance in 1869, but after that this particular club may not have continued. There are several references to performances from the early 1880s, including a mid-winter occasion with fireworks on 24 June 1882,[8] and also a note on the formation of a Moonta Mines Glee Club in 1898. The latter had 25 male voices and its conductor was L. Davey (probably James Leslie Davey). The founding members of this choir are listed in the newspaper and reveal a good collection of Cornish surnames: Andrew, Butson, Cornelius, Davey, Jolly, Phillips, Rowe, Spry, Trembath. At its inaugural concert, this choir had a 'full house' and was assisted by the Moonta Orchestra conducted by J.H. Thomas.[9]

At about the same time, despite the obvious existence of a Moonta Glee Club in the early 1880s, the following appeared in the *Yorke's Peninsula Advertiser* in 1899:[10]

> ### The Moonta Glee Club
>
> It is now six months since the glee club, which bears the above name, was formed in Moonta. It is a society for the development of all kinds of vocal music and comprises some of Moonta's ablest singers. Special attention is given to glee and solo singing, some very promising soloists have been unearthed since the inception of the club. Dr Drummond is the president, and Miss Mabel Roach the pianist, and both work most assiduously for the welfare of the club. Rapid progress has been made in glee singing and it is a pleasure to be at the practices, where all is harmony.

It is not apparent how long the 1880s incarnation of the Moonta Glee Club lasted, nor the Moonta Mines Glee Club of 1898. Nor is it clear whether the Moonta club mentioned in the above article from 1899 was a choir specific to Moonta or the Moonta Mines one that began in 1898. The only reference to a Moonta Glee Club between 1900 and the 1920s was in 1905, when the Club and other musicians from the area assisted the Maitland town band at a concert held in its aid in the town hall at Maitland.[11] Perhaps the Glee Club continued to exist, but was not as active, or not as newsworthy during this time. At some stage it must have wound up, however, and yet another incarnation emerged in the late 1920s, the *Register* reporting in December 1928 that a concert had been given by the 'recently formed Moonta Glee Club', conducted by A. Doley.[12]

This 1935 photograph of the Moonta Glee Club depicts the late 1920s incarnation referred to in 1928. The conductor, A. Doley, is seated between the two pianists, Mary Rowe and Kathleen Davey (niece of James Leslie Davey). In 1928 the choir was said to have 24 members but

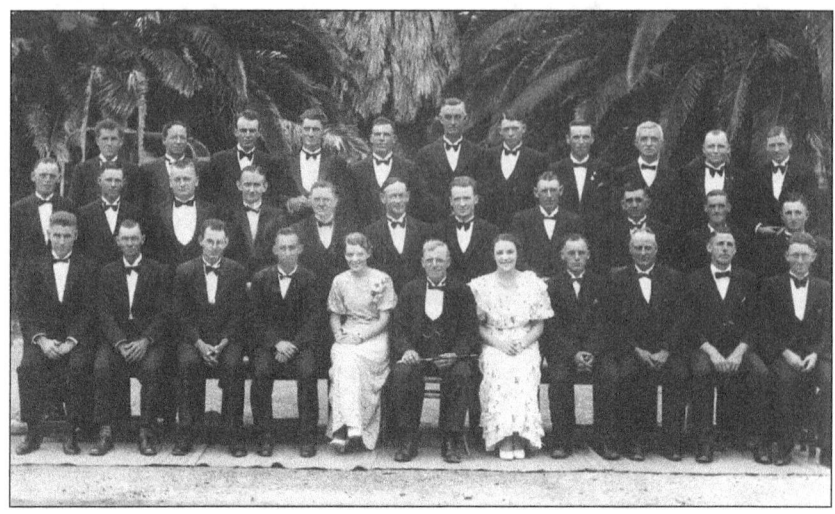

Moonta Glee Club, 1935

had grown somewhat between then and when the photograph was taken. Many reports of performances by this choir can be found on the National Library's *Trove* newspaper site, especially in the early to mid-1930s. Still with only 24 members, the Club joined with the Wallaroo Town Band, the Moonta Orchestra (conducted by Johnnie Thomas's son Carl) and a range of solo artists in a 'grand concert' in the Wallaroo Town Hall to raise money for the 'relief fund'.[13] It gave performances in Maughan Church in Adelaide and in many country towns as well as the townships in the Copper Triangle (Moonta, Wallaroo and Kadina), and participated in several music competitions, often winning first or second place. In 1936 it joined with choirs from East Moonta and Moonta Mines in a massed choirs celebration of South Australia's centenary.[14]

There were also Cornish choirs in Adelaide at various times, as Kate Neale has noted – particularly the Cornish Musical Society established more than 120 years ago by the newly-formed Cornish Association of South Australia (CASA). There was also a 'Moonta Harmony Choir', formed in Adelaide in the early 20th century, which sometimes combined with the Musical Society for performances. Eventually the Harmony Choir changed its name to 'The Cornish Carol Choir' and existed until 1992.[15] Within five years of its closure the present CASA choir was established.

Local Cornish and their Choirs

By the time the Moonta and Wallaroo mines closed down in 1923, there had been numerous choirs in the area over the years, including many church choirs, which would have allowed workers to participate in formal group singing if they wished to do so. Add to that the informal singing that is part of Cornish life, particularly in pubs, and it is to be expected that out-of-work Cornish miners from the Copper Triangle (and their Welsh 'cousins' from the Wallaroo smelting plant), who went to Adelaide looking for work, would have been pleased to find outlets for their singing.

An interesting juxtaposition of circumstances occurred in the mid-1920s that led to the development of the choir that is the main focus of this chapter. At the same time as those fleeing the closed mines and smelters in Moonta and Wallaroo looked for work in Adelaide, Holden's Motor Body Builders Ltd needed skilled workers for their recently-formed business. There had been a Holden & Co. in Adelaide from 1856, originally a saddlery. As the world moved from using horses to automobiles for transporting people and goods, Edward Holden, grandson of the J.A. Holden of the saddlery business, moved the firm's focus to the manufacture of vehicle bodies. By 1917 they were producing only vehicle components, mostly body shells.

J.A. Holden, Motor Body Builders Ltd, became a company in 1919. As its business expanded, the former miners from the Copper Triangle provided a ready work force and the Holden company hired many of them. The third circumstance that sparked the beginning of the male choir was that Clarrie Roberts' job as a tramway driver in Broken Hill had come to an end in late 1926, after which Clarrie returned to South Australia to look for work and, in 1927, he too had been hired by Holden's.

Robynne Sanderson, elsewhere in this book, has told us of Clarrie's life and musical pursuits in Broken Hill. Clarrie, born in 1882 and named Clarence Reginald Roberts, was the third of eight children born to Edward Roberts and his wife Fanny, nee Hanford. The youngest child was born in 1896 and all seem to have survived beyond infancy. The official South Australian Births Deaths and Marriage records give Clarrie's birth place as Spalding, a town about 180 km due north of Adelaide, where the family was living at the time of his birth. The five children who arrived after Clarrie were all born in Terowie, so the family must have moved there between 1882 and 1884. Spalding is in the District of Burra, which is no doubt why some sources give his birth-place as Burra. This is a farming area but there is also a slate quarry at Spalding and Terowie became an important railway town.

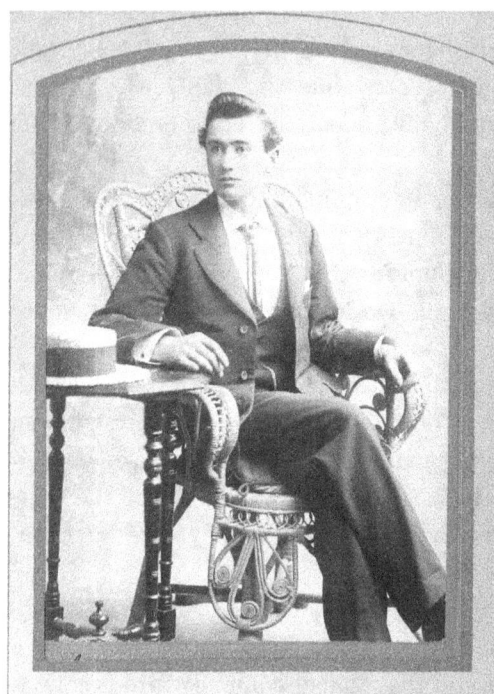

Clarrie Roberts in Broken Hill days, c. 1907

Clarrie moved to Broken Hill with his family in about 1900. Robynne Sanderson tells us of his life there as a driver on the tramway and of the many musical groups in which he was a member and often had a leading role. He married Gwendoline Birt in 1904 and had four children, all born in Broken Hill – Frank, in 1905, Mavis in 1908, Nance in 1909 and William in 1912. Clarrie and his family were very good friends with a member the first author's own family, Alfred Thomas Goldsworthy, who had married in Broken Hill in 1907 and had two children there in 1908 and 1909.

Alfred and family moved back to Adelaide in about 1915 but his and Clarrie's families renewed their friendship ten or so years later when Clarrie also returned to South Australia to live.

The story is fairly well-known that once Clarrie was employed at the Holden Motor Body Builders factory at Woodville, he realised that he was among many good singers. Just as they had sung while working down in the mines, the employees who had come from the Copper Triangle sang while they worked in the Holden workshops. It is also fairly well-known that the Cornish and Welsh have a natural ability to sing and to harmonise as they do so. As the history of the Metropolitan Male Choir

Local Cornish and their Choirs

(MMC) of South Australia relates, the proprietor of the company, James Holden, would hold social evenings for the employees at his home, and these provided the ideal opportunity for the men to gather 'around the piano for a sing-song'.[16] Soon a fledgling choir was born, with Clarrie as its conductor.

Although the choir's official history says that it began in 1928, it had performed in public several months before that, as reported the previous year in the Adelaide press:

> Membership of Holden's Male Choir is now more than 40. The choir was formed a little while ago, and last night conducted the first fixture in the form of a social evening at the King William street works of Holden's Motor Body Builders Limited. Dancing, items by individual members, and several concerted numbers provided the entertainment. [...] it is proposed to give choral entertainments, some for charity, in the near future.[17]

As early as June 1927 another article in the *News* reported that a practice hall and piano had been provided for the choir by Holden's and that Mr Roberts 'is most enthusiastic about the talent at his disposal, and hopes to make the choir a force to be reckoned with'. The choir were aiming to have 60 members 'shortly' and were already practising 'about 60 choruses'.[18] In October of 1927, at a large function in Gawler to raise money for charity, the choir joined with Holden's Silver Band, the Caledonian Society's Pipe Band and bands from Port Adelaide and Gawler 'to the infinite delight and amusement of the crowd'.[19]

The choir had already gained a considerable reputation by early in 1928: 'Holden's Male Choir, which has become widely known and appreciated because of the high quality of its entertainments, will give a concert in Semaphore Town Hall on Tuesday night'.[20] There were many reports of concerts during the rest of the 1920s and early 1930s, revealing the energies of the choir and its conductor and the considerable number of charities, for example, 'Hilton families in distress' and the Morialta Children's Home, that were helped in those Depression times. From 1928 the choir was regularly featured on radio, usually 5CL but sometimes 5CK, and by 1931 was known as the '5CL Male Voice Choir'. It had already competed in several choir contests and had gained first place at Tanunda and Adelaide.

A milestone for conductor Clarrie was that he was chosen to conduct the annual performance of the *Messiah* given by the Adelaide Harmony Society in the Adelaide Town Hall in December 1930, after the death of the previous conductor for 15 years, Samuel Gould. The choir had 140 members and was accompanied by a full orchestra and soloists. No one received any pay for this performance and all the proceeds were given to charities.[21]

In 1934 the choir, still named the 5CL Male Voice Choir, took part in Adelaide's first Choral Festival in the Adelaide Town Hall. In 1936 it joined in South Australia's Centenary celebrations, where there were 'Massed Mixed Choirs' and 'Massed Male Choirs', totalling several hundred singers. It was reported that 'the whole of the floor of the Adelaide Town Hall was filled with choristers' at one of the rehearsals for the main concert in November.[22] The choir chose South Australia's centennial year (1936) to change its name to The Metropolitan Male Choir of South Australia, which it has kept (apart from adding 'Inc.' to it in 1991).

Judging from newspaper reports, there followed many successful years for the MMC, the next 15 or 16 of them still under the baton of Clarrie Roberts. (There are inconsistent reports of when he retired, some saying 1951, others saying 1952.) Robynne Sanderson has described the successful reciprocal visits of the MMC and the Broken Hill Quartette Club choir and how these visits were very helpful to the Broken Hill singers. There are many newspaper reports of the Metropolitan Male Choir's steady stream of activities, attesting to the commitment and energy of the choir's members and its conductor. It is interesting to note that performances continued during the 1939 to 1945 war years, with an example here from the main Gawler newspaper.[23] It is also interesting to see that the choir was versatile and happy to combine with other groups and to play music from a variety of countries.

Concerts were given in a range of country towns as well as in the

---

Special Notice

Gawler Institute, Tuesday, October 31st,
GRAND SCOTCH CONCERT
with Metropolitan Male Choir of 40 voices; Scotch Piper; Dancers; Comedian and Singers.
Popular prices: 1/6 and 1/- See Handbills. Book early.

city, usually with a focus on raising money for worthy causes. The choir performed in Gumeracha, in aid of the local hospital; at the Hahndorf Institute in support of the Institute itself; at the Salisbury Institute in aid of the Congregational Church Manse Fund; and at Riverton, invited by the Country Women's Association, in aid of the town's Institute. Concerts were also given in aid of the Red Cross, one of which was held in the Methodist Hall at Allenby Gardens. In these activities the Metropolitan Male Choir was continuing the pattern set by its predecessor, Holden's Male Voice Choir, and by the choirs in Moonta described earlier.

There are reports of the choir taking part in church anniversaries, including centenaries, usually in Methodist churches but also sometimes in Congregational ones. The centenary of the Hindmarsh Congregational Church, for which the MMC and four soloists, including Clarrie's daughter Mavis, supplied the 'programme' for the Pleasant Sunday Afternoon gathering, was reported in some detail.[24] The service included a cantata called *The Martyrs*. Clarrie Roberts, along with conducting the MMC, was also conductor of the Hindmarsh Congregational Church choir. In 1950 the MMC performed in the Norwood Wesley Church, in aid of the church's Centenary Fund and in 1946 it was involved in the Methodist Church Centenary at Thebarton. Like the Holden's choir, the MMC gave frequent performances at Maughan Church's Pleasant Sunday Afternoons.

Mention should also be made of the many choral competitions and Eisteddfods in which the Metropolitan Male Choir took part. In April 1947, it was placed first in the choir competitions at Centennial Hall, while in June 1951 it was the winner of the main choir section of the Adelaide Eisteddfod. In the results of the competitions on that occasion, it is interesting to see Cornish names such as Barratt, Chappell, Dawe and Richards among winners in the junior sections. In March 1952, at the Royal Adelaide Exhibition Championships choral contest, the Metropolitan Male Choir gained first place in the male choir section, bettering the Port Adelaide Orpheus Society and the Lithuanian Choir.[25]

In later years the Metropolitan Male Choir has continued to fare well in competitions, as documented in the publication written to describe its first 70 years.[26] This small book contains a good deal of information on the choir's successes and 'noteworthy events', useful to have given the lack of accessible newspaper resources after 1954. Some ambitious larger works have been performed in combination with other choirs or the Adelaide Symphony Orchestra, such as Mahler's Symphony No. 8 at Centennial Hall in 1968, Beethoven's 9th Symphony at the opening of the Adelaide Festival Centre in 1973, and Brahms' Alto Rhapsody, sung in German with Sir Bernard Heinz conducting.[27]

Also in later years the choir travelled more extensively within South Australia and interstate, and undertook some major international tours. As an indication of the extent of these activities, co-author John Brimson, a member of the choir for over 20 years, commented that he:

> travelled overseas to England, Wales, Canada, USA, Holland, Germany, Austria and New Zealand on concert tours with the choir. Highlights were singing in the Royal Albert Hall and with many world-famous Welsh and Cornish choirs while on tour. On occasions we performed ad lib on a glacier, quaysides, railway stations, restaurants and jumbo jets, as well as in shopping centres and airports.[28]

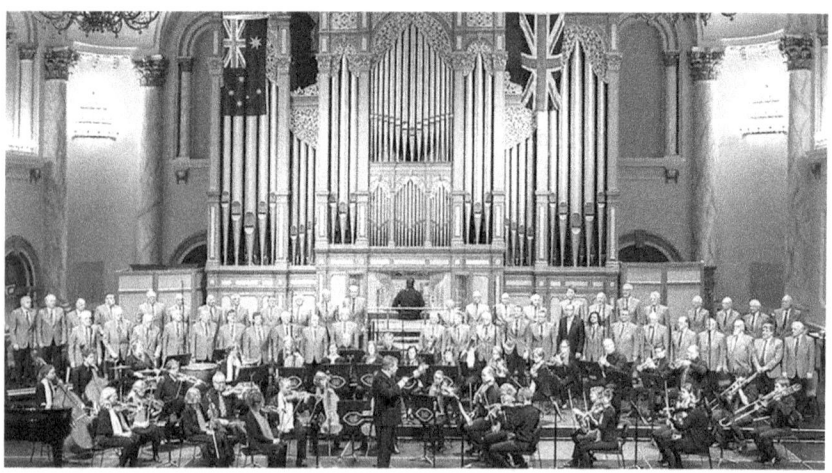

The Metropolitan Male Choir of SA, Adelaide Town Hall, 2016

For the purposes of this chapter, we are perhaps more interested in the Cornish influences at play in the choir's first 30 or so years. It is not known how many of the Holden/5CL choir members were Cornish, but there is a belief that many of them were, backed up by occasional mentions of names such as Bottrell, Hocking, Rodda and Rogers, as well as the conductor Clarrie Roberts himself, of course, and his daughter Mavis, who was the choir's pianist (and sometimes soprano soloist). Unfortunately, no complete list of early members is available nowadays and the choir has no formal archives as such, so we cannot know for certain. The fact that performances were given in many Methodist churches (Maughan Church was a favourite) and the focus on helping charities was similar to that of the Moonta choirs suggests more than an accidental link with Cornishness.

We know from newspaper reports that, back in the days when the Cornish Association of South Australia's annual meetings and reunions were notable enough to be written about, the Metropolitan Male Choir was typically featured in the program. An example is illustrated here.[29] Clearly, members of the Cornish Association felt an affinity with the choir, perhaps because of its conductor but also the likelihood that some of the members were Cornish or of Cornish descent. Several carols are recognisably Cornish, but other parts of the choir's repertoire were probably not so, as the range of choral music suitable for part singing is mostly not characteristically Cornish.

Concert for Cornish folk

A Cornish tea and concert will be held in Pirie Street Methodist Hall on Wednesday, December 9, by the Cornish Association of South Australia.

Tickets (3/6 or 2/- for concert only) will be sold at Saunders' Cafe, Adelaide Arcade, on Thursday and Friday between 2 and 4 p.m.

Carols and other items will be given by the Metropolitan Male Voice Choir.

The Metropolitan Male Choir has had some Cornish songs in its programs, for example Trelawny, Song of Cornwall and the St Keverne Feast Song, as shown in Huddleston's book.[30] The choir has visited Cornwall and given a concert together with the Bodmin Male Choir while there. And it helped host the combined Kernow Male Voice Choir, as well as performing in a joint concert with it, when the latter visited Adelaide from Cornwall in 2003. Its first conductor, Clarrie Roberts, from 1927 to 1952, was Cornish and its third conductor, Don Noblet OAM, from 1981 to 2009, had a Cornish mother, who hailed from St Agnes. A list of choir members in 1998 has over a dozen very recognisable Cornish surnames and others that could be Cornish.

Athough the choir, with its current conductor, has a stronger Welsh flavour nowadays, there is considerable evidence of Cornish influence in its earlier years – at least some of which has been maintained, through its performances on tour in Cornwall in 1994 and 2000 and its joint program with the Kernow Choir already mentioned. Further, the choir has continued to show an affinity with Cornish communities by singing for many years until very recently in the Moonta Mines Uniting Church, in an ecumenical service on the final day of the Kernewek Lowender – a Cornish festival highlight. When the MMC turned 75 in 2003, South Australian musician Timothy Sexton wrote a special song for them, entitled *One More Day*, its words evocative of Cornish life.

Notes

1. *South Australian Advertiser*, 2 December 1865, p. 3
2. *South Australian Advertiser*, 4 July 1866, p. 3
3. *South Australian Advertiser*, 12 May 1866, p. 5
4. *South Australian Advertiser*, 17 September 1866, p. 3
5. *Wallaroo Times & Mining Journal*, 24 February 1866, p. 4
6. *Wallaroo Times & Mining Journal*, 28 February 1866, p. 2
7. *South Australian Advertiser*, 24 June 1867, p. 3
8. *Yorke's Peninsula Advertiser*, 27 June 1882, p. 3
9. *Yorke's Peninsula Advertiser*, 2 June 1899, p. 3
10. *Yorke's Peninsula Advertiser*, 20 Jan 1899, p. 2
11. *The Register*, 10 October 1905, p. 3 (same article repeated in the *Chronicle*)
12. *The Register*, 24 December 1928, p. 3
13. *Kadina & Wallaroo Times*, 17 October 1931, p. 2
14. *The Advertiser*, 6 October 1936, p. 10
15. Carthew, N. (2013), 'Carols, Bands and Choirs', CASA Cornish History Seminar paper, Kernewek Lowender
16. Huddleston, M.J. (1998*), The Metropolitan Male Choir of South Australia Inc.: The First Seventy Years, 1928–1998*. Hindmarsh SA, Abbott Press
17. *News*, 18 August 1927, p. 18
18. *News*, 21 June 1927, p. 12
19. *Bunyip* (Gawler), 21 October 1927, p. 10
20. *News*, 10 February 1928, p. 10
21. Personal knowledge; Samuel Gould was the main author's maternal grandfather.
22. *Advertiser*, 10 August 1936, p. 16
23. *Bunyip*, 13 October 1939, p. 3
24. *Advertiser*, 31 March 1938, p. 17
25. *Advertiser*, 31 March 1952, p. 3
26. Huddleston, op. cit.
27. Ibid., p. 10

28 John Brimson, personal communication
29 *Mail*, 21 November 1953, p. 70
30 Huddleston, op. cit., p. 30

Acknowledgements

Grateful thanks are due to John Brimson for providing insights and resources for this paper. A member of the SA Metropolitan Male Choir for more than 20 years, John possessed knowledge of the choir that otherwise would not have been possible to locate. If he did not immediately know where to look for something himself, he knew whom to ask and how to contact them.

Thank you to Mary Walters, daughter of Clarrie Roberts' friend Alfred Thomas Goldsworthy, for the photograph of Clarrie as a young man in Broken Hill (possibly at Alfred's wedding).

Thank you to Janine Goldsworthy for the photograph of the Moonta Glee Club, 1935.

The photograph of the choir in 2016 was taken at the Adelaide Town Hall at one of its Prom concerts and is from the choir's website.

H. Lipson Hancock and the 'Betterment Principle': Health and Wellbeing at Moonta and Wallaroo Mines

PHILIP PAYTON

In the June 1919 edition of the official *South Australian Department of Mines Mining Review*, L.C.E. Gee, Chief Register of Mines, published a wide-ranging report on the 'Betterment Principle' then in operation at the Moonta and Wallaroo Mines. Building on an article penned by H. Lipson Hancock, 'Welfare Work in the Mining Industry', which had appeared the previous year in the *Australian Chemical Engineering and Mining Review*, Lionel Gee in his report described the welfare system that had reached its high point on northern Yorke Peninsula in the years before and during the Great War.[1]

H. Lipson Hancock

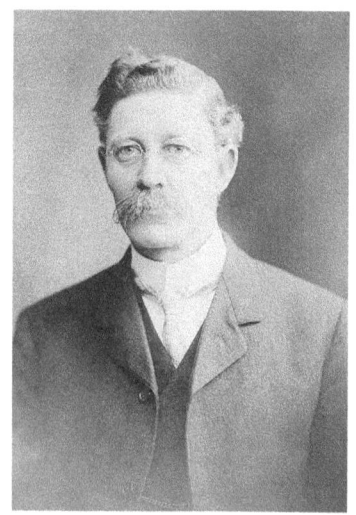

H. Lipson Hancock, who had coined the phrase the 'Betterment Principle', had become General Superintendent of the Moonta and Wallaroo mines following the retirement in 1898 of his father, Captain Henry Richard Hancock ('HRH'), who had managed the workings (first Moonta, and then Wallaroo too) for all of 34 years.[2] Although his appointment smacked of 'Cousin Jack' nepotism, H. Lipson Hancock was cast in a different mould to his father, taking 'paternalism' to new heights as he introduced ever more methodical routines and sought to rapidly modernise the mines now under his control. Although 'HRH', his father, was a 'practical miner' who had learned on the job, as had many of his contemporaries from the mines of Cornwall and West Devon, H. Lipson Hancock was 'booked learned', having studied at the Ballarat School of Mines. At times, he appeared almost obsessed with his concern for order, rationality and progress, and was often critical of traditional Cornish practices. For example, he ended the time-honoured measuring of depths in fathoms, adopting instead the foot as the standard, and opposed the equally venerable courtesy title 'Captain' for a mine manager (although he proved unsuccessful in suppressing its use at Moonta and Wallaroo).[3] Old Cornish engine-houses, with their ponderous Cornish beam-engines manufactured years before in Cornwall, were progressively replaced by new electric pumping and winding equipment, and much of the considerable infrastructural investment after 1900 was concentrated on the Wallaroo mine.[4] Two boom periods, 1905–1907 and 1911–1918, underpinned H. Lipson Hancock's 'bold and enterprising' program of development.[5]

In this context, the 'Betterment Principle' appeared an integral part of the modernising process. Initially, H. Lipson Hancock had followed his father's somewhat *ad hoc* existing welfare policies, with their emphasis on deserving cases. In 1896, for example, when he was understudying his father with a view to shortly taking over the mines' management, H. Lipson Hancock had arranged (and persuaded the company to pay for) the journey to Britain of one George Metherall, a young lad badly injured underground, so that he might undergo specialist surgery.[6] In the same year, 'HRH' himself had also organised a substantial grant to the Wallaroo Mines Brass Band.[7] H. Lipson Hancock felt that such payments were useful 'from a political point of view', winning the employees' loyalty and countering the influence of the trade union movement active on the mines.[8] Thus, when William Lathlean, another young lad, was badly mangled by the crusher at the Moonta mine, H. Lipson Hancock recommended the payment of £90 so that the unfortunate youth could be placed in the Home for Incurables in Adelaide. Likewise, he arranged the donation of land at East Wallaroo to the Wallaroo Benevolent Society for their proposed old-folks' home.[9]

The 'Betterment Principle' in action

By 1912, however, H. Lipson Hancock had decided that the present welfare system was untidy and in need of review. His efforts were soon hailed as 'best practice' in the Australian mining industry, the emergent 'Betterment Principle' seen to mirror the success of his other recent innovations in the Yorke Peninsula mines. Lionel Gee in his report, for example, noted that 1,008 men, accounting for 65.59% of the workforce at Moonta and Wallaroo, had been employed in the mines for ten years or more – a measure, he argued, of the success of the company's policies in retaining labour. Indeed, he added, only 81 men, or 5.27%, had been employed for less than twelve months. At the same time, Gee thought it significant that 1,069 employees lived in their own houses (albeit many in self-builds on the mineral leases at Moonta Mines and Wallaroo Mines), while a mere 122 occupied rented accommodation.

Moving on to the provision of facilities by the company under the Betterment Principle, Gee noted that at the Wallaroo smelting works there were baths, changing-houses, and a general impression of 'tidiness, space and light'.[10] At Wallaroo plots of land were sold freehold to employees on easy terms. In October 1912, for example, James Henry Chynoweth secured allotment No. 222 at East Wallaroo, on which to build a house, and a month later Clarence William Opie acquired allotment No. 212.[11] At Moonta Mines settlement, there was a vigorous tree-planting program to enhance the appearance and amenity value of the area, and in addition the company supported the Moonta Mines Institute, as well as providing a reference and circulating library, a billiards room, recreation hall, rotunda, tennis courts, and children's playgrounds.

Similar facilities were provided at Wallaroo Mines, including a pavilion, croquet lawns, a hockey-pitch, and a bowling green with twelve rinks and 'a good club house'.[12]

In addition to statutory benefits under the Workmen's Compensation Act, the company operated its own Club and Medical Fund, as Gee explained. Married men, for example, contributed one shilling per week to the Medical Fund and sixpence to the Club, while boys earning less than five shillings per week contributed threepence to both the Fund and Club. An adult employee unable to attend work through illness or injury could claim 20 shillings a week from the Fund for up to six months,

H. Lipson Hancock and the 'Betterment Principle'

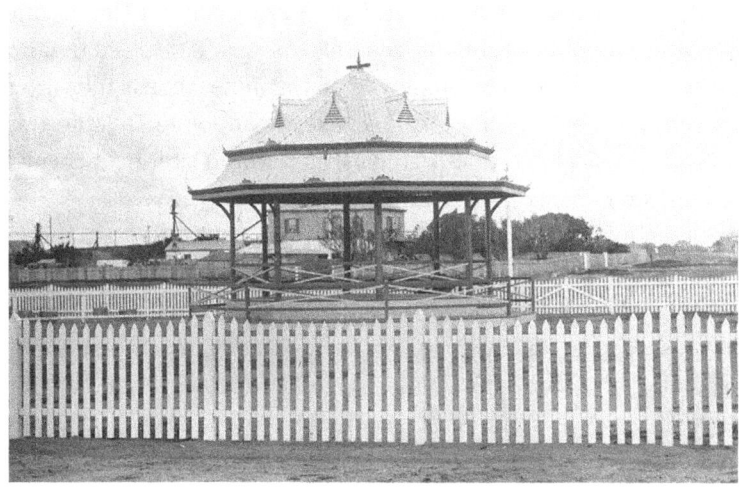

The Rotunda at Moonta Mines, c. 1908

after which he would be able to claim 10 shillings a week for a further six months. Boys would receive half these rates. Alongside these benefits, Gee also saw the sliding-scale of remuneration, introduced by H. Lipson Hancock in the early 1900s, where employees participated directly in the company's profits, as a progressive example of profit sharing and integral to the spirit of the 'Betterment Principle'.[13]

Cornish tradition

The clarification and codification of the Betterment Principle should certainly be understood as a key element of H. Lipson Hancock's modernising drive on the Yorke Peninsula mines. It created conditions that contrasted starkly with the earlier years, such as the 1870s, with the prevalence then of disease, high infant mortality, and general insanitary conditions.[14] However, despite these clear improvements, H. Lipson Hancock's Betterment Principle owed much to traditional Cornish practice that he so often regarded with suspicion. His own father, 'HRH', steeped in the tradition of the Tamar valley mines of Cornwall and Devon, had been anxious to ameliorate the worst of the conditions at the Yorke Peninsula mines, and as early as November 1864 the Moonta directors had written to him to 'agree with you as to the advisability of adopting any reasonable measure for the promotion of the social and moral welfare of the men'.[15] He arranged permission for the erection of chapels and schoolrooms on the mineral leases, and decreed that no boy under the age of 14 could be employed on the mines unless they attended night-school three times a week. Likewise, he appointed a mine surgeon and introduced a 'club & doctor' fund which would later be incorporated and enhanced in his son's Betterment Principle.

Earlier still, at the Burra mine, which was similarly dependent on Cornish mining practices, a mine surgeon had been appointed by the South Australian Mining Association (SAMA). As well as dealing with employees' sicknesses and injuries, he took a wider interest in welfare and social conditions. In June 1847, Allan Thomson, the mine surgeon, wrote to Henry Ayers, the SAMA secretary, to complain that fever was widespread in the community as a result of the 'Slaughter Houses & C., Stock Yards, and Piggeries attached to different stores, together with the chamber filth thrown out of the cottages, and that deposit in the creeks'.[16] Ayers arranged for the construction of miners' cottages (to discourage the practice of living in dugouts along the creek), and also donated land for the erection of chapels.

Here again we may detect the influence of Cornwall. 'Bal clubs' and 'doctor's pence' were a feature of many Cornish mines from at least the early nineteenth century.[17] The degree of provision varied considerably from mine to mine, and in the more remote areas it was often difficult to persuade 'bal surgeons' to reside in the mining villages. As late as 1872, 10 of 11 major mines in St Just-in-Penwith had surgeons who, wishing to avoid the wildness of the far west, preferred to live in more fashionable Penzance. As a result, it was often many hours before a doctor could be summoned and an injured man treated.[18] But other mines were more conscientious and provided a range of benefits, an outstanding example being Carn Brea Mines in the Camborne–Redruth district. As the mine's captain explained in 1864:

> I have always recommended liberality with regard to club money. We [even] apply it to pensioning off old men who are unable to work any longer on the mine, who have been there for many years . . . we always make them some allowance, and we are not particular about the injury or illness which is occasioned by their work. We treat an illness brought

on by working in the mine as a visible hurt. Then, again, out of the club we bury the men, and if a man dies from an ordinary illness, not at all connected with his duty in the mine, we always pay for the coffin. Any man working in the mine has his coffin from the mine, and that is always charged to the club at Carn Brea.[19]

At Carn Brea there was also provision for widows, and at some of the larger mines there were barbers whose services were provided by subscription to the club and doctor's funds. To some extent such activities anticipated the many friendly societies that were to flourish in Cornwall (and in Cornish communities overseas). They also reflected the religious and cultural influence of Methodism, especially as it developed in Cornwall, with its commitment to 'self-help', 'betterment' and 'mutual improvement'. There was indeed a 'distinctive Cornish hue', as Roger Burt has described it, to the many self-help institutions that had sprung up by 1850 – the Liskeard Institution, the St Austell Useful Knowledge Society, the St Austell Literary Society, the Launceston Philosophical Society, and many more.[20]

Methodism, 'Betterment' and the 'Rainbow System'

Central to such activity was the concept of 'betterment', as the Methodists expressed it, and it is no coincidence that H. Lipson Hancock incorporated this telling term in the title of his 'Betterment Principle' program. The Betterment Principle may have been an integral part of his modernising agenda at Moonta and Wallaroo, but its roots lay firmly in Cornwall. Significantly, the same might be said of H. Lipson Hancock's 'Rainbow System' of religious instruction, which was built upon equally firm Methodist foundations but also reflected his modernising imperative, as witnessed on the mines themselves and in the Betterment Principle. Methodist Union in South Australia in 1901 had made redundant the Primitive Methodist chapel on Moonta Mines, and after 1905 the building became the focus of H. Lipson Hancock's new Sunday School regime. As he wrote:

> This meant a complete reconstruction, necessitating careful thought and much wisdom, and involving considerable expense. The whole teaching arrangements had to be reorganized and suitable rooms provided,

together with the needed apparatus for teaching. Led by the present Superintendent of the School [H. Lipson Hancock himself], the teachers undertook the reconstruction.[21]

The Rainbow System was authoritarian and highly structured. It was also seen to be highly successful and by 1918 Moonta Mines Sunday School had received 7,000 visitors, with the Rainbow System adopted across northern Yorke Peninsula at Yelta, Wallaroo Mines, Agery, Paskeville and Greens Plains West.[22] The Sunday Schools were organised into numerous departments and committees, and conducted according to an unvarying code of behaviour. As H. Lipson Hancock explained:

> After the removal of hats and cloaks, under supervision, the different sections are formed into line, headed in each case by the leader of the day. The procession, to the accompaniment of music, passes through the Kindergarten room on its way to the main hall for the opening exercises, a junior teacher taking a place after every third scholar. One teacher or helper should be available, if possible, for every three scholars, but at least one for every four or five scholars.[23]

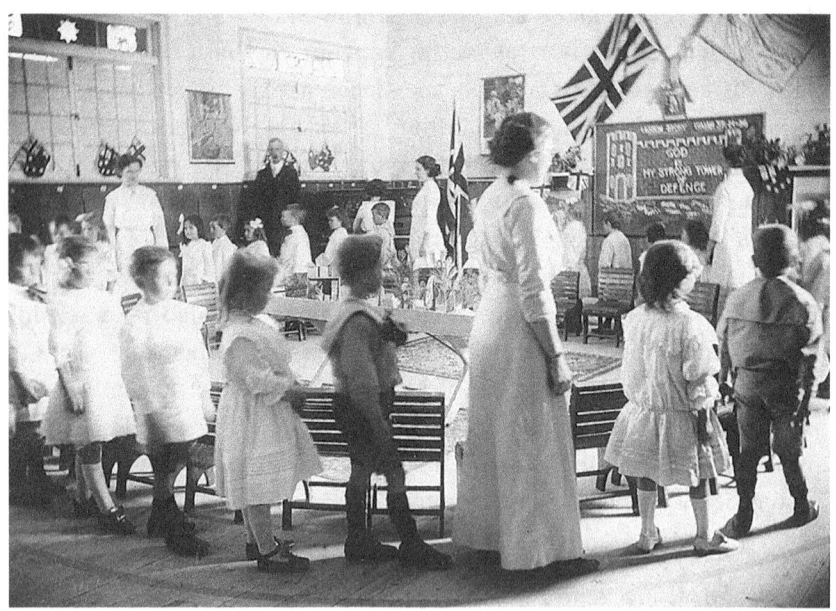

Rainbow procession marching in the Kindergarten room

H. Lipson Hancock and the 'Betterment Principle'

There is no doubt that H. Lipson Hancock saw the Rainbow System as part of his welfare work on the mines. Wellbeing in the next world was as important as in this, and the discipline instilled by the system's rigid strictures was designed to produce model young citizens. As H. Lipson Hancock had already admitted, welfare work generally could be politically useful. This was no more so than during the Great War, when the hitherto cohesive community of northern Yorke Peninsula was ruptured in the increasingly rancorous debate over conscription to the armed forces.[24] Previously, Methodism and the Labor movement on the mines had worked hand in hand but the conscription issue drove a wedge between the two. Rank and file Labor men (and women) continued to adhere to the voluntary principle, but the Methodist church – on the Peninsula and in South Australia as a whole – moved firmly behind conscription. At Moonta and Wallaroo the Betterment Principle and Rainbow System became the voice of institutional Methodism, one that H. Lipson Hancock articulated in a series of publications during the war years as he attempted to exert moral authority in difficult times. Yet the Peninsula towns overwhelmingly rejected conscription in the two referenda. Perhaps surprisingly, as Arnold Hunt observed, plainly 'the [Methodist] church's capacity to influence the thinking of its members on this issue was very limited, and in some areas (such as Moonta) was virtually non-existent'.[25]

Conclusion

It is clear that the conscription issue had undermined the strength of institutional Methodism on northern Yorke Peninsula, despite the best efforts of H. Lipson Hancock. We can speculate as to how this might have affected both the 'Betterment Principle' and the 'Rainbow System' in the years after the Great War, if mining had continued unabated. But the reality was that, with the rapid post-war decline of the mines and their closure in 1923, both were destined to disappear swiftly from the scene. H. Lipson Hancock's welfare policies might be seen as the high point of a tradition inherited from Cornwall but, like his other modernising policies at the mines, they were nonetheless short-lived, victims of rapidly changing circumstances that he could not have foreseen.

Notes

1. *South Australian Department of Mines Mining Review*, half-year ended June 1919; H. Lipson Hancock, 'Welfare Work in the Mining Industry', *Australian Chemical Engineering and Mining Review*, October 1918
2. Anon, *The Wallaroo and Moonta Mines: Their History, Nature, and Methods, together with an Account of the Concentrating and Smelting Operations*, Hussey & Gillingham, Adelaide, 1914, p. 4
3. State Library of South Australia [SLSA] BRG40/1034, Wallaroo and Moonta Mining and Smelting Company, Minute Books, 1895–1923, 19 February 1918
4. Philip Payton, *Making Moonta: The Invention of Australia's Little Cornwall*, University of Exeter Press, Exeter, 1997, pp. 181–183
5. Henry Brown, 'The Copper Industry of South Australia: An Economic Study', John Lozenzo Young Scholarship Thesis, 1937, revised 1960, p. 92
6. SLSA BRG40/1034, 23 June 1896
7. SLSA BRG40/1043, 30 June 1896
8. SLSA BRG40/1043, 18 October 1899
9. SLSA BRG40/1043, 4 November 1902; 10 June 1908
10. *South Australian Department of Mines Mining Review*, half-year ended June 1919, p. 53
11. SLSA BRG40/1043, 29 October 1912; 19 November 1912
12. *South Australian Department of Mines Mining Review*, half-year ended June 1919, p. 54
13. *South Australian Department of Mines Mining Review*, half-year ended June 1919, p. 54
14. Ella Stewart-Peters, '"To brave a thousand Cornishmen": The role of Cornish identity in Opposition to Government Intervention at Moonta Mines', *Journal of the Historical Association of South Australia*, 43, 2015, pp. 87–97
15. SLSA BRG40/543, Moonta Mines Proprietors, Out-Letter Books, 1863–69, 15 November 1864
16. SLSA BRG22/80, South Australian Mining Association, Miscellaneous Papers, 28 June 1847
17. A.K. Hamilton Jenkin, *The Cornish Miner*, 1927, republished David & Charles, Newton Abbot, 1972, p. 310; D.B. Barton, *Essays in Cornish Mining History: Volume One*, D. Bradford Barton, Truro, 1968, p. 118
18. Barton, *Essays*, p. 57
19. Jenkin, *Cornish Miner*, pp. 267–268
20. Roger Burt, *The British Lead Mining Industry*, Dyllansow Truran, Redruth, 1984, p. 123
21. H. Lipson Hancock and William Shaw, *A Sunday School of Today*, Adelaide, 1912, pp. 21–22
22. H. Lipson Hancock and William R. Penhall, *The Missionary Spirit in Sunday School Work*, Adelaide, 1918
23. H. Lipson Hancock, *Modern Methods in Sunday School Work,* Adelaide, 1916, pp. 20–21
24. Philip Payton, *Regional Australia and the Great War: 'The Boys from Old Kio'*, University of Exeter Press, 2012, pp. 139–162; Philip Payton, *One and All:*

H. Lipson Hancock and the 'Betterment Principle'

Labor and the Radical Tradition in South Australia, Wakefield Press, Adelaide, 2016, pp. 196–221

25 Arnold D. Hunt, *This Side of Heaven: A History of Methodism in South Australia*, Lutheran Publishing House, Adelaide, 1985, p. 291

Acknowledgements

The photographs included are all courtesy of the State Library of South Australia and have no known copyright restriction. The first and third in the list are part of the Hancock Collection.

H Lipson Hancock, General Superintendent of the Moonta Mines Sunday School c. 1914 (PRG 1185/7/2)

The Rotunda at Moonta Mines c. 1908 (B 21215)

The Rainbow procession marching in the Kindergarten room, Moonta Mines Methodist Sunday School c. 1914 (PRG 1185/7/15)

Sir John Langdon Bonython, a Rich and Successful Life: But South Australia or Cornwall?

JEAN PREST

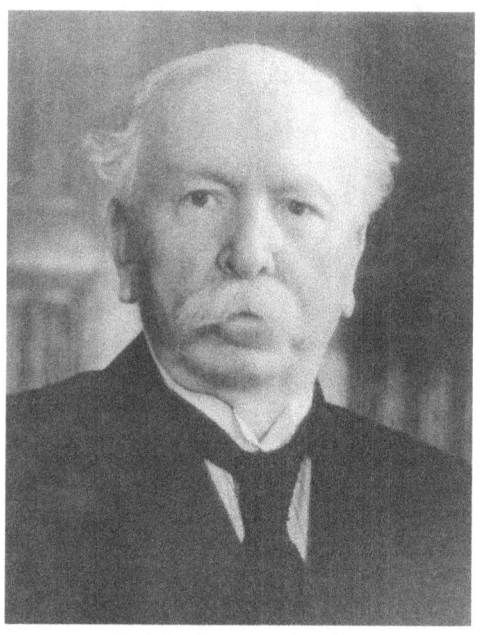

This chapter is concerned with claiming for Sir John Langdon Bonython, never a miner, the title of South Australia's most successful and revered Cornishman over his very long life from 1848 to 1939. This claim for his position of premier Cornishman must be estimated in the strength of his attachment to Cornwall, the power he wielded and, most of all, his influence over the State's and subsequently the Commonwealth's history. (Incidentally, he is referred to here as Langdon Bonython but before he was knighted he was called by his first name, John.)

Sir John Langdon Bonython, a Rich and Successful Life

How can the strength of his Cornishness be estimated? At first it must seem extremely flimsy. Born in London, Bonython left Cornwall in 1854, when he was six, to come to South Australia with his mother and father and his older brother. They were assisted migrants, though not without some capital. And his father, George, was born in 1820 and baptised at Charlotte Town, Prince Edward Island, Canada, where *his* adventurous father, Thomas Bonython, had migrated when the last of the land owned by the family in Cornwall was sold. Young George was sent back to England, unaccompanied when only seven, to be raised by his maternal grandfather, John Harris Langdon, in London. He was an architect and appears to have been far more influential in George's life than George's own father. The family still has a handsome lithograph of Grey's Hospital upon which they had worked. This architectural training served George well in the new town of Adelaide. A devout Methodist, he worshipped all his life at Pirie Street Methodist Church, which he helped to build. The lovely staircase in Adelaide's Town Hall is reputed to be his work, as were five or six grand houses between Wakefield Street and Hutt Street.

Arriving in the colony of South Australia twenty-four years after its foundation, there was the added pleasure of finding that Grandfather Thomas Bonython had preceded them. I must assume that they had always corresponded and that probably Grandfather Thomas had made the second migration via London. His little grandson, John Langdon Bonython, now had in Australia a Cornish grandfather and grandmother awaiting him. His own connection with Cornwall had been brief but these grandparents were Bonythons and Methodist and, to make them even more acceptable in the colony, which they had reached fourteen years ahead of George and his family, this grandmother could claim her family's connection with John Wesley, for her grandfather had become one of his ministers. No better connection could be made.

She was a formidable influence on the little John Langdon Bonython. She, and not his mother, told him tales of Cornish traditions and of the beauty of its landscape, its romantic literature and its heraldry and, most of all, of the great estates which he might one day reclaim. There is much evidence of the deep ambition to return to his Cornish origins with these lands in sight. His own grandson, Eric Glenie Bonython, was brought up in his grandfather's home when his mother and father, Hugh Bonython, died before he was four. Eric's book, which attempts to trace the family history as far back as the Norman Conquest, is a tribute to the care and kindness of Sir Langdon and his wife, Polly. In the book he refers frequently to what he calls 'grandfather's only hobby', which was tracing his Cornish lineage.

Langdon Bonython finished his schooling with Headmaster Thomas Burgan, and became a reporter on the *South Australian Advertiser*. South Australia's planners had provided for a newspaper at the very outset of the colony. It was called the *South Australian Register* and was owned by Robert and William Kyffin Thomas who were printers.[1] It wasn't until 1858 that their principal leader writer, John Henry Barrow, was tempted away to set up the *Advertiser*. He was a great mentor for the budding journalist. Bonython was possessed of much energy and drive and, in his first decade with the paper, he became an expert Hansard reporter and worked in almost every other department of the paper. Nevertheless, after Barrow died (according to Bonython), he offered King, the remaining partner, £25,000 for a share in the business. He was only 26 at the time and had a young family.

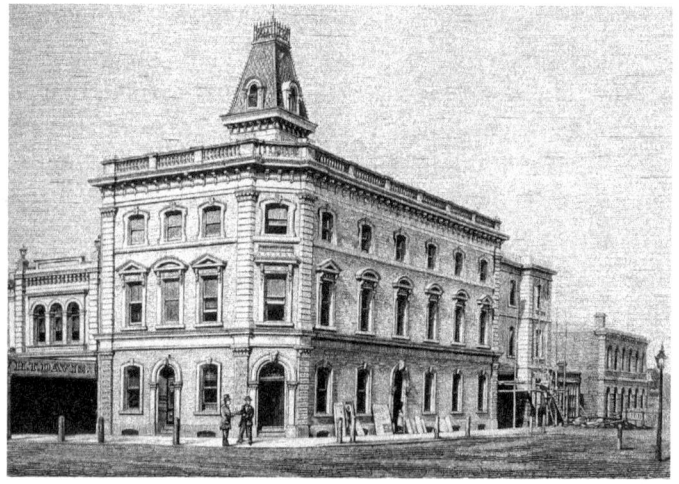

The *Advertiser* building, Adelaide, c. 1905

It was an enormous sum. Warren Bonython, his grandson, once spoke of the great love his grandfather had for his grandmother Anne, Thomas's wife. Did she, by then a widow, offer that sum? Or was it George, his father? A third possibility is that John Langdon himself had made such a sum on the Exchange, dabbling in mining shares. Though no gambler, he certainly had inside information about the rise and fall of prices and he paid people like the geologist, Pleitner, for information. However, the offer was sharply refused – something he never forgot. He waited, and by the Indenture dated 19 June 1880, John Langdon Bonython became a junior partner with general charge of the literary staff and correspondence. By 1893 he owned the paper outright until he sold it in 1929, 36 years later.

He also had great success in the field of education. It began in the same year in which he took over the *Advertiser,* when he wrote a number of editorials about the impact of compulsory education upon the growth of newspapers. He wrote:

> Happily, primary education is vastly more common than it was twenty-five years ago and every year it is decreasing the percentage of the population unable to read.
>
> The press has contributed in no mean degree to the forces which have brought about this most desirable change. The press has also been a most persistent and consistent advocate of popular education as well as being itself a popular educator. The press has promoted education and education has multiplied the readers of the press and so increased its usefulness.

Involved initially in his own children's primary school, he soon came to be appointed Chairman of the Adelaide School Board. He remained so for the next eighteen years. It was clear from the carefully compiled statistics that the children were learning to read and to be able to recite the multiplication tables, but many parents came before the Board begging for free places. The issue of free education in the decade after the passing of the 1875 Act continued to be very divisive and even the *Labor Advocate* berated the miners of Moonta who demanded it. 'No greater curse can fall upon a people than this spirit of dependence,' its editor thundered. It was not until 1891 that free education first appeared on the South Australian Labor Party Platform. South Australian children had to wait another two years for Cockburn, then Minister for Education, to provide it.

Bonython was also building a large support base as a champion of the teachers, and wrote much about John Anderson Hartley, a King's College

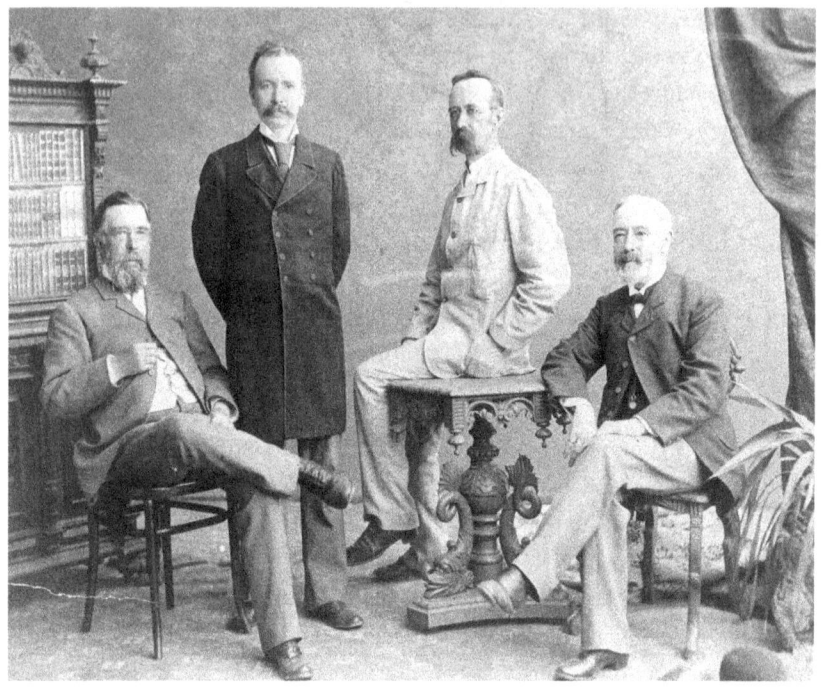

Bonython (second from left) and Hartley (second from right), 1891

science graduate who came to South Australia to be the first Headmaster of Prince Alfred College. Hartley and Bonython had much in common and their Methodist faith was a special bond. Hartley eventually created and controlled the South Australian Education Department.

Mention should also be made of Charles Henry Pearson, a brilliant scholar, Fellow of Oriel College and Professor of modern history at King's College, London. In Adelaide for only four years, he maintained a correspondence and friendship with Cockburn and Bonython who watched with great interest his future career in Victorian politics. They also watched his involvement with the Royal Melbourne Institute of Technology (RMIT), which was rather different in its origins from Adelaide's. Annely Aeuckens explains the origins of South Australia's School of Mines compared to that of RMIT, which was conferred from above:

Adelaide, by virtue of its dominant position, tended to monopolise the intellectual and social life of the colony. This had a significant effect on areas such as education and particularly technical education, which was supported by a consensus of interest in the capital city as a means of aiding agricultural and industrial development in the colony. Indeed, technical education was not so much a product of economic growth as an instrument used to promote it; anticipatory rather that derivative.

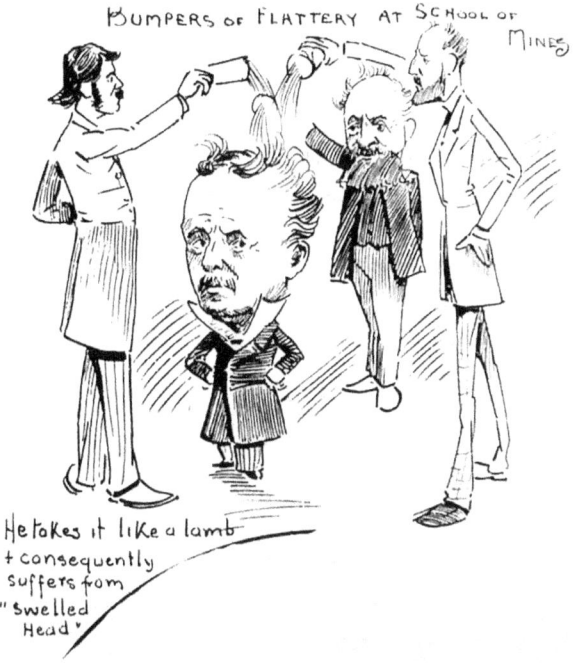

It was thanks to Cockburn, Minister of Education in the Downer Government in 1886, that a nine-member board, which included Bonython, was set up to investigate technical training – but in the end it was Premier Playford who made the decision to establish the School of Mines and Industry. When Bonython became President he made it his empire. Evidence of the Protestant work ethic has always gone down well in South Australia and Bonython certainly earned the accolades which came his way. And his experience with the rapidly growing School of Mines proved useful when he added to his load the Chairmanship of Roseworthy Agricultural College.

By the 1890s South Australia had survived a dangerous decade. The population was growing and it was literate. Education played a vital role not only in the expansion of newspaper readers. What Bonython did at this stage was dangerous but brilliant. South Australia had been granted responsible government in 1856 but between then and 1890 had had no less than 29 premiers, averaging about one every year. (It was as though, having received responsible government, South Australia's political world had been settled for ever.) But in the 1890s Sir John Cockburn came to office for two years and with a very brief flurry by Playford, Holder and Downer, the remainder of the 1890s belonged to Charles Cameron Kingston.

Bonython, in his early years was a radical. He made a lifetime friend of Cockburn and their closeness was sustained by the fact that, with Bonython's support, Cockburn went to London as Agent-General. He never returned but the two men wrote to one another every fortnight without fail for over 30 years. It was a wonderful and strange friendship. Cockburn was a well-connected doctor and an Anglican. He was erudite and charming and rather 'way-out'. His Opposition in Parliament called him 'Mr. Fanciful Notions' and it was apt. But some of those 'notions' were very practical too. For example, he favoured Votes for Women and Arbor Day, which he established on every school's calendar, and a School of Mines.

The other and more dominant figure in the 1890s was Charles Cameron Kingston, son of Sir George Strickland Kingston, a surveyor who served, some thought disloyally, under Colonel Light in the very early days. Kingston was a wild boy but a brilliant law student and draftsman, recognised by Sir Samuel Way, Chief Justice of South Australia, a member of the Privy Council and Chancellor of the University. But Kingston's private life and marriage was anything but respectable and his attempted duel with pistols against Sir Richard Butler and then divorce proceedings, involving another Member of Parliament's wife, shocked the citizens of Adelaide. However, Bonython supported him and stood to gain even more from this loyalty had Kingston survived longer to serve the Commonwealth Parliament. It was said that in the 1890s Cockburn visited Bonython by day and Kingston by night for the *Advertiser*'s support.

Sir John Langdon Bonython, a Rich and Successful Life

In this last decade of the nineteenth century the Kingston government enacted a vast amount of progressive legislation. Probate and succession duties, progressive land values and absentee taxes, village settlements, adult suffrage and an electoral code, free education, married women's property Acts, close settlement (land purchase), regulations to the State Bank Act, protective duties, early closing, factory Acts, workmen's compensation Acts and industrial arbitration were all part of his program.

The year 1894 saw the circulation of the *Advertiser* double that of the *Register* and the former was henceforth ahead with advertising revenue. Furthermore, Bonython was a great innovator. He used Supplements to make room for additional news matter and photographs, especially in the *Chronicle* and the *Express* which he also published. He was willing to spend huge sums of money on better and faster presses and his reduction of the cost of the paper to a penny from the moment he acquired it showed his understanding of the demographics of the time.

John Hirst's book, *Adelaide and the Country*, indicates clearly that Adelaide continued to govern the rural areas between 1870 and 1917 and even after country men predominated in the House of Assembly. It is no wonder that Bonython became a leading figure in a highly centralised system of government or that he won the circulation battle with the *Register*, which he so often characterised as 'old womanish' [sic] and out of date. Bonython was a proponent of a centralised public health system, a police force and poor relief. He called for elegant buildings, centralised control of planning and civic and municipal parks and gardens in keeping with a fine and dignified metropolis which was all possible for a capital of a small state with an exceptionally homogenous society. As he helped shape Adelaide, he grew to love it.

By 1900 he had been running the *Advertiser* for fifteen years. The whole operation was working smoothly with W.C. Crookall in charge of the printing and the running of the office, F.T. Robertson as associate-editor, A.H. Young and C.R. Wilton as leader writers and J.H. Martindale, H. Sexton and O.L. Peacock among a number of very competent, senior journalists. Moreover, his eldest son, Lavington, had begun in the business department and his second son, Hugh, was showing promise as a reporter. Furthermore, in 1898, together with J.R. Fairfax, he was knighted. They were the first newspaper proprietors to be so honoured. Not only were his publications being recognised but his influence in gaining the support of the Premiers Kingston in South Australia and Turner in Victoria via his own friend, David Syme, owner and editor of the *Age*, to support the elevation of South Australia's Chief Justice, Sir Samuel Way, to a seat on the Judicial Committee of the Privy Council in England illustrated the power he wielded.

So, in 1900 he took himself, his wife Polly and his two unmarried daughters on a grand tour of Europe. The highlight for him was to see for himself the Bonython estate in Cornwall. It was by then a great Gothic ruin. (Today it is being heroically restored by a South African couple, the Nathans.) Bonython had already subscribed to an altar window in the Cury Church and so was welcomed. He also met a number of families to whom he had written in the course of his earlier attempts to trace his family and to recover their possessions. These people included the Godolphins, the Rashleighs, the Ennis and the Trefusis families and the Vyvyans. The Vyvyans had at one time bought 'Bonython' and had sold it to a Mr Lyle, who promptly departed for New Zealand leaving it tenanted. When he died his daughter inherited it and though she had not the income to support it she stubbornly refused to part with it. To quote great-grandson John Bonython in 2006:

> What about the land? Great Grandfather had never given much consideration to that question, a vital one if one lived in Cornwall. The post 1880's agricultural slump had left land an unsatisfactory investment but had not removed its social significance. I don't think Great Grandfather realised this. Remember Lady Bracknell? 'Land gives one position but prevents one from keeping it up'. That's all that can be said about land.

Not being able to acquire Bonython was Sir Langdon's greatest disappointment.

Upon his return to South Australia, Bonython took the unexpected step of standing as an Independent for the new House of Representatives. He was not a very enthusiastic federalist as John Bannon has shown. He compared the *Register's* seventeen editorials on federation to the *Adveriser's* fourteen. A little of the continuing rivalry between these newspaper editors crept in here. Will J. Sowden was an advocate of Free Trade and was consistently anti-Labor by comparison to Bonython. But he was native-born and Bonython was not. He was an early member of the Australian Natives Association and Sir Langdon was not, although his son Lavington joined. Bonython never exhibited populist enthusiasm for Australia in the way that Barton and Deakin did. And although both Sowden and Bonython considered themselves Cornishmen, Sowden was a member of the Adelaide Club and Bonython was not.

Some of his negativity might also be attributed to his love of Cornwall. Because of Cornwall he never felt or even understood the kind of Australian nationalism that Russell Ward wrote about or that the *Bulletin* represented. His garden in the Adelaide hills, his Carminow, was filled with bluebell dells and imported rhododendrons. Consequently he never heard the birds. Nor did he admire his environment. 'Send me a nice landscape, preferably of Cornwall and, indeed, if you can get it cheap, left over from the Royal Academy show' would have been his call and was what he wrote to his friend, Cockburn. His values were imported and, like the vast majority of Australians at that time, he accepted unthinkingly the arrangement of a Commonwealth within the Empire.

Bonython's editorials in the lead-up to the crucial vote for Federation harped continually on cost. He had been party over the long, preceding gestation period of the constitution. And South Australia provided outstanding delegates to debate the powers of the Upper and Lower Houses. He himself had attended the 1890 Convention and the 1898, both times taking on Hansard reporting shifts. In the end he was able to take on trust whether the federation could bring in Western Australia or what a financial burden Tasmania would be and who would control the River Murray waters and many other imponderables, but his nagging worry was always cost. For answers he turned to the New South Wales Government Statistician, T.A. Coghlan. The *Advertiser* was filled with long articles containing so many figures that no one could have interpreted them! Yes-No Reid became the nickname for the New South Wales Premier who became fourth Prime Minister of Australia, but it might equally have applied to Bonython. Despite this the people of South Australia voted nearly four to one to adopt the Constitution. Belief in the Senate's role as a States' House helps explain why.

Bonython came in second only to Kingston in the ensuing election for the House of Representatives. Kingston had assured him he had the support of the Labor men in South Australia though he stood as an Independent. Subsequent Prime Ministers treated him with kid gloves but though he worked as conscientiously as ever he was not at ease in the role of Parliamentarian. At one point he wrote to Cockburn: 'I could have made a good speech but hadn't the pluck to make it and now the opportunity is gone. I feel disgusted with myself. This is a constant experience on my part.'

He voted for progressive measures and always claimed that he had got the Federal Parliament to take the cost of the Northern Territory off South Australia's hands. Certainly, he was the first to introduce such a measure but had to wait until 1911 to have it enacted. He had also while in Parliament helped to establish the Commonwealth Literary Fund, chairing it from 1908 to 1929. The largest call upon his time was as a Royal Commissioner on Old Age Pensions in 1905–1906. And all this was done with overnight train travel to and from Melbourne while Parliament was sitting, while otherwise keeping his normal and enormous number of hours at the newspaper. These train journeys did however provide useful confidences which produced insightful articles and breaking news! He was always ahead of the game – and the *Register*. It is no wonder that in 1906 he decided not to stand for the seat of Barker.

Instead, he took a much-deserved break with Polly and the girls and his youngest son, Frank, who was still a schoolboy and had to be left with friends in London while the Bonythons and the Cockburns toured the Continent. Then they all went down to Cornwall. He certainly enjoyed the company of the Rashleigh brothers and visited them at Mevagissey. On this visit he gave the Cury Church a peel of bells and to Truro a large sum which saw a gallery in the County Museum and Art Gallery named after him. His always enquiring mind saw him investigate technical education at the Royal Institution of Cornwall, of which he was elected President in 1931.

At what point in his life did Bonython give up the idea of returning to Cornwall and buying an estate? This we will never know. Perhaps his wife, Polly, may have said 'no' to the idea on this visit. They were a devoted couple. Her maiden name was Marie Louise Frederica Balthaser and this also helps to explain why, when war broke out, there was never any expression in the *Advertiser* of the violent racist epithets so hurtful to good Barossa citizens. Bonython served in the Great War the way he knew best. The friendships he had forged in the Federal Parliament saw him called on again and again, understandably with his radical reputation and the rise of Labor Prime Ministers like Fisher and Hughes. The Australian Soldiers Repatriation Fund Board of Trustees was set up in 1916 with Bonython as the South Australian Trustee. Thus he resumed the exhausting trips which took him regularly to Melbourne. The Fund closed in 1917 but Bonython was retained to serve on a new Commission for Repatriation with very broad powers. Eventually, in 1920, a Commission of three salaried men and an army of public servants took over the whole pension structure. By then the guidelines had been laid down.

During the war Bonython's early radical leanings received their first blow. Newspaper publication, though hindered by censorship and severe paper shortages, rose hugely in number but so did costs. In the middle of the war Mr Justice Isaac Isaacs heard the case of the Australian Journalists Association and others, initiated in December 1916 and heard in Melbourne in February, March, April and May 1917. Bonython was furious to discover that his own men had joined in this case. (Nevertheless he regarded Isaacs, who was to preside over the Federal Arbitration Court, as an old friend and amicably endured six hours of his company on the train trip to the Adelaide hearing and then entertained him at Carclew [his home in North Adelaide] and Carminow [his 'country' house at Mount Lofty], both properties bestowed with historic Cornish names.) Needless to say, the *Advertiser* displayed a very clear understanding of the case. But his relations with the unions were souring and they had by this time their own paper. He had failed completely to understand Deakin's acknowledgement of the new power play in his second Government. And news of the Russian Revolution raised more alarm bells.

The last two decades of his long life saw a transition from his political position as an advanced radical to a conservative one. At the state level early Labor premiers such as Verran and Vaughan had discussed their difficulties with the Caucus with Bonython, as Prime Minister Watson had at the federal level. All persuasions still courted him for the coverage his paper afforded but privately he came to fear the direction that was being taken. Like many of his contemporaries he spoke of Britain as 'home' and revered its class structure, its Empire and its political traditions.

This state of mind was reinforced by the third and last trip he made to Britain in 1924. The year before, he had accepted a Commonwealth appointment to the British Empire Exhibition which was to be held in London the following year. Sir John Bice was the South Australian appointee and the two men went to Melbourne for the first meeting. There Bonython learnt that the Duke of Devonshire was to preside over the exhibition with U.F. Wintour as general-manager receiving £5000 and expenses – and rarely there! Bonython thought it an even greater waste of money when a soldier-secretary was appointed for South Australia at £1200 when he could have been got for £350.

He justified the exhibition itself because he believed that it could make money in a country where, he believed, 250,000 people would attend a football match each Saturday. Even in his own state 32,000 turned out for the Australian Rules match between Western Australia and South Australia. Throughout the 1920s Sir Langdon found it incomprehensible that people could be so involved in sport, but he provided greater and greater space for it in the columns of his paper. He entertained at Carminow a number of people connected with the exhibition and they all seemed to be planning to be in London in 1924.

But in November Sir John Bice died. He was a Cornishman and had served on the School of Mines Council. Sir Langdon was, at this stage, complaining of being overwhelmed with work and was greatly worried by the rejection of the Australian stud rams by Britain because of concern for rinderpest in Western Australia. He was still determined to go because he dearly wanted to see his grandson, John (later a founder of Santos), admitted to Cambridge. Two further tragedies made the trip much less one of pleasure and more an escape. Of his three living sons, the second, Hugh, had died after a long illness in 1915. The youngest, Frank, who also worked on the *Advertiser,* but on the accounting side, died in September 1923 aged only 38. Four months later his beloved Polly died. It was his eldest daughter, Mary Elsie, married to Herbert Angus Parsons, who rallied her father and persuaded him to keep to the original plan but accompanied by her son and Lavington's. The three sailed off on the TSS *Aeneas* and upon arrival went immediately to Cornwall. By July he had introduced them to polite society and we find them listed at the Duchess of Devonshire's reception in London. Altogether they spent five months abroad. But Miss Lyle still refused to sell the former Bonython property and, it seemed, he now had to be content with his own Carclew and Carminow in South Australia.

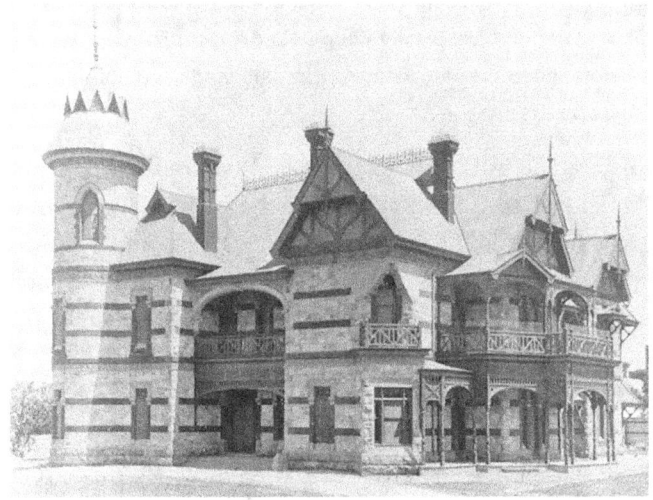

Carclew, North Adelaide, 1897

It should not be the mere possession of wealth which makes him the most notable Cornishman in South Australia, but his long history of philanthropy can allow him that claim. Throughout his life he gave generously to a vast number of causes. His links with the University were marked by his endowment of a Chair of Law and his subsequent gift of $50,000 to build Bonython Hall – its Gothic design and heraldic adornments were his choice. His largest single gift was $100,000 for a marbled Parliament. It is also true that during the Great Depression he not only paid the wages of the public servants but contributed generously to the establishment of the Kuitpo Colony. And there are many more instances one could cite.

In his latter years he continued his long hours at the paper, enjoyed his regular visits to the Cornish Association of South Australia which he, together with Sir James Penn Boucaut, had established in February 1890, and he continued to collect books and pictures about Cornwall. He had sold the *Advertiser* for £1.25 million in 1929. This was a vast sum at that time. And it is no surprise that a reading of his will in 1939 reveals that the trustees were directed to set aside from the residuary estate the sum of £20,000 (in English sterling) for:

> the purchase of that portion of the Bonython estate in the Parish of Cury in the Duchy of Cornwall in England and comprising 700 acres or thereabouts which has usually been held or occupied with the mansion house belonging to the said estate or the said lands and hereinafter called the Bonython estate.

If the estate had not been acquired in 21 years the whole sum was to pass to his eldest son, Lavington. If his heart was always in Cornwall, nevertheless he was laid to rest in South Australia and accorded a huge public funeral. Two more generations later the last of the direct line, John Rutherford Bonython, died in Cornwall in 2004, having spent all his adult life there.

Note
1   The *South Australian Register* changed its name to the *Register* in 1900 and the *South Australian Advertiser* changed its name to the *Advertiser* in 1889. For simplicity I have used *Register* and *Advertiser* to refer to these newspapers.

Selected reading
Bonython J.L., Papers, PRG/1–9, Mortlock Library, South Australia
Bonython J.L. & Co., Business Records, BRG 10, Mortlock Library, South Australia
Commonwealth Parliamentary Debates and Papers, 1901–1906, 1914–1920
South Australian Parliamentary Debates and Papers, 1890–1939
Aeuckens, Annely (1989), *The People's University: The South Australian School of Mines and Industries and the South Australian Institute of Technology 1889–1989.* South Australian Institute of Technology, Adelaide
Bannon, John (1998), Trust in the Hands of the People: South Australians, the Press and the First Federal Referendum. *The New Federalist*, No. 2, December
Bonython, Eric Glenie (1966), *The Bonython Family: Histories of the Families of Bonython of Bonython and Bonython of Carclew.* The Griffin Press, Netley, SA
Hirst, John (1973), *Adelaide and the Country 1870–1917.* Melbourne University Press, Melbourne
Howell, P.A. (2002), *South Australia and Federation.* Wakefield Press, Kent Town, SA
Jaensch, Dean, (ed.) (1986), *The Flinders History of South Australia Political History.* Wakefield Press, Netley, SA

Prest, E.J. (2011), *Sir John Langdon Bonython: Newspaper Proprietor, Politician and Philanthropist.* Australian Scholarly Publishing, North Melbourne (see for source material)

Richards, Eric (ed.) (1986), *The Flinders History of South Australia Social History.* Wakefield Press, Netley, SA

Acknowledgements

The photographs in this paper were all included in my book on Sir John Langdon Bonython (see Selected Reading).

The photograph of Bonython is from the private collection of the Wilson family, used with permission.

The photograph of the *Advertiser* building comes from Eric Glenie Bonython's 1966 book on the Bonython family (see Selected Reading). The photograph of Bonython and Hartley is from the State Library of South Australia collection, image no. B 4967; it is in the public domain.

The cartoon, *Bumpers of Flattery*, is from *Quiz*, 14 April 1898.

The photograph of 'Carclew' is from the State Library of South Australia collection, image no. B 5344, photographer Ernest Gall; it is in the public domain.

One False Move: The Bravery of Leon Goldsworthy GC, DSC, GM

JAN LOKAN

It was possible that the war would simply not have been won without him.

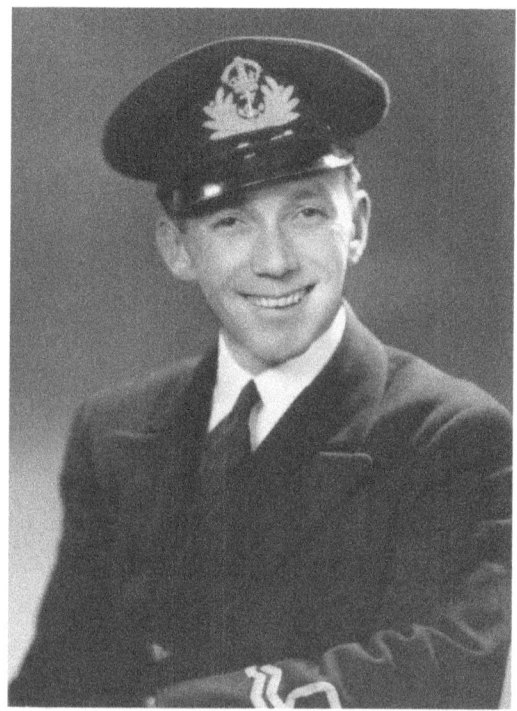

The above statement was made in a tribute to Leon Goldsworthy when he died in 1994, referring to his service in the Royal Australian Naval Volunteer Reserve (RANVR) in World War Two. There is no doubt that he altered the course of many people's lives.

One False Move: The Bravery of Leon Goldsworthy

Leonard Verdi Goldsworthy was born on 19 January 1909 in his parents' house at Broken Hill, the second son of Alfred Thomas and Eva Jane Goldsworthy and younger brother to Eric. He was rarely called Leonard – his family called him Len, but he was known as Leon in most of his everyday life, and was 'Goldie' to wartime mates and many press reporters. For the purposes of this paper, he will be referred to as Leon. And yes, his mother was an opera enthusiast, which is where the 'Verdi' middle name came from.

Alfred Thomas Goldsworthy was a Moonta boy who moved to Broken Hill in the early 1900s, in his 20s, when it had become harder to make a living as a miner in the Copper Triangle. He had some success in Broken Hill and stayed there for about 15 years. He met his future bride, Eva Jane Riggs, there and married her in June 1907. Eva was another South Australian, born in Gawler South, who had gone to Broken Hill with her parents some years earlier. Alfred and Eva had two children in Broken Hill in quick succession: Eric James, born in 1908 and Leon, born in 1909. (Two more sons were also born there, but died as babies, one in 1911 and the other in 1913.)

Before addressing Leon's life further, the very unusual circumstances which led to his having the surname 'Goldsworthy' are outlined here. They began with his great-grandmother Mary back in Cornwall. She was born a Goldsworthy and had an illegitimate baby in 1835. Although her parents would not accept her coming back to their home after the baby's birth, the infant, Thomas, was given her surname. For a while they survived in poor houses, but by the time Thomas was six years old, she and he were back in the Goldsworthy household. He was only five years younger than Mary's youngest brother (which has led to numerous family trees erroneously placing him as being another brother). The 'putative' father (Thomas VIAL) was ordered by the Truro Court of Petty Sessions to pay 1/6 per week for his upkeep, but ran away from his home and never paid.

Thomas came to South Australia by himself in 1855 and married Cornish-born Grace Williams, nee Dunstan, in Kensington, South Australia, in February 1859. Their first child (of nine), a girl named Mary Elizabeth, was born in December of the same year. She married in 1879 and her oldest child, Alfred Thomas, was born in July 1880. Unfortunately (or perhaps fortunately) for Mary, her 'husband' (William JAMES) turned out to be a bigamist and the marriage was not a marriage at all. Mary Elizabeth was thus a single parent and the baby Alfred, as the reader will have guessed by now, grew up with 'Goldsworthy' as his surname.

Returning to Leon's story, he was what might be called a 'weedy' child, small and inclined to sickness. Between the ages of five and six years he contracted diphtheria, a serious illness even today, but an extremely serious one in those days. Children never went to hospital, but were nursed at home, with a yellow flag attached to the front gate to let people – friends and relatives – know there was diphtheria in the house.

Leon became very ill, so a nurse was sent to help care for him. A few days later the nurse held a mirror to his mouth but no breath was detected and no pulse, so she pronounced him dead. His mother could not accept this and screamed that she saw his eyelid flicker. The mirror test was done again and a slight smear appeared, and a faint pulse. From then on, the nurse called him 'The Resurrection'.

His recovery was very slow and he was bedridden for so long that he lost the ability to walk. Their doctor in Broken Hill advised Alfred and Eva to go back to South Australia and take Leon to Adelaide for a holiday at one of the beaches. While there, they were to place him in the sea and massage his legs daily. It worked! In those days, around 1915, there was none of the medication, nor physiotherapy treatment, that would have helped him back to full health. Leon's sister Mary has often wondered if this was the start of Leon's love of the sea. She also thinks it interesting that no one else in the family ever learned to swim.

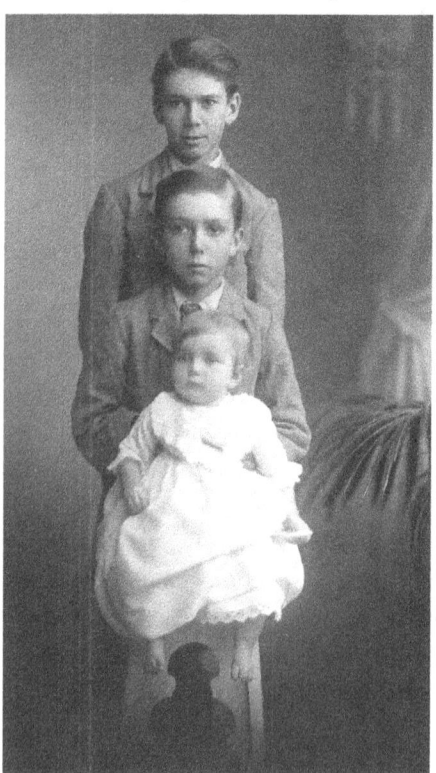

Eric, Leon and Iris in 1919

One False Move: The Bravery of Leon Goldsworthy

Not long after this episode the family returned permanently to South Australia, first to Moonta, where the first daughter, Iris, was born in 1918 and the boys went to Moonta Primary School. A few years later the family moved to Kapunda, where both Eric and Leon attended Kapunda High School. Then another move was made to Woodville, where Mary was born in 1925. Leon then attended the School of Mines and the University of Adelaide, where he studied Electrical Engineering and Physics. One of his close friends at the university was Marcus (later Sir Mark) Oliphant.

While the family lived in Woodville, Leon joined a gymnasium to do gymnastics and wrestling to strengthen his body. Mary can remember that, as a small child, she went to a gymnastics display where she saw Leon standing on his hands and going on them up and down a flight of stairs. She also remembers seeing him perform on the overhead rings, at which he was very good.

Leon finished his university course in the Depression years, when employment was very scarce; he was fortunate that the University of Adelaide took him on as a technician in the Physics Department. During this time he managed to find a job at Rainbow Neon Lights in Sydney, which led to a transfer to Perth with the same company in 1931. Apart from the war years, he remained with them until he retired.

Leon married Maud Edna Rutherford in Perth in November 1939, a few months after war was declared. He tried to enlist in the navy in 1940 but was rejected because of his size. He was a little over 5ft 4ins (160 cm) in height, weighed about 50 kilograms and wore a size 4 shoe. He then tried both the air force and the army. The air force also rejected him because of his size, and he was not acceptable to the army because he had hammer toes. So, what did he do but have the offending toes removed! Meanwhile his daughter, Pamela, was born in November 1940.

Then in the following year everything happened at once: all three forces wanted him. Not surprisingly, as it was the one he had applied for first, Leon chose the navy and joined The Royal Australian Naval Volunteer Reserve (RANVR). Two months' training at HMAS *Cerberus* in Victoria followed, after which he was transferred to the Admiralty in England with the rank of Acting Sub-Lieutenant. A few weeks later, he was sailing up the River Mersey in the north-west of England and, as they came into anchor, a small grey mine sweeper went past. Not long afterwards there was a muffled booming explosion from the fog in the distance; the mine sweeper was destroyed and Leon and some of his fellow sailors were thrown off their feet.

This event had a profound effect on Leon. He resolved to make use of his academic training and requested to enter the 'Rendering Mines Safe' (RMS) Unit at HMS *Vernon*, at Portsmouth on the south coast. He also felt that his physical strength coupled with slight build could be an asset. He did not have to wait long for a vacancy.

HMS *Vernon* was established before World War One, and was known as the 'Torpedo School'. It was where research and development were done to produce new mines for the allies but also to study captured German mines to understand how they worked. Following on from the increasing prevalence of mines during World War Two, *Vernon* had assumed responsibility for mine disposal and development of procedures to disarm them. To do this, they had to succeed in capturing some. This work was known to the Germans, who began to place booby traps in their mines to make them harder to capture. A few months before Leon applied to the RMS Unit, a German bomb being studied exploded, killing five staff members and injuring many. Air raids were heavy also and the establishment was hit several times. One bomb demolished an entire building and killed 100 people. Personnel were thus reluctant to be associated with the program there.

Leon was undaunted and began training at *Vernon*, and was surprised at how scanty the training was. When he was fitted into the smallest diving suit they had, he disappeared into the body of the suit. One then had to be adapted to fit. He found that expert personnel were few, with many never living to tell of the mistakes they had made. He had confidence in his electrical engineering and physics training, which he now found to be highly useful. He also benefited greatly from his gymnastics and wrestling training, which had given him a strong, wiry body and very strong wrists.

Two other equally foolhardy Australians had also joined the RMS Unit – Stuart Mould of NSW and Hugh Syme of Victoria. One day the three of them were called to delouse a new type of German explosive device, which functioned as either a mine or a bomb and consisted of photo-electric cells behind a glass dome. It would explode if the dome was

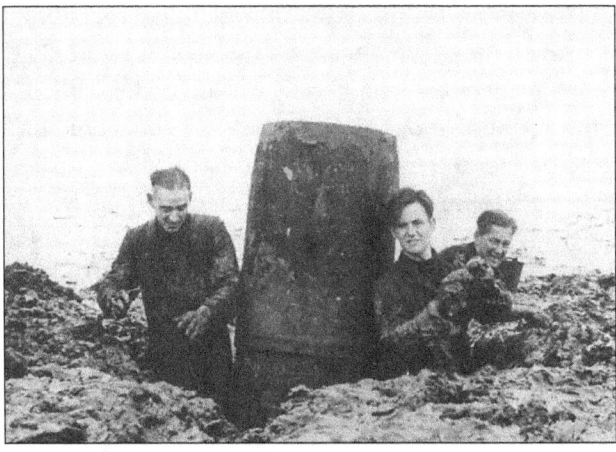

The unexploded mine/bomb. Below: What do we do next?

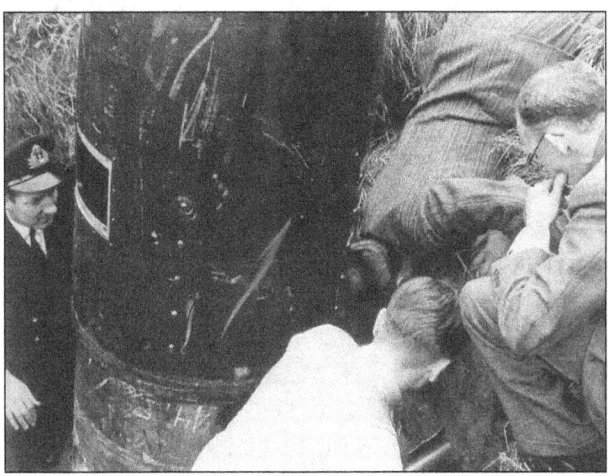

removed and sunlight filtered in. One had not detonated when it hit the ground on a beach, which allowed research scientists to see the principle on which it functioned. The three Australians succeeded in disarming the mine. Photographs show the kinds of situation that mine disposers often had to deal with.

Later, Leon, Mould and another Australian, Lieutenant Anderson, were asked to develop a diving suit that would be resistant to magnetic mines, and give freedom of movement. Leon suggested that it carry its own oxygen supply. When finished, it did have its own oxygen cylinder. In

August 1943, Leon donned the new suit, which had revolutionised naval diving, to recover a mine off Sheerness, in Kent. It was only the second time that such a mine had been rendered safe underwater. Many mines had short fuses, and had one been activated, Leon would have had just 17 seconds to defuse and escape.

On another occasion Leon nearly drowned when he was wearing the suit. He had signalled to be pulled to the surface and the launch rocking and bucking in the choppy sea caused him to rise unevenly. Somehow, he fouled the ladder and smashed his helmet against the hull. Water poured in and bubbles rose to the surface. Luckily his diving attendant realised he was in trouble, dived in, grasped the nearly drowned Leon and hauled him aboard semi-conscious. Typically, after a recovery period and a new helmet, Leon went down again to complete his task. On yet another occasion he disarmed an acoustic mine off Milford Haven in Wales. It had lain in the water for more than two years and all efforts to sweep it had failed. Using the same diving suit, Leon successfully removed the fuse and the primer and later recovered the mine intact.

For his work in 1943, especially in disabling the Sheerness mine, Leon was awarded the George Medal in April 1944 'for gallantry and devotion to duty during a hazardous enterprise' and was Mentioned in Despatches twice in August that year. He also won the George Cross (the non-military equivalent of the Victoria Cross) in September 1944 'for gallantry and undaunting devotion to duty' for his skill and courage in recovering mines in Britain between June 1943 and 1944. These events earned him a promotion to Lieutenant Commander.

In 1944 when the French port of Cherbourg was badly needed for the Normandy (D-Day) campaign, Leon dived to a depth of 17 metres to deactivate a new German 'K type' mine – the first of its kind to be discovered. He completed the delousing amid enemy gunfire and bombs, and depth charges dropped regularly by the Allies to fend off German U-boats. For this he was awarded the Distinguished Service Cross, 'for bravery in the face of the enemy', in January 1945, making him the most highly decorated Australian navy officer in World War Two. In all, he de-loused 304 enemy mines.

All mines once laid were in a highly dangerous state and Leon's work often had to be done in a bulky diving suit, with touch the only sense available, as murky water made it impossible to see. Leon was constantly exposed to situations from which there was no escape, where one false move with an unknown mechanism could mean instant death. His nickname 'Ficky' among his mates was derived from his reputation as a 'Mr Fixit.' He was wounded once when a German parachute mine and its aluminium case exploded prematurely and he was hit in the back, injuring his spine. He spent three months recovering from his injuries, but continued with his work after he recovered.

It was the mine known as an 'oyster' mine that was his most difficult, and possibly the most dangerous. It would explode when the water pressure around it changed. A ship passing overhead could trigger it, but Leon rose to the challenge and deloused the mine. Danger was a constant companion. On another occasion, when searching for a parachute mine on the bed of the River Thames, he thought he had reached the end of his life. A 'well' of stones had to be sunk and as their weight increased the walls were forced to the bottom. When Leon lowered himself into the well he could only use his touch, as it was too murky to see. The well swirled with coarse sand which, had it been allowed to settle, would set like concrete. Jet hoses kept the sand from packing. Halfway down Leon realised the hoses had broken down, and within seconds the sand began to set. His body started to stiffen. He had almost given up when luckily emergency hoses broke the sand-particle tomb and he shot to the surface, propelled by the build-up of oxygen in his suit. Once again, after a recovery period, he went down to finish the job and, using only the sense of touch, he disarmed the mine.

As the war in Europe was nearing its conclusion, Leon was loaned

> **MOST DECORATED AUSTRALIAN NAVY MAN**
>
> From Australian Associated Press, London
>
> With the award of the DSC Acting-Lieut-Commander L. V. Goldsworthy, RANVR, of East Perth (WA), has more decorations than any other officer in the Australian Navy.
>
> He was the first officer in any of the services to be awarded within nine months the George Cross, George Medal, and the DSC, and also to mention in despatches and promotion.
>
> The latest award is for gallantry in hazardous operations in face of the enemy. Goldsworthy shares with two other Australian naval officers, acting-Lieut-Commander J. S. Mould and Lieutenant H. R. Syme, the distinction of being awarded both the George Cross and the George Medal.

to the US Navy's Mobile Explosive Investigation Unit, to advise them on their impending invasion of the Philippines and Borneo. Leon's work was on Japanese mines and booby traps. These were altogether different from the German mines and he had to learn all over again. He was one of the first to enter the caves of Corregidor that were mined by the Japanese. For his work for the American Navy he was awarded two medals, but the Australian Government of the day, adhering to policy, refused him permission to accept them! Finally, after he had returned to London, the news that the war had ended flashed over the radio.

Leon was invested with his medals on two occasions by King George VI at Buckingham Palace, once in 1944 and once after his return to London in 1945. His notable wartime career led to his portrait being painted by official war artist Harold Abbott; the portrait still hangs in an annexe to the Hall of Valour at the Australian War Memorial (AWM) in Canberra.

Early in 1946, Leon sent a telegram to his mother, saying 'Arriving Adelaide tomorrow 10.30 am by troop train, hope to see you'. His sister Mary's husband Alf took the day off work and took Mary and her mother to the Adelaide Railway Station by 10.00 am. Alf went to find out which platform the train would be arriving at, but came back and said 'nobody knows of a troop train arriving here'. There were also reporters and photographers at the station, no doubt also looking for the same troop train. Alf then questioned the Station Master, who also knew nothing about a troop train. After several phone calls the Station Master discovered that the train had gone to Keswick (a station just beyond the metropolitan area). He called a taxi for Alf and his family, very hard to get in those days owing to petrol rationing.

The family arrived at Keswick, hoping the train would still be there, and finally found Leon. Much talking amid the train tracks ensued, particularly about his ribbons and wondering which colour bar represented which decoration. The oak leaf awarded for being Mentioned in Despatches, that had to be worn with the colour bars, wasn't visible. He said 'it's there' and lifted his lapel – he had tucked it underneath. Suddenly Leon looked dismayed and they realised the reporters and photographers they had seen at the Adelaide Railway Station were now there. Leon would not answer their questions, saying he couldn't remember. After much

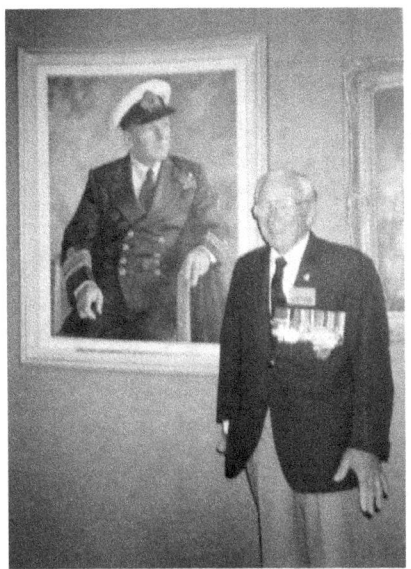 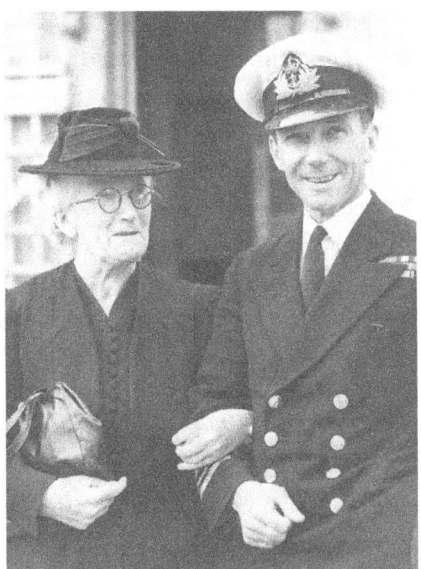

Leon, bedecked with medals, next to his portrait in the Australian War Memorial, and with his mother at Keswick station.

persuasion he consented to having his photo taken with his mother. The photo appeared on the front page of the *News* that day. The train continued on to Perth where all on board were to be discharged.

After the war, the Commonwealth Victoria Cross and George Cross winners formed an Association and Leon was appointed its Vice-Chairman. They met twice a year in London. While they were there the Queen invited them all to Buckingham Palace for lunch. At one of these luncheons they all assembled with the Queen for a photograph, a copy of which hung back in Australia in Leon's lounge room. Leon was sitting in the front row next to the Queen.

Broken Hill had claimed Leon as its own because it was his birth place, even though his home was there for only about six years before his family returned to South Australia, and he later spent most of his adult life in WA. In 1966 the Broken Hill Navalmen's Club raised funds, with the help of their wives, to erect a Sea Scouts Hall in his honour. Once it was finished, they invited him to come to Broken Hill to open 'Goldsworthy Hall', which he duly did.

Once, on holiday in South Australia, staying with his older brother Eric, Leon thought he would try and catch up with his friend Sir Mark Oliphant, from university days, who was Governor of South Australia at the time; he rang Government House and found Sir Mark at home. Sir Mark said 'I have a day off, come and have lunch here'. So Leon spent a day reminiscing of days gone by. He found one remark of Sir Mark's upsetting: he had said to Leon, 'You helped save lives, I helped destroy them'.[1]

South Australia honoured Leon by naming a street in Glenelg North, 'Goldsworthy Crescent'. WA has honoured him by naming a ward in one of the major hospitals after him, and by placing a plaque in the footpath of St George's Terrace, Perth.

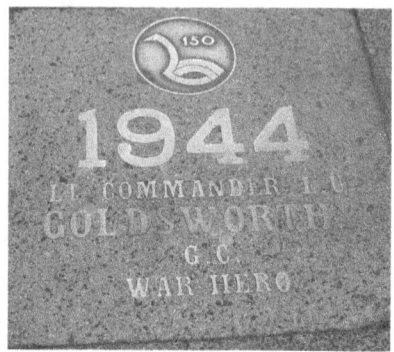

Plaque on St George's Terrace, Perth

When our new federal Parliament House was opened on 9 May 1988 in Canberra, Leon received an invitation to attend. The invited guests were assembled either side of the red carpet. The Queen, who was to open Parliament House, came along the red carpet with Paul Keating, our then Prime Minister, followed by all the Parliamentary dignitaries. Suddenly the Queen left the group and came over to Leon saying, 'I think we have met before, nice to see you again'. He felt very honoured that she remembered him.

Leon was chosen to lead the ANZAC Day Parade in Perth in 1989. The *West Australian* newspaper of 25 April reported the occasion:

> There are times – like today – when Leon "Goldie" Goldsworthy remembers the years he was a mere heartbeat away from death. Australia's most highly decorated ex-naval man will also recall his mates as he leads his fellow servicemen along St George's Terrace on the ANZAC Day march.
>
> 'I look forward to the annual reunion, of meeting old friends, and seeing who is left,' he said. 'I might not be able to make it next year.'

One False Move: The Bravery of Leon Goldsworthy

Twelve medals – including the George Cross, the Distinguished Service Cross and the George Medal – bedeck the chest of the small man who carried out one of World War 2's most harrowing jobs. He spent 5 years disarming German and Japanese mines on land and under water. At 80, Leon Goldsworthy, of South Perth, is modest about the dangers he experienced.

After studying at Adelaide University, he worked in the neon sign industry, moving to Perth in 1931. When war broke out, he joined the navy, was commissioned as sub-lieutenant and went to Britain. He said his civilian technical training and gymnastic and wrestling workouts helped him through some close calls. Once, he was blown up underwater. His spine was injured and he had blackouts until an operation eased the problem.

'Some people were afraid to die in those times, others didn't give a blooming hoot,' he said.

Which category did he fit into? He wouldn't say – especially today.

Leon died on Sunday 7 August 1994. His funeral was a full Naval Service, which Mary and her husband flew to Perth to attend. The Navy contingent, a 50-escort party, comprised a naval band, a 12-sailor firing party marching with reversed rifles, six coffin bearers and an insignia bearer. At the conclusion of the service the Last Post was played, followed by a gun salute and then one minute's silence and Reveille, a very impressive service. This took place, on a wet day, at Perth's Karrakatta

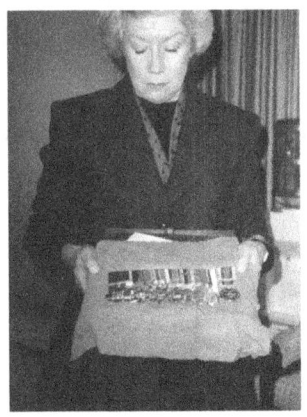 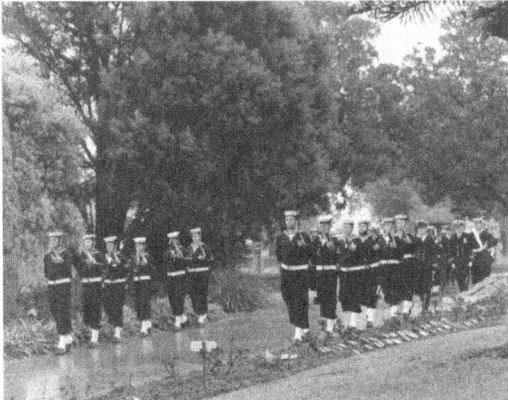

Leon's funeral; his daughter Pamela with his medals, and the Naval Escort

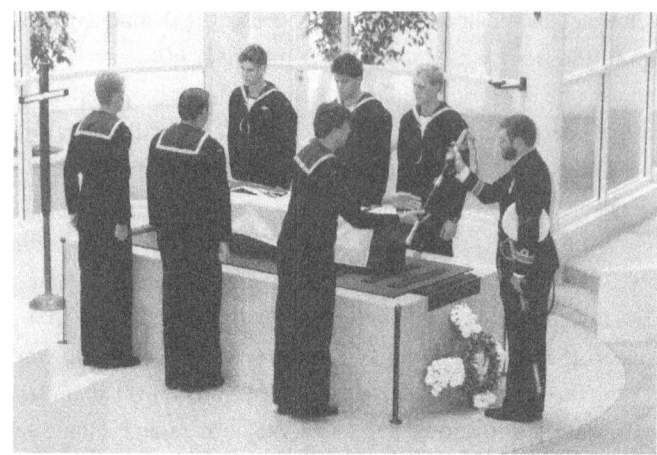

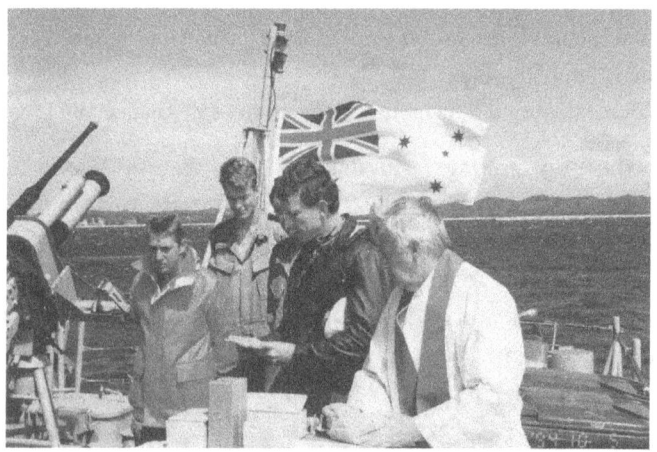

The coffin and sword, and the burial at sea

Cemetery, but Leon's ashes were scattered at sea from a warship on 5 October 1994 in Cockburn Sound out from Fremantle. The service was conducted by Chaplain Alan Stubbs of the Royal Australian Navy.

Further accolades were accorded to Australia's most decorated Naval Officer in WW2. In 1995, on the 50th anniversary of peace in the Pacific, Australia Post chose eight heroic Australians from WW2 to appear on two sets of 'Australia Remembers' stamps, four per set. Leon, chosen for his heroism in mine disposal, was in the second set. The others in his set were Leonard Waters, Australia's only World War 2 Aboriginal

One False Move: The Bravery of Leon Goldsworthy

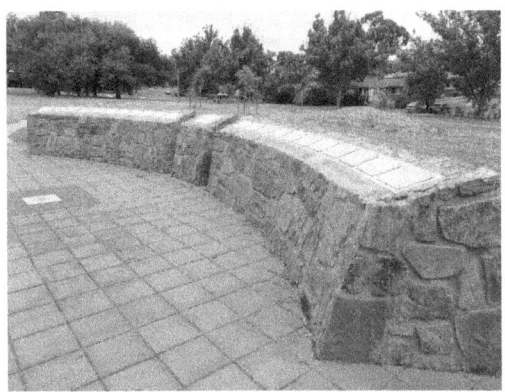
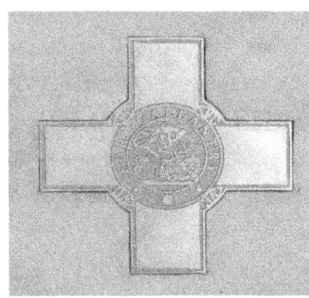

Pedestals with plaques in George Cross Park, Canberra, and the George Cross, For Gallantry, which is set into the path

fighter pilot, Sister Ellen Savage, Australian Army Nursing Service, who was aboard the hospital ship *Centaur* when it was attacked by a Japanese submarine and Chief Petty Officer Stoker Percy Collins, who was involved in the Battle of Crete, serving on HMAS *Strahan*. Leon's daughter, Pamela, was invited to launch the set of stamps in Perth.

A Memorial Plaque was erected in Western Australia's Garden of Remembrance, and also a stand-alone Memorial Plaque on the walkway to the Cross of Sacrifice in King's Park State War Memorial, Perth.

There were eight RANVR Officers, all very brave men, who were engaged in mine disposal in England during World War Two, including Leon. They were awarded a total of four George Crosses and 10 George Medals, but Leon's Distinguished Service Cross and Mentions in Despatches made him Australia's most highly decorated. In 2001, the Commonwealth Government established a park in Canberra to honour those who were awarded a George Cross. It has over 20 mounted plaques, two of them explanatory and the rest devoted to individuals who were awarded the Cross in World War Two.

The details of Leon's wartime experiences have come from his own notes and his sister's memories, supplemented by naval historians or biographers who wrote recollections for the many obituaries that appeared in August and September 1994, especially those in the London *Daily Telegraph*, the Sydney *Daily Telegraph Mirror*, the *West Australian* and the *Australian*. The following is from the *West Australian*:

But Goldsworthy remembered the 'Sheerness Job' as his first successful underwater rendering task, a job that took him beneath an isolated stretch of the River Thames, and almost got him killed by Royal Air Force fighters using the river to test their guns before flying off to France. It was this job in which Goldsworthy had to work with his hands thrust through a fishing net to delouse the mine, that contributed to his George Cross. But it was not the only one, hundreds followed and when D-Day finally came Goldsworthy was there on the beach to tackle some of the most intricate mines Hitler's experts had fashioned. So how did Lieutenant Commander Goldsworthy avoid the hand of death when it claimed the lives of so many RMS men?

It was possible that the war would simply not have been won without him.

Goldsworthy appreciated that the principle of expendability should apply equally to all parties engaged in the mass madness of warfare. But he knew too, that his position was unique. Intense specialisation, coupled with luck had developed him into an officer who could not be replaced – the loss of whose life and knowledge . . . could be a serious setback to the Allied anti-mine works.

He was credited with delousing over 300 mines and bombs during World War 2. By his example and courage, Goldsworthy was a great inspiration to his team of sea divers who worked with him on these dangerous assignments. He was also a great inspiration to his family and will always be remembered as a gentleman, a great Australian and as an example to us all.

He was truly a Cornish descendant who changed our world. Considering that he nearly died as a small child makes his achievements even more remarkable.

Final accolade

In February 2015, to mark the 40th anniversary of the introduction of the Australian Honours system, the Royal Australian Mint released a 'Cross of Valour and Australian George Cross' coin as part of the 'Australian Bravery' collectible series (not for circulation). The coins are gold-plated over fine silver, using a rare technique to strike them. When the

Australian Honours system began in 1975, the Australian George Cross became the Cross of Valour. The names of the George Cross winners are on the front of the coin, together with a miniature effigy of Queen Elizabeth (as shown), and the those of the Cross of Valour winners are on the back. Leon Goldsworthy's is the innermost name in the top left quarter of the photograph.

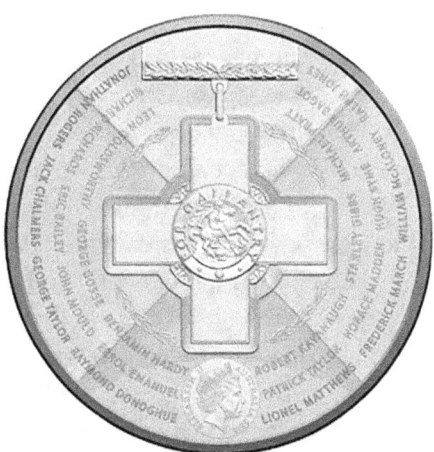

Notes

1. Sir Mark Oliphant, known as Marcus in student days, became a skilled nuclear physicist, engaged in research first at the Rutherford Laboratory in Cambridge where he and the team he worked with managed to split the first atom in 1932. In 1937 he became Professor of Physics at the University of Birmingham, where colleagues realised in 1940 that Uranium 235 could be used to make an atomic bomb. Oliphant, representing an influential British committee, was sent to the USA in 1941 to urge the US's Uranium Committee to consider the importance of developing an atomic weapon, which would require enormous resources to accomplish. He also visited US physicist friends who backed him up and, because of his efforts, the US established the Office of Scientific Research and Development. After Pearl Harbor this Office initiated research at Columbia University in Manhattan to begin the work. In 1943 Oliphant was sent as a British delegate to the project, which by then was called the 'Manhattan Project' and had moved to a dedicated laboratory in New Mexico. Oliphant, however, spent most of his time in the US working on research at Berkeley University, trying to refine Uranium 235 for peaceful purposes. He returned to England in April 1945.

   No one at the time knew how disastrous such a bomb would prove to be and, after its use, Oliphant said he 'would not have pressed for its creation if he had known'. He developed a strong anti-nuclear stance from then on.

   Source: www.notable biographies.com/supp/Supplement-Mi-So/Oliphant-Mark.html

Acknowledgements and sources

The family history information given in the early part of this paper was researched in Cornwall by the author and was documented and published by her in 2018, in *Goldsworthys then and now: Family stories from Moonta Reunion, 2014.*

Photographs used in this account mostly belong to Leon's family, but those of the plaque on St George's Terrace, Perth, and in George Cross Park, Canberra, were taken by the author.

The photographs of mines come from *One False Move, story of 'the Australian mine defusers in World War II'*, by Robert Macklin (Hachette, Sydney, 2012) – who in turn obtained them from Leon's own collection, now possessed by his daughter, Pamela Stynes.

The photograph of Leon and his mother on Keswick Railway Station comes from the front page of the Adelaide *News* of 6 April 1946, with an accompanying story on p. 3.

The author has one of the Bravery coins and photographed it, but chose to use the image from the Royal Australian Mint brochure, which shows the names more clearly.

The author is indebted to Leon Goldsworthy's daughter Pamela and to his sister Mary Walters (who died only last year) for information on and insights into Leon's life and exploits, as well as for the family photographs used. Thanks are also due to mutual second cousin Allan Goldsworthy (deceased) for giving me his extensive collection of press cuttings about Leon's heroism, and especially Leon's many obituaries, featured in the UK and USA as well as in Australia. The descriptive material on Leon's wartime accomplishments comes from all of these sources.

Creative Cornish:
An Australian Literary Heritage

ROSANNE HAWKE

This chapter discusses some Cornish-Australian writers, including journalists, poets and novelists from the early days of European settlement, showing how Cornish themes and characters have been treated by both Cornish and non-Cornish writers. A search for personal identity often brings writers to examine their Cornish roots, and so present-day authors are also explored here, with special attention given to contemporary children's writers.

> *A youth and maiden loved each other amid much opposition from their parents. This persecution succeeded so that the youth was forced to leave Cornwall and emigrate to a distant land. In their secret cove the lovers met for the last time and vowed under the moon that they would meet each other again in three years whether they were alive or dead.*
>
> *Time passed and the three years expired. One moonlit night when the sea was as glass the young girl sat on a rock near the cove. A passer-by, a crone, called out to her to be careful for the rocks were dangerous when the sea rose. But she wasn't heard, and then the crone noticed a young sailor appear by the girl's side with his arm about her waist.*
>
> *The crone relaxed and sat awhile since the girl had help at last. She watched the loving pair as the tide arose and washed about them, and she was frightened again for they made no effort to move to safety. Instead they appeared to float upon the water. She heard their voices, but no hint of terror, just singing:*
>
>> *I am thine,*
>> *Thou art mine,*
>>> *Beyond control;*

> *In the wave*
> *Be the grave*
> *Of heart and soul.*

Into the sea sank the lovers. The old woman scrambled closer and called again and it was as if they turned and looked her full in the face, smiling like angels. Then they kissed each other and disappeared.

The body of the maiden was found in the morning in a nearby cove. The news finally reached Cornwall that the young man had died far away at sea on that very night.

This is a story from Robert Hunt's 1881 collection of Cornish folktales (p. 247) and is retold in my own young adult novel *The Messenger Bird* (2012, p. 7). How and why does Cornish folklore appear in a modern young adult novel? It comes from a search for roots and identity.

Let us look first of all at the Cornish writers of early settlement times. Alan M. Kent and Gage McKinney's *Reader in Global Cornish Literature* (2008) gives 138 entries of Cornish literature; some are from Australia. Poems about the Burra and Kapunda mines are mostly anonymous and mostly unhappy; a poem called 'The Emigrant's Sabbath' by Revd. T.D. Murray in South Australia in 1848 compares the mines with Cornwall and shows the lack of Christian comfort in the new world (p. 33). The narrator in 'The Miner in Foreign Parts: Australia', written in 1902 by Mark Guy Pearce, remembers what he left behind and how he has sent his mother enough money to keep her for a half year (p. 127). Cousin Sylvia's poem 'Lucky Find: 1845' celebrates the discovery of copper at the Burra mine and makes a comparison with Madron Well in Cornwall. I wonder if writing a century later in about 1943 can make the memories sweeter (p. 169)?

Some early Cornish writers were journalists, such as Sir John Langdon Bonython, who was sixteen when he started with the Adelaide *Advertiser*, became editor in 1884 and its owner in 1893. His obituary stated he was a pioneer and master builder of Australian journalism. Some aspects of Bonython's life are described in Jean Prest's chapter in this book and a very comprehensive story of his life can be read in Prest's excellent biography of him (2011). Frederick Vosper, also a journalist, became sub-editor of the Charters Towers *Northern Miner* and later formed his own labour weekly, the *Republican* (Payton, 2020, p. 320). According to Kent and McKinney's anthology, South Australia's Harry Kneebone (1876–1933) became one of the finest journalists and politicians of his generation (2008, p. 257).

The *Northern Star*, the first country newspaper in South Australia, and its successor, the *Kapunda Herald,* faithfully served the mid-north and Kapunda area. The *Northern Star* was first published in 1860 and became a voice for the Cornish (Payton, 2020, p. 194). It printed news from Cornwall and even published letters and stories in Cornish dialect. Besides J.S. Pearce, who was a correspondent for the Adelaide *South Australian Register,* other notable writers who resided in Kapunda included Sir William John Sowden (1858–1943). His parents were both Cornish, and he was a journalist and newspaper editor who lived in Kapunda before 1867. He later worked as a reporter on the *Yorke's Peninsula Advertiser* and was associate editor of the *Port Adelaide News* (Hawke, 2009, p. 16). Burra did not get its own newspaper, the *Northern Mail* (soon renamed the *Burra News*), until 1876 but it also served its Cornish readership well.

Novelist Alice (Grant) Trevenen Rosman (1882–1961) was born at Kapunda, daughter of Trevenen Rosman. When young, Alice built card-houses and invented tales of their inmates for her sister Mary. Her early stories appeared in the *Observer, Chronicle* and *Southern Cross* newspapers. She worked as a journalist and wrote over nineteen novels, many during the Depression. They were among the top best-sellers in Canada and the United States of America for four successive years (Hawke, 2009, p. 16).

Some Cornish influences can be detected in early Australian adult fiction. In Catherine Martin's *Silent Sea* (1892), for example, the villain is a Cornishman. Martin deploys a stereotypical comic portrait of Cornish miners, although she portrays their mining practices in detail. Trevaskis, the mine manager, is shown more as a desperate man than an evil one. He is possibly the most important character in the novel, yet he is still the villain. His name, of course, is instantly recognisable as Cornish.

Patrick White, in *Voss* (1957), created Laura Trevelyan as one of the main characters; a character whom the critic C.D. Narasimhaiah (1988) argues is an exile, just as Patrick White himself is an ambivalent exile

(p. 59). Laura's discontent is discussed (White, 1957, p. 68) and she admits to being a poor immigrant (p. 403). She says early in the novel that this is not her country, although she has lived in it, and yet by the end she is 'perfectly at home in the environment to which she no longer expected to belong' (p. 410). Trevelyan is another well-known Cornish name, although the only other 'Cornish' characteristics she exhibits are her dark hair and her psychic ability to know when her lover, Voss, is in trouble.

In *A Fringe of Leaves* (1972) Patrick White portrays Ellen Roxburgh as a reformed Cornish country girl – a 'lady by adoption'. This novel shows how the Cornish were considered in the nineteenth century. Ellen's English husband says: 'Who would have thought that a crude Cornish girl could be made over to become a beautiful and accomplished woman' (p. 107). But always Ellen's Cornishness is just below the surface, in her language and in controlling her emotions: 'while her Cornish self struggled to restrain its temper' (p. 197). Yet it is this same Cornish character that enables her to survive shipwreck, life with Indigenous people, and the consequent disillusionment that the removal of her society brought (Hawke 2005b, p. 25).

Veitch's *Spindrift* (1980) is an engrossing narrative about the life of Mary Bryant, the daughter of a Cornish fisherman, who was sentenced to deportation to Botany Bay in the First Fleet. The resilient character of Mary Bryant is sympathetically portrayed in this novel. References to Cornwall in *Spindrift* include the phenomenon of ghosts (p. 3), while Cornwall itself is depicted as remote (p. 4). Cornish wrestling, fairs, (p. 20) and smuggling are incorporated into the story. Prejudice against the Cornish is illustrated when Will Bryant engages in a tussle with officer Casson, who declares: 'By God, I'd love to prick you with t'other end! Give me reason to do it, Bryant, just one small reason to stick you like the smooth smuggling Cornisher you are!' (p. 67). Later, when Mary says she is glad Will is Cornish like herself, Bryant replies: 'Aye. And to hell with all foreigners, especial the English' (p. 54).

'Cornishness' in *Spindrift* is interpreted by other characters as duplicitous and wily (p. 65); an Irish convict calls Will a 'damn Cornisher' (p. 75). Mary Bryant's story is told with compassion, but other characters in the book reveal how the Cornish generally were perceived: as remote, 'other', on the wrong side of the law, cunning. Thomas Keneally's portrayal of Mary Bryant in *The Playmaker* (1988) is subtly different. Besides stressing her Cornish resilience, Keneally shows her as having a 'tribal' disposition (p. 185) and paints her as a Cornish witch, able to exorcise evil and bad dreams, usually by having sex with the one afflicted (p. 178). In all, there are some thirteen books dealing with Mary Bryant in either historical fiction or non-fiction listed on the world-wide-web, the most recent being Craig Scutt's *Mary Bryant: The Impossible Escape* (2007).

A famous Cornish–Australian novel is Phyllis Somerville's *Not Only in Stone* (published in Adelaide in 1942; republished 1984). This story is written in Cornu–Australian dialect which, as the Cornish would say, "ee could be gettin' used to directly'. Set in South Australia's 'Little Cornwall', northern Yorke Peninsula, this is the story of Polly Thomas, of her strength and courage as she arrives in from Cornwall with her family in 1865. *The Days of May* (1981) by Mervyn Wyke Evans is also an unashamedly Cornish novel, depicting the real-life May family which emigrated to South Australia in the nineteenth century. This novel and Phyllis Somerville's *Not Only in Stone* portray the newly arrived Cornish migrants in a landscape very different from their own, demonstrating how they make their life within it while keeping their identity and culture intact.

Contemporary writing with Cornish themes

There are many Cornish descendants in Australia today who write but not all may refer to their Cornish roots: for example, Peter Goldsworthy, and acclaimed critic and writer, Kerryn Goldsworthy (a contributor to this book). There is not room here to discuss each of these contemporary writers, so a few will suffice. Author and academic Nick Jose's literary novel, *The Paper Nautilus* (1987) is set on South Australia's Yorke Peninsula, where Jack Tregenza, at the wedding of his niece Penny, thinks back on his family life. This story has an intriguing structure, finishing at Penny's conception, unravelling as a nautilus shell and just as delicately. Contemporary writer of adult historical fiction, John Fletcher, in his novel, *A Far Country* (2000), writes openly of the Cornish, including Cornish miners who worked at the Burra Burra mine and at Kapunda. Fletcher has admitted that his Cousin Jack credentials are alive and well!

Other writers include the award-winning poet and storyteller Jill Gloyne (1999) with her short story, 'The Stranger from Lostwithiel', a ghostly tale of a Cornish migrant and lost love, set on Kangaroo Island. Bruce Pascoe, poet and author of 26 books, says both his Cornish and Indigenous ancestry inform his writing: 'He takes his wry humour from his Cornish ethnic roots' (Cornish Australians, 2009). Poet John Blight's Cornish ancestors arrived in 1851. Like Pascoe, Blight was also of Indigenous descent yet he too stressed how his Cornish background influenced his style (Blight, 1987). Tony Brooks has produced a trilogy called *Curve of the Earth* (2003), which centres around two Cornish mining families who migrate to Australia and settle in Wallaroo and Moonta. Jennifer Carter, writing as Mary Talbot Cross, has published *The Foundling* (1998) and *Fortune's Fool* (1998), both set in Burra during the mining days. Roger Norris-Green's novel *Outcast* (2007) has as the main character Primitive Methodist preacher, Nathan Mattingley. Cornish names like Treloar and Pellow abound, as the book is set in early Moonta.

More recently Fiona McIntosh has written a saga called *Fields of Gold* (2010) inspired by her family history, set in Cornwall and India. Jack Bryant flees trouble in Penzance and hopes to start his life anew in India's mines. Cheryl Hayden's novel (2013) *The Christmas Game* tells the story of the Cornish Prayer Book Rebellion in 1549 in defence of Cornwall's identity, language and religion. Reviewer Michael Chappell considers that this is an engrossing reading of the events of 1549, 'bloody events which involved the lives of thousands and cost the Cornish 11% of the population' (2013). Queensland writer Kate Morton's best-selling novel, *The Forgotten Garden* (2008) is a family saga spanning Australia and Cornwall. It has all the elements of a typical Cornish tale, with a house on the Cornish coast, storytelling, secrets and a century old mystery. It is rather gothic and very Cornish.

Children's and Young Adult Fiction
Some children's novels employ Cornish names, or maybe the story is set by the sea, as in many traditional Cornish novels, or perhaps the tale is set in a part of Australia that is known as a 'Cornish area', such as Yorke Peninsula. Certainly, I believe our identity is connected to place; I feel

Creative Cornish: An Australian Literary Heritage

more 'at home' living as I do near Kapunda and Burra, where I know my family's ancestors lived.

Max Fatchen was adamant that his Cornish ancestry shone through his writing, especially in his sea faring adventure, *The Spirit Wind* (1973). 'I was conscious of my Cornish background when I wrote that,' he told me. The sea is brilliantly evoked, but no one else may know such scenes were inspired by a Cornish love of the sea. There is no mention of the Cornish in the novel. Although Boori Pryor, of Cornish and Indigenous descent, has chosen to explore his Indigenous heritage rather than his Cornish one, he is a creative storyteller; perhaps the Cornish influence is subliminal? Alison Croggon, born in Cornwall but living in Australia, besides being a successful poet and theatre critic, has written fantasy novels for young adults called the *Pelinor Quartet*. There are bards in the novel and some place names sound reminiscent of Cornish places but there are no overt Cornish themes. Fiona McIntosh's fantasy novels for children, for example, *The Whisperer* (2009), also are excellent stories for young people; although not dealing overtly with Cornish identity, they also add to the collective creativity of Cornish descendants.

Emily Rodda, best selling Australian children's author, asserts that her Cornish ancestry has affected her writing, albeit in an indirect way. Although there is no mention of Cornish themes in her fantasy series *Rowan of Rin* (2004), the people in the novel are immigrants, just as the Cornish were. Rowan, the unlikely hero, knows that the answer to many of their problems lies in the past (p. 135). He discovers on one of his adventures to the coast, that 300 years ago the folk of Rin had come from far away – yet they had had no memory of this past. Even so, he thinks, 'I do not feel like a newcomer … this is the only home I know' (p. 103). In Rodda's series *Deltora Quest* (2000), there may not be any direct reference to Cornishness either, yet there is the sense of a descendant life played out in a landscape that is not one's own. The grappling with belonging in this landscape is portrayed quite plainly. Rodda's brilliance in telling a story (a particular Cornish trait, perhaps) shines, as does her use of fantastical creatures and settings.

D.M. Cornish, another Cornish descendant, writes fantasy novels for young people and his stories, for example, *The Monster Blood Tattoo*, are extremely creative as well as being self-illustrated. 'I know of my

Cornish background of course,' he states, 'but I haven't knowingly written in a Cornish way as I'm not aware of all the culture' (personal communication, 2013). Yet there is a long streak of storytelling in his family, and he likes monsters.

Some novels highlight the supposed magical nature of Cornwall: its superstitions, myths or folklore. In my novel, *Sailmaker* (2002a), the story of Tom Bawcock's Eve, there is a correlation between the fishing village of Mousehole in Cornwall and a town on Yorke Peninsula, South Australia's 'Little Cornwall', where the townsfolk are sandbagging to stop the lighthouse island from melting away. The images of the storm in *Sailmaker* have a Cornish feel of ruggedness and wildness:

> The wind's so strong we can't walk upright. Even in the dark I can see white, flying up on the side like whipped sugar being flung off a giant fairy-floss machine. There's no way he'll survive in a sea like this. (Hawke, 2002a, p. 132).

Other indications of Cornishness used in *Sailmaker* include the name of the tour guide, Mr Pengelly, the fact that the sailmaker is an old sea dog whose great-grandfather was Cornish, and the recounting of a ghost story. Although the ghost story is based on local folklore of Edithburgh on the Yorke Peninsula, it also echoes Cornish stories.

Gillian Rubinstein's *Beyond the Labyrinth* (1990) is also set on Yorke Peninsula and the main character's surname is a Cornish one, Trethewan. Brenton Trethewan is described as small and dark, like his Cornish forebears, a stereotype that is still widely accepted: 'Brenton has inherited the dark colouring and slight build of some remote Cornish ancestor, along with other traits that make him both stubborn and dreamy' (p. 4). According to Elliott-Binns (1955, p. 62), being stubborn, detached, and imaginative are Cornish character traits. Perhaps this could stretch to dreaminess as well? Rubinstein seems to be evoking a Cornish character here. Brenton is the only one able to read the mind of the alien in *Beyond the Labyrinth* – a reference to a supposed Cornish 'feyness'. There is also a reference to 'Jack the giant killer', a Cornish folk story, where Jack kills the giant at St Michael's Mount (p. 5).

Rubinstein goes a step further in her next novel, *At Ardilla* (1991). When I first read this story, exploring the feelings of an intense and talented girl called Jen (accepted as a generic name for Cornish women), I had a distinct recollection of Cornwall. The story is set in a house by the sea, Ardilla, which itself becomes one of the 'characters' in the story. Jen and her sister and their friends had their own 'Club' in the past – a secret ritual using chants and totems that established a special belonging to Ardilla. But this year there are strangers at Ardilla, and the magic is threatened.

Magic and sea – is that not Cornwall?, we are entitled to ask. The sea *is* Cornwall, insists Denys Val Baker (1980, p. 122), and Cornwall is a haunted land (p. 144). Rubinstein explained that 'I spent all my holidays as a child in Cornwall' (personal communication, 2002), and the experience has influenced her work. As Denys Val Baker has argued, a person would have to be blind and deaf not to react to the atmosphere of Cornwall (p. 144). Although Rubinstein says her Cornish connection is tenuous, unconsciously or not, Cornish atmosphere and influence have flavoured her writing enough for the astute observer to notice (Hawke, 2005b, p. 29).

Legends

Wolfchild (2003) is my novel based on the Cornish legend of the lost land of Lyonesse. This was the name given by romantic poets to the fertile stretch of land between western Cornwall and the present-day Isles of Scilly. It was previously called Lethowsow, its Cornish name. According to the *Anglo-Saxon Chronicle*, in the year 1099 there was a very high tide which inundated whole villages in southern Britain, and many researchers believe this may have also flooded the stretch of land between Cornwall's Land's End and the Scillies, leaving only the peaks showing (Thomas, 1985, p. 275). According to legend, Trevelyan on his white steed was the last man to reach the coast of Cornwall alive, and the Trevelyan family still have on their coat of arms a white horse emerging

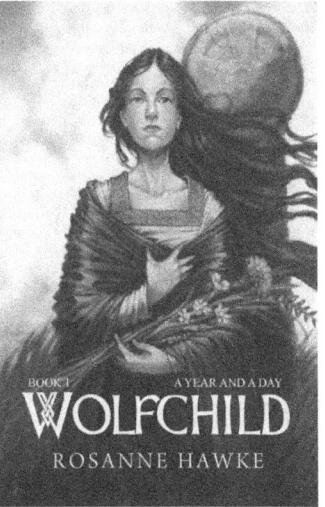

from the sea. This tale interested me so much that I wrote a story incorporating it.

It is 1099 in *Wolfchild,* and a 12-year-old girl, Morwenna, lives with her family on Lethowsow. Raw is a runaway serf who must stay hidden for a year and a day to become free. He hides in a cave in the high places which are believed to be King Arthur's final resting place. The novel brims with references to Cornish atmosphere, the sea and weather, the people's love of story telling, Morwenna's singing and feyness, the mix of superstition and religion. Yet it seems it will take a while before the English world accepts the Cornish assertion that they are not English: despite all the Cornishness displayed in *Wolfchild*, a reviewer could still describe the novel as 'an intriguing mix of English folklore and medieval history' (Huber, 2003).

Folklore

My novel *Across the creek* (2004) uses Cornish folklore in an Australian setting, an abandoned copper mine, perhaps the most Cornish setting that an Australian could devise. Aidan Curnow (the name derived from Kernow, the Cornish word for Cornwall) is drawn into a land called Trevalia when he steps across the creek, which runs through an abandoned mine near his town. In Trevalia, Aidan is led by a piskey named Raff and encounters haunting music; he travels underground through the old mine tunnels until he finds a green lake and meets the Lady of that land, and the spriggans. Aidan finds his friend Jenice has been living there with some other lost children.

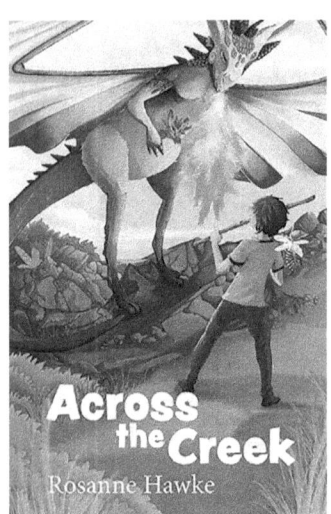

It was believed in Cornwall that some piskies went 'beyond the seas', and it is this idea that I built upon in *Across the Creek*. What if these spriggans had come with the Cornish people who emigrated to South Australia in the 1840s to work in the mines at Kapunda and Burra, then later at Moonta on northern Yorke Peninsula? There is a fire-breathing dragaroo that the spriggans have bred, and it is the symbol in the novel of Cornish culture in Australia – two cultures forming a different entity. The dragaroo is neither dragon nor kangaroo, nor does it function well as either; an indication of the assimilation that Cornish immigrants endured.

The idea of lost children is based on the Cornish story, *The Lost Child of St Allen* (Hunt, 1881, p. 86). When the boy was found he told everyone how he was lured by music into a dark grove and found himself at the edge of a lake. A beautiful lady led him to an underground cavern that was built of crystal and supported by glass pillars. This has influenced the Lady's cave in *Across the Creek,* except I have kept the landscape Australian – the crystal pillars became quartz and the lake is the remains of an open cut mine at Kapunda.

The Cornish once believed 'fairyland' was the place where souls went for particular reasons, and I have tried in my novel to be true to most of the laws of Cornish faery land; for example, in the passing of time, the types of beings located there, and the ways of escape. However, I also wanted to meld the old with the new: Aidan is a Cornish descendant from the 21st century, and calls himself Australian. He does not care much for magic, and manages to escape the clutches of the dragaroo by his own laconic character and intellect. Aidan is thus a product of his Cornishness but it is the sum of the two, his Cornish-Australian character, that gets him out of Trevalia (Hawke, 2005a, p. 135).

In Tricia Springer's *Piskey Trouble* (2005), Joey Simons finds that trouble follows him when a hole appears in the school oval. It is believed to be an old mine shaft. This story is based on Cornish folklore regarding the darker side of piskies – that of causing mischief, especially to those who do not believe in them. The reader discovers many piskey details: when Joey leaves the milk out, the piskies drink it and it curdles (p. 35). He finds other people can be piskey-led just as he is. As well as giving a background to the Cornish in South Australia, Springer's author note states that Cornish customs and traditions have continued to influence the Australian towns in which the Cornish lived (p. 64). She suggests that many of the works accredited to the piskies could be explained naturally, but she prefers the Cornish ability to make a good story.

Remembering history

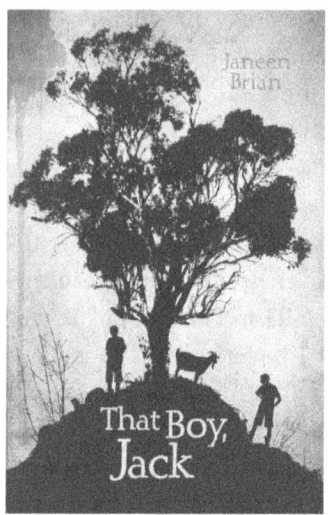

A recent Cornish children's novel is Janeen Brian's *That Boy Jack*. In the novel, Jack Pollock promised his friend Gilbert they would work in the Moonta mines together, but when Gilbert is forced to leave school to work Jack discovers he has a fear of going underground. The novel portrays Cornish immigrants with some Cornu–Australian speech, as in 'thank ee', 'me handsome', 'they be going', 'that do make me happy'. Brian explained that she did not drop 'h's from words like 'handsome' so as to make it easier for a modern young audience to read. There are Cornish surnames: Oates, Pascoe, Goldsworthy; folklore is included, for example, the story about the piskies taking the horses from the farmer's yard, as well as the song 'Going up Camborne Hill'. We taste Cornish fare, even figgy hobbin (raisins in lumps of dough). Jack goes to church at Moonta and they have a bonfire on 24 June. The story is an accurate portrayal of life in the Moonta mines in 1874, showing the Cornish as respectable, resilient, hard working people who contributed to the economic development of South Australia at great sacrifice to their families. This novel is a welcome addition to the small body of Australian Cornish titles to help children know their history and heritage. Brian has discovered her own Cornish heritage in recent years, and the novel *That Boy, Jack* has helped her explore her own identity. She states: 'Knowing the threads that bind me today grew from a village (which I've since visited) in Cornwall, also wove their stories and lives around the mines of Moonta and are part of me today, gives me a joy of belonging' (personal communication, 2004).

Tricia Springer's *Boy of the Mines* (2005) is another historical novel showing the life of Cornish miners in Moonta on northern Yorke Peninsula. Whereas Brian's novel covers the difficulties of everyday life and school life, 'a time which had dramas often steeped in basic problems of work, health and water' (Brian, personal communication, 2004), this story shows what the pickey boy's life that Brian's protagonist desires would have been like. In *Boy of the Mines,* Henry Harper's father dies in the mine. Henry becomes a pickey boy, sorting the ore as it comes to the surface. His mother says his eleven pence will not be enough for them to live on, so she takes in washing, using a mangle that the mine provides for widows (p. 10). The book shows the difficult life in the mine cottages, with lack of water, bullying, friendship, chapel, saffron buns and pasties, mention of Captain Hancock the mine manager, and even the taming of a nanny goat to pull a billycart in a race. And of course, Cornish names occur, such as Penhall and Trenwith.

Cornish identity

Two novels for young people that show the effect of discovering one's Cornish ethnic identity are *Splashback* by Errol Broome (1996) and my own, *Zenna Dare* (2002b). *Splashback* is the story of Ned Manford and how he feels he does not fit in his family; for a start, he hates water on his head and his father was a star swimmer! His mother says he is not his father's son, meaning in his aversion to water, but Ned takes it literally and he is sure he was adopted. When he goes rowing with his friend Kip and jumps off the jetty, he misses and cracks his head on the edge of the dinghy, before dropping into the sea. When he is pulled out he has slipped into a different time. He has been rescued by a whaling boat bound for Cornwall.

Splashback depicts Cornish life in Fowey in the nineteenth century. Superstitions and sayings are also included to indicate Cornish culture. For example, the ship cannot leave on a Friday. Ned thinks, 'There were things these people believed that no one ever explained' (p. 49). There are also references to Cornish folklore: 'leave the magic to the piskies' (p. 57). When Ned slips back to his own time, nothing has changed but he knows he has. He has met his ancestors, and found a sense of his ethnic identity and thus his place in his family.

Zenna Dare (2002b) is a young adult story with multiple issues, and readers often only see the one of reconciliation. Not many reviewers or critical writers have opened up the issue of the Cornish identity that Jenefer Tremayne discovers, maybe because she discovers so much else: a belonging to a rural area, a family secret and a relationship with Caleb, an Indigenous boy, when she had never met an Indigenous person before.

Zenna Dare deals with Cornish identity and how important it is to know one's heritage, yet with not dwelling too much on the differences.

For me, *Zenna Dare* began in the finding of a photo of my grandmother and a postcard of an opera singer. Imagine if they were one and the same! I started creating two women in different centuries: Jenefer and Gweniver. I too am a Cornish descendant and *Zenna Dare* became my journey as much as it was Jenefer's. In this case searching for roots led to inclusion of historical material in *Zenna Dare*, as well as Cornish culture, folk stories, names and Kernewek (Cornish language) phrases. With Caleb's understanding and support, Jenefer successfully unravels a mystery but she discovers much more than a family secret: she finds an ethnic identity that she never knew she had, learns of reconciliation and second chances, and brings together an estranged family. She now knows she belongs: a Cornish descendant but also an Australian and she can embrace Australian culture, in all its diversity, with confidence. In my novel *The Last Virgin in Year Ten* (2006), 14-year-old Caz is at first not comfortable with her Cornish heritage, unlike her friend Matthew Tallack who is a King Arthur enthusiast. As her relationship with Matthew progresses and she finds the courage to stand against her peer group, so does her acceptance of who she is.

Exile

The Messenger Bird is my most recent work with a Cornish theme, and in it Nathaniel, who lives in 1887, visits Tamar in the present day. Nathaniel is part of that assimilation into an Australian culture often described by Philip Payton. He calls himself a 'native Australian'; he is the first of the 'Anglo' generation born on Australian soil. He is a son of Australia, yet he knows where his family came from, and he studies to build upon what his father has achieved on the land. His grandfather was first a miner at Burra, and then was able to buy land at Allendale North. The land was

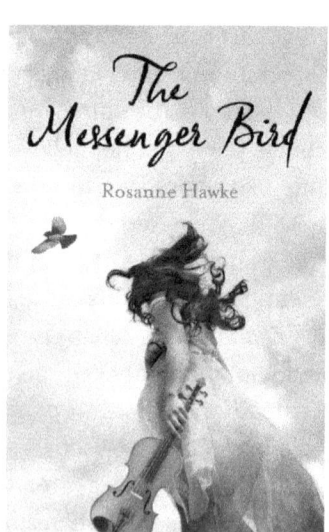

important to all his family, but Nathaniel wants more: an education and his music.

In a low moment, Nathaniel tells Tamar that we are all exiles in this world until we arrive in heaven (Hawke, 2012, p. 200). His father felt he had been exiled from Cornwall as he was a child when he came – he had no choice. But Australia is Nathaniel's country now. He tells Tamar that there is no point in keeping alive the old – you just need to know where you came from to understand your origins, and then you make it into something to fit the new – we can belong here (p. 134). Nathaniel is born of the Cornish diaspora, but he does not want to look back. He wants to belong but it does not dominate him. It is like author Sophie Masson's experience. She states: 'It's as if I belong to the world, as if the kingdom is itself both within and without me, linked to other people' (1996, p. 139). Nathaniel's Methodist beliefs allow him to think this way too, and to show a typical Cornish resilience in 'making do'.

Nathaniel's family still has bonfires on 24 June, reflecting their Cornish heritage. He attends chapel and sings in the choir and does not drink, for temperance sake. Tamar's family does not observe any of these things – and this is where Nathaniel says the old ways have changed. In *The Messenger Bird* we can see the old culture and how it has been reduced. All Tamar knows of Cornishness is festivals and pasties, old mines, and her name. Yet the knowledge that Nathaniel brings helps her with a sense of confidence, healing and belonging that she feels growing within her.

Researcher Emma Bennett states that my novels encourage readers to discover their own identities, and provide a strong foundation from which young people can begin their research into the Cornish in Australia (2012, p. 177). I would add that the other children's writers I've included here also provide a platform for exploring Cornish identity in Australia. I hope other writers will be similarly inspired and add to the Cornish–Australian body of literature for children.

Kernewek

An important, though less accessible, area of Cornish influence in children's literature in Australia is the work of Lillian James who writes children's short fiction in Kernewek, the revived Cornish language. Author Lillian James is also a bard of Cornwall, is very aware of her

Cornish identity and calls herself a Cornish Australian. Her stories have an Australian setting and theme, for example, *An Boekka* (1998), 'The Red Dragon', is about bushfires; *Sagh Leun a Gregyn* (1991), 'A Bagful of Shells', is set on Yorke Peninsula with a storm and abalone poachers. *Kamm ne Bell* (1990), 'A Step too Far', is set in Moonta where Mandy, the protagonist, falls down a mine shaft. James says she writes to add to the body of Kernewek literature for children and students of the language to enjoy (personal communication, 2004). James' recent publication, *Anethow Ostralek* (2012), the collected stories of Lilian James, gives us her body of work in one volume.

Conclusion

Historian Elliott-Binns wrote almost seventy years ago that the Cornish people were emotional, imaginative, with startling contrasts of mood haunted by memories and the past, had a love of soil, and a love of music (1955, p. 62), a literary imagining that remains powerful today. Add to that some superstition, strong religious beliefs, and a sense of adventure and you have an idea of 'Cornish characteristics' and what good storytellers the Cornish are, many having been creative in the literary field. As we have observed, the Cornish have also been written about (not always kindly), and they have written about themselves. While there is not as much Cornish–Australian literature as Australian–Irish, for example, and although many creative Cornish descendants have written fiction without Cornish themes, of late more authors of Cornish heritage have discovered their own family history, resulting in recent fiction that serves to explore their Cornish identity.

References

Bennett, E. (2012), 'Cornish-Australian identity and the Novels of Rosanne Hawke'. In Payton, P (Ed.). *Cornish Studies: Twenty* (pp. 166–179). Exeter: University of Exeter Press

Blight, J. (1987), *John Blight*. VHS Recording. Sydney: Australia Council

Brian, J. (2013), *That boy, Jack*. Newtown, NSW: Walker Books

Brooks, T. (2003), *Curve of the Earth*. Henley Beach: Seaview Press

Broome, E. (1996), *Splashback*. St Leonard's, NSW: Allen & Unwin

Chappell, M. (2013), 'Review of *The Christmas Game*'. Amazon website

Cornish Australians (2013, March 4), in *Wikipedia*. Retrieved March 18, 2013, from http://en.wikipedia.org/wiki/Cornish_Australian

Croggon, A. (2002), *The gift*. 'Pelinor Quartet', no 1. Camberwell, Vic: Penguin
Elliott-Binns, L.E. (1955), *Medieval Cornwall*. London: Methuen
Evans, M.W. (1981), *The Days of May*. Adelaide: Rigby
Fatchen, M. (1973), *Spirit Wind*. London: Methuen Children's Books
Fletcher, J. (2000), *A Far Country*. Milson Point, NSW: Random House
Gloyne, J. (1999), 'The Stranger from Lostwithiel'. *The Nautilus Shell*. Kangaroo Island: Jill Gloyne
Hawke, R. (2012), *The Messenger Bird*. St Lucia, QLD: University Queensland Press
Hawke, R. (2009), 'Kapunda Cousins'. *Cornish Communities in Australia*. Adelaide: Cornish Association of SA, pp. 1–21
Hawke, R. (2006), *The Last Virgin in Year Ten*. South Melbourne: Hachette
Hawke, R. (2005a), 'Jack and Jen in Oz: Cornish Identity in Australian children's literature'. In O'Neill, P. (Ed.). *Exile and Homecoming, Papers from the Fifth Australian Conference of Celtic Studies*. Sydney: The Celtic Studies Foundation, University of Sydney
Hawke, R. (2005b), *Jack and Jen in Oz: Cornish identity in Australian children's Literature and some Observations on the Genesis of Glanville Park*. Unpublished PhD thesis, Adelaide: University of Adelaide
Hawke, R. (2004), *Across the Creek*. South Melbourne: Lothian
Hawke, R. (2003), *Wolfchild*. South Melbourne: Lothian
Hawke, R. (2002a), *Sailmaker*. South Melbourne: Lothian
Hawke, R. (2002b), *Zenna Dare*. South Melbourne: Lothian
Hayden, C. (2013), *A Christmas Game*. Redruth, Cornwall: Palores
Huber, R. (2003), 'Angels and Rats', *Viewpoint* 11, Spring, p. 21
Hunt, R. (1993), *The Drolls, Traditions and Superstitions of old Cornwall* (1881). Felinfach: Llanerch Publishers
James, L. (1990), *Kamm Re Bell*. Truro, Cornwall: Kowethas an Yeth Kernewek
James, L. (1991), *Sagh Leun a Gregyn*. Truro, Cornwall: Kowethas an Yeth Kernewek
James, L. (1998), *An Boekka*. Truro, Cornwall: Kowethas an Yeth Kernewek
James, L. (2012), *Anethow Ostralek*. Truro, Cornwall: Kowethas an Yeth Kernewek
Jose, N. (1987), *The Paper Nautilus*. Ringwood, Vic: Penguin
Keneally, T. (1988), *The Playmaker*. London: Hodder & Stoughton
Kent, A. & McKinney, G. (Eds) (2008), *The Busy Earth: A Reader in Global Cornish Literature 1700–2000*. St Austell: Cornish Hillside Publications
Martin, C. (1995), *Silent Sea*. (1892). Sydney: University of NSW Press
Masson, S. (1996), *Borderland*. Children's Book Council Conference Papers
McIntosh, F. (2010), *Fields of Gold*. Camberwell, Vic: Penguin
McIntosh, F. (2009), *The Whisperer*. Sydney: HarperCollins
Morton, K. (2008), *The Forgotten Garden*. Crows Nest, NSW: Allen & Unwin
Narasimhaiah, C.D. (1988), 'Gifts of exile'. In Bennett, B. (Ed.). *A Sense of Exile*. (pp. 57–65). Perth, WA: University of Western Australia
Norris-Green, R. (2007), *Outcast*. Moonta: Roger Norris-Green
Payton, P. (2020), *The Cornish Overseas: A History of Cornwall's Great Emigration*. Exeter: University of Exeter Press

Prest, E.J. (2011), *Sir John Langdon Bonython: Newspaper Proprietor, Politician and Philanthropist*. North Melbourne: Australian Scholarly
Rodda, E. (2000), *Deltora Quest: Forests of Silence,* no 1. Norwood: Omnibus
Rodda, E. (2004), *Rowan of Rin: The Journey.* Norwood: Omnibus
Rubinstein, G. (1990), *Beyond the Labyrinth.* Ringwood, Vic: Penguin
Rubinstein, G. (1991), *At Ardilla.* Norwood: Omnibus
Scutt, C. (2007), *Mary Bryant: The Impossible Escape.* Fitzroy, Vic: Black Dog
Somerville, P. (1984), *Not Only in Stone* (1942). Adelaide: Wakefield Press
Springer, T. (2005), *Boy of the Mines.* Mooroolbark, Victoria: Loranda
Springer, T. (2005), *Piskey Trouble.* Mooroolbark, Victoria: Loranda
Talbot Cross, M. (1998), *Fool's Fortune.* Victoria: Shalimar Press
Talbot Cross, M. (1998), *The Foundling.* Victoria: Shalimar Press
Thomas, C. (1985), *Exploration of a Drowned Landscape.* London: Batsford
Val Baker, D. (1980), *The Spirit of Cornwall.* London: W.H. Allen
Veitch, A.S. (1980), *Spindrift.* Sydney: Angus & Roberson
White, P. (1960), *Voss.* London: Penguin
White, P. (1976), *A Fringe of Leaves.* London: Penguin

Further relevant publications

Hayden, C. (2002), 'Cousin Jack: Postmodern Hero or Problem Child? – finding Cornish Identity in 21st century Australia'. *Australian Celtic Journal,* 8, pp. 27–80)
James, L. (1990), *Kevrin an Glus-hwytha.* Truro: Kowethas an Yeth Kernewek
James, L. (1995), *An Dhragon Rudh.* Truro, Cornwall: Kowethas an Yeth Kernewek

Acknowledgement

Thank you to Walker Books Australia for the use of the cover of *That Boy Jack* –

Cover image credits:

(grunge background) © Andrii Muzyka/Shutterstock.com;

(goat silhouette) © Klaus Kaulitzki/Shutterstock.com;

(boys/mountain silhouette) © Engin Hakki Bilgin/Shutterstock.com;

Walker Books Australia

Cousin Jack and his Economic Niche

CHERYL HAYDEN

Introduction

In 2001, as a part of my Cornish Studies research (University of Exeter), I surveyed the members of Australian Cornish associations in an attempt to understand how and why a culture made almost invisible by its absorption into the white Anglo-Celtic majority was today being celebrated so enthusiastically. Who, I wanted to know, was behind it and what drove their passion?

I sent bundles of surveys to Australia's Cornish associations, all of which encouraged their members to participate. Of my surveys, 190 (23 per cent) were returned, representing 13 per cent of total estimated Cornish association membership and providing me with sufficient quantitative and qualitative data from which to extract results and propose conclusions (Hayden, 2002).

One of the key findings, although not surprising, was the power of Cornish mining as a precursor to attracting 21st Century Australians to their Cornish identity, often over and above other (and arguably more dominant) ethnicities appearing on their family trees. What was quite unexpected was the apparent role of the female descendants of these miners in passing on an interest in the almost exclusively masculine part of our heritage. This chapter presents that part of the research project that relates directly to this finding and the theory that endeavours to explain it.[1]

The Survey
Findings and snapshot
More Australian women than men (69 and 55 respectively) participated in the survey. The average ages were 62 for women and 66 for men, most respondents were married – more men than women – and the women were more likely than the men to have a spouse who also identified as Cornish. Of the 124 Australian-born respondents, 116 identified as Australian (105 exclusively) with others saying they also identified as British, English or Cornish, while four gave more particularised identities such as 'Cornish-Australian' or 'Celtic-Australian'. Eight did not identify as Australian, despite being born here.

Based on the most common responses to the survey questions, the 'average' member of a Cornish association in Australia is a 62.5 year-old woman who joined the association because of her interest in Cornish history and culture. She may not have Cornish-born grandparents, but can certainly identify at least two Cornish-born great-grandparents, at least one of whom was a miner. However, she identifies as Australian and sees no need for public displays such as the wearing of Cornish tartan or marching in parades.

Australians and their Cornish heritage
More interesting, however, is the historical nature of the Cornish ancestry with which Australians identify. Ancestry, of course, is historical by definition, but for a significant number of the Australian survey respondents, locating a Cornish-born ancestor required delving into the 19th Century. Of the 124 Australian-born respondents who are the subject of this analysis, a vast majority (90 per cent) did not have Cornish-born parents and half had no Cornish-born grandparents. The 62 (50 per cent) who *did* have Cornish-born grandparents reported a total of 97, and these comprised: 43 paternal grandfathers, 22 paternal grandmothers (including 16 couples), 16 maternal grandmothers and 16 maternal grandfathers, including nine couples (see Table 1).

The men among the respondents were far more likely to have a Cornish-born paternal grandfather (53 per cent) than a maternal grandmother (nine per cent), which seemed to indicate a paternal bias among men when selecting an identity. While women did not demonstrate this extent of numeric bias, further data analysis showed they were far more likely to have been influenced by a female grandparent than a male grandparent, and also more likely to have a miner among their ancestors. Of all respondents, 69 per cent had a miner among their ancestors.

Australians and their Cornish-born grandparents

Cornish Grandparents	Men (n= 55)		Women (n= 69)		Total G'parents	% total (n=97)
	No.	%	No	%		
None	19	35	43	62	-	-
Paternal grandfather	29	53	14	20	43	44
Paternal grandmother	13	24	9	13	22	23
Maternal grandfather	5	9	11	16	16	16.5
Maternal grandmother	6	11	10	14	16	16.5
Total grandparents	53		44		97	100

Table 1. Exactly one half of survey respondents had no Cornish-born grandparents. The 62 who did identified a total of 97 Cornish-born grandparents and, of these, the paternal grandfather was most common, and much more likely to be identified by male respondents.

Not only does our Cornish heritage stretch back beyond our recollection of Cornish-born ancestors to the days of Cornish mining prowess, it is interesting to note that for most people in the survey, Cornish ancestry comprised no more than 25 per cent – the equivalent of one grandparent or two great-grandparents. Despite this, 67 per cent of the Australian men and 46 per cent of the Australian women said their Cornish heritage was the most important to them, citing a number of reasons such as its numeric dominance, their knowledge of this heritage, their surname, or the influence of one particular parent or grandparent. Even among the Australians, however, there are variations, particularly along gender lines, with men more likely to be influenced by paternity – after all, it is the men who tend to keep their surnames, and Cornish names are often particularly recognisable – while women were more inclined to refer to 'special' or 'emotional' aspects of identity. The women were also four times more likely than the men to say their Cornish heritage was *less* important to them than that of another ethnic group, perhaps suggesting that their participation in the Australian Cornish community had been influenced by a partner or husband. What is apparent, however, is that the size of the Cornish branch of the family tree does not appear to be significant when it comes to choosing an identity. So, if size does not matter, what does?

The economic niche and Cornish particularity

Miners, farmers – and what about the fishermen?
'*Cornishmen are fishermen, Cornishmen are miners too* ...'[2]

The Cornish might very well be renowned as fishermen in Cornwall, but in Australia they are miners – of the Australian-born survey participants only one person identified a fisherman among his ancestors. So if they are not fishermen, and if farmers are not well represented, it remains the task of the miner to drive our enthusiasm for our Cornish identity. This 'particularization' of identity and the occupation of an economic 'niche' mark the works of Taylor (in Alcock et al., 1979) and Smith (1991). They suggest that a blinkered view of identity that enhances one part of the group at the expense of others results in a narrow view of the group as a whole, and in the Australian Cornish community, this has happened in spades.

Australians have participated in the process of 'particularization' to the extent that Cornish identity in Australia is markedly different from that in Cornwall, and the economic niche is working as a powerful force in favour of the miner.

In the Australian context, the main 'victims' of this trend have been farmers. Despite being the second largest ancestral occupational group identified by survey respondents, farmers seem to lack the particularity needed to convince contemporary Australians to identify with their Cornish heritage. While 31 per cent of respondents identified a Cornish farmer among their ancestors, and farming made up 17 per cent of all listed occupations, the farmer was overly dependent on the presence of a miner in the family for recognition. This is revealed by the fact that while there were only 2.3 times more miners than farmers identified in the survey, Australians were *five times* more likely to identify with their Cornish background if they had a miner and no farmer than they were if they had a farmer but no miner (Table 2). And it became quite apparent from the survey results that in Australia, Cornishmen are not fishermen at all.[3]

Our Cornish-born ancestors and their occupations

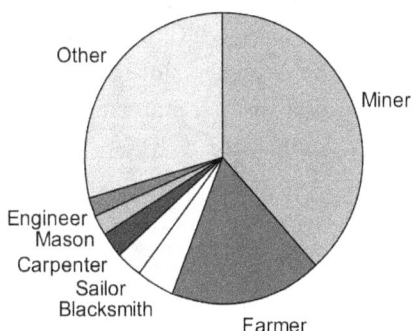

Figure 1. The 124 Australian-born survey respondents identified the occupations of 224 individuals and, of these, 86 were miners. In all 44 different occupations were mentioned.

Miners and farmers among our Cornish-born ancestors

	Men (n = 55)		Women (n = 69)	
		%		%
Mining ancestor	38	69	48	69
Farming ancestor	19	35	20	29
Miner (but no farmer)	25	45	33	47
Farmer (but no miner)	8	14	4	6

Table 2. Respondents identified 2.3 times more miners than farmers (86:39) but were five times more likely to identify a 'miner only' than a 'farmer only'. Interest in Cornish heritage falls away markedly, especially among women, in the absence of a miner.

These findings are strangely compelling. Could it be that women were more inclined than men to be drawn to the particularity of a distinctive and very masculine mining culture? Was there something about women and the way culture is passed down through the generations that was breathing new life into the myth of Cousin Jack?

Female particularity and the search for Cousin Jack
More Australian female than male respondents to this survey confessed to being drawn to 'special' or 'particular' aspects of their Cornish ancestry and the statistics show that they certainly went looking for it. After all, as we have seen, among survey respondents, they were

far less likely than the men to have had a Cornish-born grandparent and therefore less likely to have heard the accent and heard stories of 'home'. The women who *did* have Cornish grandparents had a fairly even distribution among the four possible grandparents, while the men overwhelmingly identified Cornish paternal grandfathers. So while paternity – perhaps carrying with it a distinctive Cornish surname – appeared to be driving Australian men, women were conducting an entirely different search in the quest for an authentic identity.

The nature of women's search patterns is seen again among those who say their Cornish heritage is the most important. There were 50 Australian women in this category and 46 per cent were from Victoria – and of these, 87 per cent had a mining ancestor. The corresponding figure for South Australia was 86 per cent. By comparison, of the Australian men in this category there was no particular or disproportionate affiliation with any State or Territory, nor with a mining ancestry. Once again, then, mining is shown to be a potent influence among women eager for a definable and 'authentic' heritage.

So, among those Australians who identify with their Cornish heritage, what we have is this:

- Australians – especially women – are more interested in their Cornish heritage if it involves mining.
- Men are less particular about the nature of their Cornish identity, but tend to draw on their paternal ancestry.
- Women are more likely to be interested in their mining heritage if it occurs on the maternal side of their family.
- The pull of a mining heritage is particularly potent among women who were born in Victoria or South Australia.

It can be argued, then, that Australians of Cornish descent are well and truly engaged in an extremely particularising process when it comes to their ethnicity, and women appear to be the driving force behind it.

Explaining the quest – why here? why now?
Homogenised, normal human beings
The search for authentic roots and a particular identity is not unique to the Cornish diaspora and not unique to Australia, but in what we

commonly refer to as the 'western world' it does appear to have emerged at a particular point in time: during the era of emergent globalisation and, in particular, of multiculturalism.

In Australia, the influx of southern and eastern European immigrants, and later, Vietnamese refugees, provided the 'Anglo-Celtic' community with a new and visible batch of 'others'.[4] In the tradition of Said's Orientalism (1991), the presence of these groups provided urban 'white' British Australia with a mirror with which to examine itself, determine what it was and what it was not, and to then assert its 'pure white' (Dyer, 1997, 22) superiority. This furthered the process of Anglo-Celtic homogenisation and created a heightened sense of being the embodiment of 'normal human beings' or, as Dyer (p. 3) puts it: 'not of a certain race ... just the human race'. The Cornish were among those in Australia to not only have all the privileges of being 'white' but also 'without ethnicity' – and 'without culture' (Frankenberg, quoted in Dyer, 1997, 9). Their Protestantism making them even 'less ethnic' than Catholics (Ibson, 1981, 284), Cornish Australians were perfect candidates for inclusion in this 'cultureless' group, which then developed a *'me-too'* mentality in the quest for ethnicity (Dyer, p. 10). Here, then, we have a paradoxical situation in which the majority, having traded on the power of its white, non-ethnic position as the purest representation of the human race, now sensed that its very colourlessness reflected poorly and palely against the 'culturally rich' minorities who had 'a kind of guarantee of authenticity' (Hall, in King, 1993, 43).

Among the academics to have pondered over the nature and timing of major cultural shifts during the latter part of the 20th Century, three have suggested times that place mass migrations as a forerunner to postmodernism and to confirm the latter's role in creating a shift towards the 'certainties' of the past. Hobsbawm (quoted in McGuigan, 1999, 81) says the 1960s marked the starting point for the rise of identity as an issue of political debate, and certainly this would coincide with the arrival of many southern Europeans to Australia. Harvey (1992, vii) has identified 1972 as the beginning of the postmodern era, which was marked by a 'sea-change in cultural as well as in political-economic practices' and Baudrillard (quoted in McGuigan, 150) suggested that 'history took a turn in the opposite direction' some time during the 1980s, a notion supported by Sardar's comment (albeit made of 'non-western' cultures) that to survive postmodernism requires 'moving forward to tradition' (quoted in McGuigan, 91). It is perhaps worth noting the origins of South Australia's Kernewek Lowender in the early 1970s (which preceded most of this).

Becoming 'ethnic'

For the Cornish to now reassert their identity was problematic. Having identified as 'proto-typical Anglo-Saxons' and 'British' they were now, not surprisingly, faced with the widespread notion that there were few meaningful distinctions between the white ethnic groups (Ibson, 1981, 285). Another problem was that the Cornish in Australia had hinged their identity almost exclusively to a mining industry that belonged to the 19th Century and a religion that officially 'died' in 1977 (Gillman, 1988, 91), and indeed, it must be noted that, in Australia, Methodism is linked with the Cornish and particularly with the Cornish-based mining communities.

Nevertheless, the condition of postmodernity with the numerous identities and roles it foisted upon people created the need, especially among those who were 'without culture' or 'without roots' to locate the ethnic roots to which they 'ineluctably, organically' belonged (Dixson,1999, 51). This search reflected the belief that *"whence we came'* is central to the definition of *'who we are"* (Smith, 1991, 22), and provided 'yet another defence mechanism against anomie and alienation' (Zubrzycki, 1992, 18).

The other issue in communities such as the Australian-Cornish community is that many of us have multiple 'ethnicities' on our family trees to choose from. The idea that who we are is ineluctably connected to 'whence we came' is fraught with difficulty when we come from so many different places. Our roots might be Cornish, but as the survey results showed, most respondents identified as Australians whose most recent Cornish-born ancestors were grandparents, if not great-grandparents. They also identified a raft of other ethnic groups as being among their ancestors. We might, for example, also be descended from Scottish and German immigrants. We can, if we choose, select to identify as Cornish–Scottish–German: as Robertson has pointed out, there is no limit to particularism, uniqueness, difference and otherness (in King, 1993, 76–80). This, however, is problematic, if not akin to schizophrenic. The solution, then, for many people in diasporic populations is to select one identity which is deemed more meaningful than the others.

More meaningful than the rest

Of interest here is the decision-making that leads a polyethnic person to choose to identify with their Cornishness rather than their Scottish or Welsh or English heritage. According to Harvey (1992, 303), 'the assertion of any place-bound identity has to rest at some point on the motivational power of tradition,' a notion that suggests that a culture's 'degree of distinctiveness' (Taylor, in Alcock et al., 1979, 24) may have something to do with the reasons people might be inclined to identify more closely with one 'ethnie' rather than another. For the Cornish in Australia, this could be found in their 'economic niche', which in turn satisfied the need of minorities to 'seek to preserve only what they regard as the superior elements of their traditional culture' (Taylor, 25).

For the Cornish, there is no more superior 'superior element' than their mining prowess, whether it be in the copper mines of South Australia or the gold mines of Victoria. Cornish Australians are privileged in this regard – no other white Anglo-Celtic group has such a highly specific, highly tangible and highly heroic economic niche upon which to hinge their identity. No wonder we are drawn to it.

Why women?

As noted above, the survey data present a powerful argument to suggest that Australian women are particularly adept at passing on the heritage associated with a highly masculinised Australian-Cornish mining culture.[5] One reason for this may lie in romantic suggestions such as du Maurier's (1967, 109) that old engine houses are 'memorials to daring and courage'. For those with no first-hand experience of the dangers, grief and poverty often associated with mining – the average Australian female survey respondent was born in 1939 and therefore more likely to be familiar with du Maurier than with life in a mining community – this 'down side' may have given way to nostalgic notions of heroism.

Another reason may lie in 'normal' socialisation processes. Survey figures suggest that women, being particularly influenced by the maternal grandmother and more likely than men to inherit and display the family artefacts that help us understand ourselves, are in turn more likely to be influenced in a secondary sense by the life and culture of the maternal grandfather. He is a far more potent purveyor of 'Cornishness' than is the paternal grandfather. On the other hand, the Cornish paternal grandmother, while being more numerous than each of the maternal grandparents, appears to be more dependent on marriage to a Cornishman for any influence she has in terms of passing on her own Cornish heritage. This only accentuates the extent to which the men in the survey are influenced by their paternal grandfather regardless of his occupation or the occupation of his own forebears.

Another clue to discovering why Australian women have been such a potent force behind the myth of Cousin Jack may lie in the life experiences of those very women. The women who responded to the survey had an average age (in 2002) of 62 years. Born at the beginning of World War Two, educated in the 1940s and '50s (when, along with peace, women were being sent back to their kitchens and laundries) and married in the early 1960s, had they spent much of their lives devoted to raising children only to reach 'retirement' without the identity of profession or occupation? Certainly, there would have been retired professionals among this group. However, it is quite likely that it was the men – not the women – of the survey cohort who went into retirement with the comfort of an occupationally-defined identity (their average age was 66 years). Could it be, then, that while men were likely to be perfectly comfortable with their identities and their place in the world, women felt the need to search the past for an ethnically-based identity that was well-defined, tangible and authentic? As we have seen, a Cornish identity is perfectly able, and more so than many others, to provide this.

Conclusion

Australians of Cornish descent – and in particular, Australian women – have grabbed on to the 'economic niche' occupied by the Cornish miner to create and express a well-defined identity. Indeed, one has to wonder whether anyone would be expressing their Cornish identity in Australia at all if Cornish migration to this country had been for a more diverse purpose. With that in mind, and given the apparent importance of the Cornish miner to Cornish identity in Australia today, it is perhaps worth looking at Tregenza (quoted in Payton, 1987, ix), who observed that the view that all 'nineteenth-century Cornish migrants were miners or connected with mining was a misleading, if not dangerous myth'.

Certainly, in the context that there were many Cornish people who are just as Cornish as the miner, this is a valid and important point. But why stop at occupation? We might even change the focus from occupation to religion or gender. But Payton's raising of this issue in the context of an occupationally defined study (that of the farmer) is itself a response to the importance of occupation to Cornish identity. Sadly, for the heritage-building prowess of the Cornish farmer, it would appear from the survey that he just does not have what it takes: he did not occupy an 'economic niche' that would form the basis of identity – pioneering farmers came from everywhere. And while it might be argued that so too did miners come from 'everywhere', the Cornish held a special place within this economic niche and their Australian descendants have ardently and successfully made it theirs.

And so we have a situation where Cornish identity in today's Australia is very much tied up with the myth of Cousin Jack and his ownership of a distinctive economic niche. It makes him a powerful character, undertaking difficult and dangerous work, he is driven by a God-fearing, Protestant work ethic and his legacy – in the form of industrial heritage – is there for us to admire. For those of us who grew up feeling too white and too cultureless in a multicultural society, he provides precisely the sort of identity we wanted to find when we went looking for authentic and tangible roots. Today, 150 years after his 'great emigration' he is being celebrated like never before. The extent to which this has narrowed perceptions of what it is to be Cornish, and the extent to which this narrowing might be considered dangerous or disadvantageous, really lies in the way we choose to use it.

Notes
1. Details of the entire survey can be found in Hayden (2002).
2. My recollection of graffiti, South Crofty Mine, Cornwall, 2000.
3. Issues relating to the implications of different notions about Cornish identity are covered in Hayden (2002)
4. According to Koch (2001) Australian Aborigines were largely invisible to urban Australians.
5. It should be noted that while women played a large role in 'above-grass' activities in Cornish mines, of 630 Cornish female workers who had assisted passage to New South Wales between 1837 and 1877, only eight were mine workers (Lay, 1998, 145; see also Paterson, 1993, 138; Payton, 1987, 134).

References

Alcock, A.E. , Taylor, B.K., Welton, J.M. (1979), *The Future of Cultural Minorities*, MacMillan, London

Dixson, M. (1999), *The Imaginary Australian: Anglo-Celts and Identity – 1788 to the present*, University of New South Wales Press, Sydney

Du Maurier, D. (1967), *Vanishing Cornwall*, Penguin Books, Harmondsworth (reprinted 1972)

Dyer, R. (1997), *White*, Routledge, London

Gillman, I. (1988), *Many Faiths One Nation – a Guide to the Major Faiths and Denominations in Australia*, William Collins, Sydney

Harvey, D. (1992), *The Condition of Postmodernity*, Blackwell, Oxford

Hayden, C. (2002), 'Cousin Jack: postmodern hero or problem child?' *Australian Celtic Journal (8)*, Celtic Council of Australia & University of Sydney, pp. 27–80

Hobsbawm, E. & Ranger, T. (eds) 1983, *The Invention of Tradition*, Cambridge University Press, Cambridge

Ibson, J. (1981), 'Virgin Land or Virgin Mary? Studying the Ethnicity of White Americans' in *American Quarterly*, 33 (3)

King, A.D. (ed.) (1993), *Culture, Globalization and the World-System: contemporary conditions for the representation of identity*, MacMillan, Basingstoke

Koch, T. (2001), *'Facing the Demon'* in The Courier-Mail, November 24, p. 27

Lay, P. (1998), *One and All: The Cornish in New South Wales*, Heritage 2000 Plus, Queanbeyan

McGuigan, J. (1999), *Modernity and Postmodern Culture*, Open University Press, Buckingham

Paterson, R. (1993), 'Cornish Heritage on the Northern Yorke Peninsula: The Cousin Jenny Contribution' in *Journal of the Historical Society of South Australia, no 21*

Payton, P. (1987), *The Cornish Farmer in Australia*, Dyllansow Truran, Redruth, Cornwall

Payton, P. (2000), 'Re-inventing Celtic Australia' in Hale, A. & Payton P. (eds), *New Directions in Celtic Studies,* University of Exeter Press, Exeter

Payton, P. (2001), email correspondence, 18 October 2001

Said, E. (1991), *Orientalism*, Penguin Books, London

Smith, A.D. (1991), *National Identity*, Penguin Books, London

Zubrzycki, J. (1992), 'The Search for Roots and Nationalism in Multicultural Australia: A (partly autobiographical) essay in Social Theory' in McRobbie, A. (ed.) *Arrivals, Departures, Achievements: Essays in Honour of James Jupp*, Australian National University, Queanbeyan

Acknowledgements

This chapter is part of the larger article cited above (Hayden, 2002). It is used here with permission from the Celtic Council of Australia and the University of Sydney, publisher of the *Australian Celtic Journal*.

Acknowledgements

The publication of this book would not have been possible without the generous support of the Cornish Association of South Australia, which is gratefully acknowledged. The editors are also indebted to Wakefield Press, especially publisher Michael Bollen, whose customary enthusiasm for South Australian history prompted his ready embrace of this volume, and Michael Deves, whose design work and typesetting have been of the usual high standard associated with Wakefield. The several contributors to the volume are also thanked for revisiting and revising papers that had been delivered at previous Cornish Association seminars during the Kernewek Lowender festivals, in some cases more than ten years ago, to produce the chapters that grace this book.

Contributors

Philip Payton

Philip Payton is Emeritus Professor of Cornish & Australian Studies at the University of Exeter, where he was formerly Director of the Institute of Cornish Studies, and is Professor of History at Flinders University as well as Honorary Professor at the Australian National University. He is the author or editor of more than sixty books, most on Cornish themes. Recent volumes include *Cornwall in the Age of Rebellion: 1490–1690* (University of Exeter Press) and *Vice-Regal: A History of the Governors of South Australia* (Wakefield Press). He is an Honorary Life Member of the Cornish Association of South Australia, and is a bard of the Cornish Gorsedh. His bardic name *Car Dyvresow* means 'friend of exiles'.

Greg Drew OAM

Greg is an expert on South Australia's mining history and heritage and has published a number of books on the subject. He holds an MSc and Dip Ed from the University of Adelaide and was employed as a geologist for 30 years by the State Government.

Greg developed a network of interpretive walking trails at mining heritage sites throughout South Australia and beyond, including the Burra Mining Museum and the Broken Hill Living Museum Project. He recently managed South Australia's Abandoned Mine Project, responsible for identifying risks at abandoned sites. He set up the South Australian Mining History Group in 2011, which has since had regular quarterly lectures on and several excursions to the South Australian mining landscape.

Contributors

In 2019 he was awarded an OAM for service to mining as an historian and was made a bard of the Cornish Gorseth (with name *Drew a Sydhni*, 'Drew of Sithney') for promoting the knowledge of mining technology and commitment in the Cornish diaspora.

Keith Johns OAM

Keith Johns was raised on a farm near Port Pirie and attended schools in Crystal Brook, Port Pirie and Adelaide. He graduated in Science at the University of Adelaide, majoring in geology under the direction of Sir Douglas Mawson. He joined the Geological Survey of South Australia, engaging in a wide range of projects concerned with mapping, mineral exploration and development, becoming the government's Chief Geologist in 1972. He served as Director-General of the Department of Mines and Energy from 1983 to 1992. In 2009 Keith was awarded an OAM for 'Services to mining & mining history'.

In retirement his main interest has centred on aspects of mining history and heritage, inspired by his Cornish ancestry. His forebears, who were miners and farmers, arrived in the Colony of South Australia in 1839.

Kate Neale

Born and raised in Cornwall, Kate Neale's research focuses on Cornish music and culture, exploring broader themes of identity, heritage and community construction through musical performance. Her Arts and Humanities Research Council-funded PhD was co-supervised at Cardiff University and the Institute of Cornish Studies at the University of Exeter. It concentrated on the transfer of Cornish Christmas carols to diasporic communities in California and South Australia, with a particular focus on the development and deployment of heritage narratives.

Since returning to Cornwall in 2018, Kate has continued researching and presenting her work on community carolling practices both at home and abroad, alongside working in communications and involvement in a range of voluntary roles. She was made a bard of the Cornish Gorsedh in 2019, taking the bardic name *Gwandryades An Mordrik* ('Lowtide Wanderer').

Moira Drew

Moira Drew has been engaged in family history-related research for about 30 years. She became intrigued by the story of the Ninnes Grave near Maiden Gully, Bendigo and the death of her great-great-grandmother Maria Ninnes and her two youngest daughters shortly after their overland journey from Burra in early 1852. This led to a study of various aspects of overland travel from South Australia to the Victorian goldfields in the 1850s and creation of the Overland Gold website to share her findings. In 2013, after the Kernewek Lowender festival in South Australia, she led a convoy retracing one of the routes taken by those travellers.

Moira coordinates the Friends of the Ninnes Grave group, continuing the previous work to ensure the grave was protected within a housing development. More recently she liaised with the local Council to ensure the natural bush reserve surrounding the grave is maintained. She qualified as an archivist in 1999 and until 2021 was Archivist with the Australian Red Cross.

Kerryn Goldsworthy

Kerryn Goldsworthy was born and raised on Yorke Peninsula, living on the farm established by her Cornish great-great-grandfather. A graduate of the University of Adelaide, she was a lecturer in literature at the University of Melbourne for 17 years before returning to Adelaide to make a living as a freelance writer and reviewer. She has served on the judging panels of many literary prizes including the Miles Franklin Literary Award, and was the inaugural Chair of the Stella Prize judging panel, from 2013–2015. She won the 2013 Pascall Prize for arts criticism and the 2017 Horne prize for her essay 'The Limit of the World'. Her most recent book is *Adelaide,* in the NewSouth 'Cities' series.

Cheryl Hayden

Cheryl Hayden is a former journalist, teacher and public servant and has had a life-long interest in her Cornish heritage, which comes from both sides of her family. In recent years, she has explored 16th Century Cornwall and in 2019 was awarded a PhD in Creative Arts (Flinders University) for her research into Cornish involvement in counter-Reformation treachery during the reign of Elizabeth I. This followed a Master of Creative Industries at Queensland University of Technology and the publication of her novel, *A Christmas Game* (2012), which imagined the Prayer Book Rebellion of 1549, and the completion of a Master of Cornish Studies at the University of Exeter in 2002. The chapter concluding this book relates to her dissertation for that degree.

Robynne Sanderson
Robynne Sanderson worked in the mining industry in Broken Hill and then at Broken Hill TAFE, where she was Head Teacher of Information Technology. She currently works in a bookshop and is also in her second year of Cornish language study.

Robynne has been involved in music in Broken Hill throughout her life, including as organist at St James Church since 1982 and playing clarinet in the Civic Orchestra for over 30 years. She has directed the 'Community Voices' group since 2005, including teaching several songs in the Cornish language.

Robynne was Broken Hill's Citizen of the Year in 2018 for her wide-ranging involvement in music and local history, especially research into Broken Hill's Cornish heritage. She regularly presents talks on this topic and has been a member of the Cornish Association of South Australia since 2014. In 2021 the London Cornish Association awarded Robynne the prestigious Paul Smales Medal for promoting Cornish culture outside Cornwall.

Jan Lokan
Jan Lokan has Cornish origins traced back to Crowan in the early 1600s. Her forebears were 'tinners', then copper miners. Her great-grandfather brought his family to Moonta Mines in 1864, but soon opened a much-needed school for miners' children. Jan is an Adelaide University Arts graduate and later gained a PhD in Education in Ottawa, Canada. Her working life was in educational research, first in Canada and then with the Australian Council for Educational Research in Melbourne. She has many publications in that field and was awarded a Centennial Medal for services to educational research in 2003. In retirement she has followed her interests in Cornish history, organising the SA Cornish

Association's biennial history seminars for 15 years. She became a bard of the Cornish Gorsedh in 2018, with the name *Myrgh Golsery* ('daughter of Goldsworthy'), using the 17th C form of the name.

John Brimson

For anyone familiar with Redruth, Cornwall, John Brimson entered the world 'two doors west of the Red Lion Hotel'. His parents were from Devon and Dorset but his maternal grandmother was Cornish. His schooling was in Plymouth, followed by two years of National Service in the RAF in various parts of Britain. He was a choir boy from age seven and an adult choir member from age 12, later taking principal roles in many Gilbert and Sullivan operas. He lived in Saltash, Cornwall, before his work as an insurance agent took him to Kenya for two years, then back to the British Midlands. There he undertook 'voice' studies at the Birmingham Conservatorium, under a principal singer from the Glyndebourne Opera. His next work transfer was to St Helier in the Channel Islands, from where he and his wife Audrey decided to migrate to Australia as '£10 Poms'. John died in April 2019; music was a feature of almost his entire life.

Jean Prest

Jean Prest grew up in the middle of Penfold's vineyard near Adelaide. Her athletic father, Ern Wadham, was a winner of the annual 'Bay Sheffield' foot race (akin to the Stawell Gift) and played Australian Rules football for South Australia before the national league was established. Her mother was Cornish, descended from the Jolly and Blewitt families.

After completing Honours and Masters degrees in political science at Adelaide University, Jean embarked on a PhD with Professor Douglas Pike as supervisor, only to abandon it upon marriage. Three children, three grandchildren and 50 years later she completed a PhD at the University of Melbourne, on which this chapter is based.

Jean tutored in the History Departments of Adelaide, Western Australia and La Trobe universities for many years and was Head of Middle School at Methodist Ladies College Melbourne for a decade. An avid reader and keen tennis player, she has also enjoyed travels to many parts of the world.

Contributors

Rosanne Hawke

Rosanne Hawke (*Myrgh Trevelyan*), a fourth generation Cornish-Australian, has written over 30 books for young people, including *The Messenger Bird*, winner of the 2013 Cornish Holyer an Gof award for Young Adult literature. *Across the Creek* won this award for Children's Literature in 2005. She holds a PhD, which explores Cornish–Australian literature, from the University of Adelaide. She was awarded a bardship in 2006 for services to Cornish culture and literature by promoting Cornish identity, especially among young people.

Rosanne has taught creative writing at Tabor Adelaide and in 2009 won an Australian Learning and Teaching Council Citation for Outstanding Contribution to Student Learning. She is the 2015 recipient of the Nance Donkin award and is a Carclew, Asialink, Varuna, and May Gibbs Fellow. Her latest Young Adult novel with Cornish themes is *Flying Blind*.

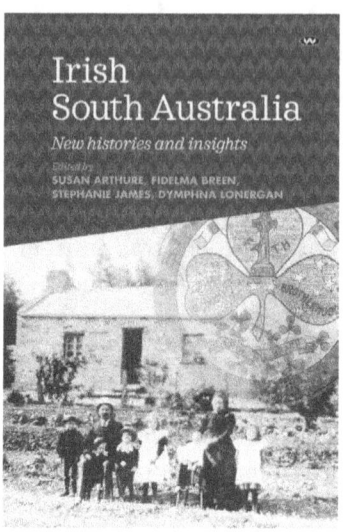

Irish South Australia
New histories and insights

*Edited by Susan Arthure, Fidelma Breen,
Stephanie James, Dymphna Lonergan*

Its capital is named after German-born Queen Adelaide, its main street after her English husband, King William IV, so it is not surprising that little is known about South Australia's Irish background.

However, the first European to discover Adelaide's River Torrens in 1836 was Cork-born and educated George Kingston, who was deputy surveyor to Colonel Light; the river was named in turn for Derryman Colonel Torrens, Chairman of the South Australian Colonisation Commission. Adelaide's first judge and first police commissioner were immigrants from Kerry and Limerick.

Irish South Australia charts Irish settlement from as far north as Pekina, to the state's south-east and Mount Gambier. It follows the diverse fortunes of the Irish-born elite, as well as doctors, farmers, lawyers, orphans, parliamentarians, pastoralists and publicans who made South Australia their home, with various shades of political and religious beliefs: Anglicans, Catholics, Dissenters, Federationalists, Freemasons, Home Rulers, nationalists, and Orangemen.

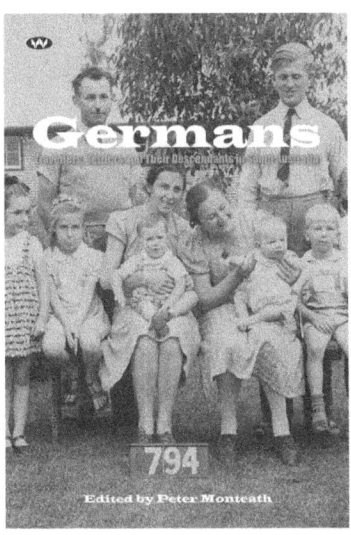

Germans
Travellers, settlers and their descendants in South Australia

Edited by Peter Monteath

From Beehive Corner and Bert Flugelman's polished balls in Rundle Mall to the vineyards, churches and cemeteries of the Barossa Valley, tangible signs of South Australia's Germans are everywhere to be seen. Too often, however, 'the Germans' are regarded as a single group in the state's history. The truth is more complex and intriguing.

Those who came during the colony's first decades mostly spoke a common language, but were divided by differences of country, culture and class. They were farmers from Silesia and Brandenburg, missionaries from Dresden, liberals from Berlin, merchants from Hamburg, miners from the Harz mountains or erudite graduates from some of the best universities in the world. They brought an astonishing variety of knowledge and talents, and were destined to make a difference in many fields.

No less varied have been the experiences of their descendants and more recent arrivals. Germans have been praised as model citizens, even as over-achievers. But at times they have also been accused of divided loyalties or barefaced treachery.

Wakefield Press is an independent publishing and
distribution company based in Adelaide, South Australia.
We love good stories and publish beautiful books.
To see our full range of books, please visit our website at
www.wakefieldpress.com.au
where all titles are available for purchase.
To keep up with our latest releases, news and events,
subscribe to our monthly newsletter.

Find us!

Facebook: www.facebook.com/wakefield.press
Twitter: www.twitter.com/wakefieldpress
Instagram: www.instagram.com/wakefieldpress

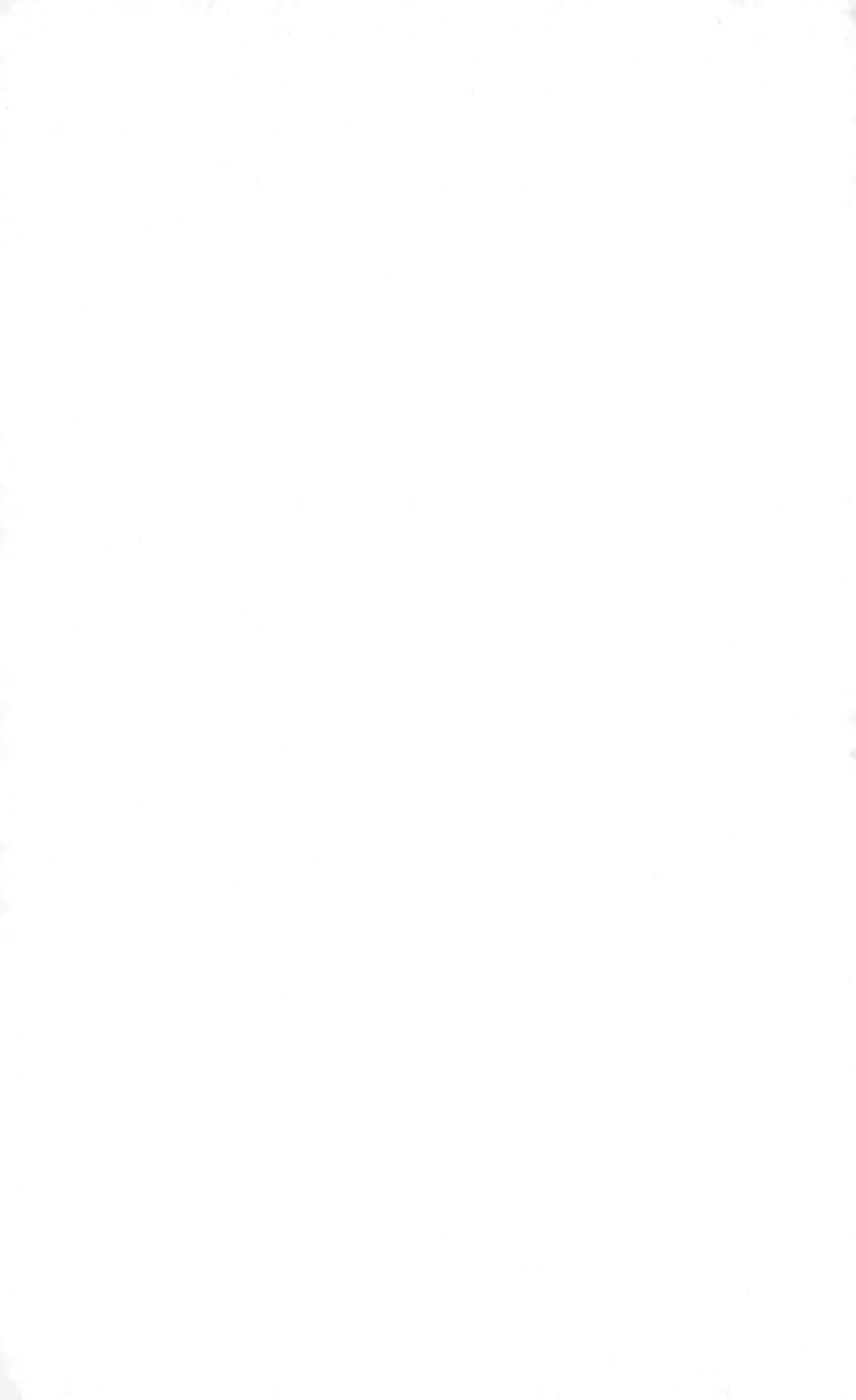

www.ingramcontent.com/pod-product-compliance
Lightning Source LLC
Chambersburg PA
CBHW071019240526
45469CB00006BD/1997